Schools of Magic

CRITICAL EXPLORATIONS IN SCIENCE FICTION AND FANTASY
A series edited by Donald E. Palumbo and C.W. Sullivan III
Earlier Works: www.mcfarlandpub.com

61 *The Fabulous Journeys of Alice and Pinocchio: Exploring Their Parallel Worlds* (Laura Tosi with Peter Hunt, 2018)

62 *A* Dune *Companion: Characters, Places and Terms in Frank Herbert's Original Six Novels* (Donald E. Palumbo, 2018)

63 *Fantasy Literature and Christianity: A Study of the Mistborn, Coldfire, Fionavar Tapestry and Chronicles of Thomas Covenant Series* (Weronika Łaszkiewicz, 2018)

64 *The British Comic Invasion: Alan Moore, Warren Ellis, Grant Morrison and the Evolution of the American Style* (Jochen Ecke, 2019)

65 *The Archive Incarnate: The Embodiment and Transmission of Knowledge in Science Fiction* (Joseph Hurtgen, 2018)

66 *Women's Space: Essays on Female Characters in the 21st Century Science Fiction Western* (ed. Melanie A. Marotta, 2019)

67 *"Hailing frequencies open": Communication in* Star Trek: The Next Generation (Thomas D. Parham III, 2019)

68 *The Global Vampire: Essays on the Undead in Popular Culture Around the World* (ed. Cait Coker, 2019)

69 *Philip K. Dick: Essays of the Here and Now* (ed. David Sandner, 2019)

70 *Michael Bishop and the Persistence of Wonder: A Critical Study of the Writings* (Joe Sanders, 2020)

71 *Caitlín R. Kiernan: A Critical Study of Her Dark Fiction* (James Goho, 2020)

72 *In* Frankenstein's *Wake: Mary Shelley, Morality and Science Fiction* (Alison Bedford, 2020)

73 *The Fortean Influence on Science Fiction: Charles Fort and the Evolution of the Genre* (Tanner F. Boyle, 2020)

74 *Arab and Muslim Science Fiction* (eds. Hosam A. Ibrahim Elzembely and Emad El-Din Aysha, 2020)

75 *The Mythopoeic Code of Tolkien: A Christian Platonic Reading of the Legendarium* (Jyrki Korpua, 2021)

76 *The Truth of Monsters: Coming of Age with Fantastic Media* (Ildikó Limpár, 2021)

77 *Speculative Modernism: How Science Fiction, Fantasy and Horror Conceived the Twentieth Century* (William Gillard, James Reitter *and* Robert Stauffer, 2021)

78 *English Magic and Imperial Madness: The Anti-Colonial Politics of Susanna Clarke's* Jonathan Strange & Mr. Norrell (Peter D. Mathews, 2021)

79 *The Self and Community in* Star Trek: Voyager (Susan M. Bernardo, 2022)

80 *Magic Words, Magic Worlds: Form and Style in Epic Fantasy* (Matthew Oliver, 2022)

81 *Discovering Dune: Essays on Frank Herbert's Epic Saga* (eds. Dominic J. Nardi and N. Trevor Brierly, 2022)

82 *Nnedi Okorafor: Magic, Myth, Morality and the Future* (Sandra J. Lindow, 2023)

83 *Science, Technology and Magic in* The Witcher: *A Medievalist Spin on Modern Monsters* (Kristine Larsen, 2023)

84 *Analyzing* Adventure Time: *Critical Essays on Cartoon Network's World of Ooo* (ed. Paul A. Thomas, 2023)

85 *Schools of Magic: Learning in Children's and Young Adult Fantasy Fiction* (Megan H. Suttie, 2023)

Schools of Magic
Learning in Children's and Young Adult Fantasy Fiction

MEGAN H. SUTTIE

CRITICAL EXPLORATIONS
IN SCIENCE FICTION AND FANTASY, 85
Series Editors Donald E. Palumbo *and* C.W. Sullivan III

McFarland & Company, Inc., Publishers
Jefferson, North Carolina

This book has undergone peer review.

ISBN (print) 978-1-4766-8059-0
ISBN (ebook) 978-1-4766-4904-7

Library of Congress and British Library
cataloguing data are available

Library of Congress Control Number 2022058573

© 2023 Megan H. Suttie. All rights reserved

No part of this book may be reproduced or transmitted in any form or by any means, electronic or mechanical, including photocopying or recording, or by any information storage and retrieval system, without permission in writing from the publisher.

Front cover: Owl on tree in misty forest under full moon at night (Shutterstock/New Africa)

Printed in the United States of America

*McFarland & Company, Inc., Publishers
Box 611, Jefferson, North Carolina 28640
www.mcfarlandpub.com*

Thank you to everyone who helped make this book happen.

To quote The Tragically Hip:
I, I am of you,
And you are in everything I do

Table of Contents

List of Abbreviations	viii
Preface	1
Introduction: A Framework for Analyzing Fantastic School Stories	7
1. Ordinary Wizarding Levels: High-Stakes Standardized Testing in J.K. Rowling's *Harry Potter* Series	33
2. Not a Bent Penny More: Capital in Patrick Rothfuss's *Kingkiller Chronicle*	68
3. Imperial Institutes: Portal Fantasies and Education in Lev Grossman's *Magicians* Trilogy	95
4. Nothing Exactly Like a Lesson: Legitimate Peripheral Participation in Terry Pratchett's "Tiffany Aching" Quintet	125
Conclusion	160
Chapter Notes	167
Bibliography	183
Index	197

List of Abbreviations

In each chapter following the Introduction, abbreviated forms are used for the in-text citations of works in the series under consideration. By chapter, these are as follows:

Chapter 1: For works in the *Harry Potter* series by J.K. Rowling
    Stone—*Harry Potter and the Philosopher's/Sorcerer's Stone*
    Chamber—*Harry Potter and the Chamber of Secrets*
    Prisoner—*Harry Potter and the Prisoner of Azkaban*
    Goblet—*Harry Potter and the Goblet of Fire*
    Order—*Harry Potter and the Order of the Phoenix*
    Half-Blood—*Harry Potter and the Half-Blood Prince*
    Deathly—*Harry Potter and the Deathly Hallows*

Chapter 2: For works in the *Kingkiller Chronicle* series by Patrick Rothfuss
    Name—*The Name of the Wind*
    Wise—*The Wise Man's Fear*

Chapter 3: For works in the *Magicians* trilogy by Lev Grossman
    Magicians—*The Magicians*
    Magician King—*The Magician King*
    Land—*The Magician's Land*

Chapter 4: For works in the "Tiffany Aching" quintet by Terry Pratchett
    Wee—*The Wee Free Men*
    Hat—*A Hat Full of Sky*
    Wintersmith—*Wintersmith*
    Midnight—*I Shall Wear Midnight*
    Shepherd's—*The Shepherd's Crown*

Preface

What is magic?
What is education?
And what does the one have to do with the other?
In fantasy narratives which feature the protagonist's education, the answer to this last question is: quite a lot.

Magic, simply put, is power over others, over the world, over the outcomes of your actions; education, similarly simplified, is the process by which an individual gains the skills and knowledge thought necessary to participate and excel in society. An education in magic, then, is intended to equip students with literal power to shape, control, and succeed beyond the institution. Magic is power, and schools teaching magic are a means of distributing—or denying—that power to individuals.

This book examines the subgenre of the fantastic school story, where the distribution of magical power via education is not only an important societal concern but also the cornerstone of the narrative. The combination of the mundane and the magical within this subgenre offers remarkable opportunities for authors, critics, and readers alike to critically examine the process and products of education, as well as the position of the educational institution within the broader fantastic society. As discussed in the Introduction, the defamiliarization of fantasy makes visible elements of education which are so pervasive and accepted they have become invisible in our everyday world, inviting and encouraging us to consider both the magical examples before us and the mundane counterparts on which they draw with an attention we might not otherwise pay to these elements. As a result, looking at how skill and ability in magic are distributed through the educational institutions which provide instruction in magic is akin to examining the ways in which power is distributed or denied through education in mundane schools, the educational institutions in our own world that

Preface

concern themselves with teaching far less fantastic subjects and skills. This examination is an important and necessary undertaking as we collectively seek to improve educational experiences and outcomes and undo the systems of discrimination and oppression which run parallel to and in our systems of instruction.

In the Introduction, I present a framework for approaching the fantastic school story holistically as a subgenre in its own right. Fantastic school stories inextricably combine the traditions of fantasy literature and of the school story genre with the issues and concerns of representing education, and each element must be understood as operating simultaneously and in relation to one another, producing a whole more nuanced and complex than the sum of its parts. I argue that this combination offers unique opportunities for representing complex concepts, foregrounding difficult issues, and socializing readers into either a critical or a complacent mindset in relation to the ideas and structures depicted—particularly those structures which comprise or inform the "hidden curriculum" of the educational institution and its practices, which is made readily available for critical consideration through the subgenre's defining characteristics. Using Jane Yolen's novella *Wizard's Hall* as an illustrative example, I introduce key questions for interrogating the hidden curriculum in fantastic school stories, drawn from the work of Michael Apple and Nancy King: What underlying meanings and ideologies are transmitted along with the formal content? How do teachers and administrators filter and distort knowledge? How do societal norms and expectations filter and distort knowledge? Whose interests shape and inform educational institutions, processes, and outcomes? How do schools distribute social, cultural, and economic capital in relation with one another?

Following this critical introduction to the framework for analyzing fantastic school stories, the remaining chapters each explore a series of fantastic school stories through this lens, centering the key questions for analyzing the "deep structures" of the education depicted. Each chapter explicates the issues addressed in a fantastic school story series and the ways in which the subgenre's possibilities are employed to foster in readers either an uncritical acceptance of the societal norms and structures depicted or a critical awareness of and even challenge to the problems and injustices brought forward by the text's combination of the magic and the mundane.

Preface

There are innumerable texts and authors which could—and have, and should, and will be—analyzed within the framework for understanding fantastic school stories set out in this book, including, but by no means limited to, the works of authors such as Libba Bray, Trudi Canavan, Roald Dahl, Ursula Le Guin, Nnedi Okorafor, Tamora Pierce, Philip Pullman, Rainbow Rowell, and Diana Wynne Jones. Here, in addition to Jane Yolen's novella, the works of J.K. Rowling, Lev Grossman, Patrick Rothfuss, and Terry Pratchett are examined. These five authors and their works have been selected to represent the subgenre of fantastic school stories in establishing the interdisciplinary framework for analysis because they are all prototypical, traditional examples of important aspects of the subgenre. These British and American authors and texts reflect the distinctly British origin and subsequent American evolutions of the school story genre, the largely white, Eurocentric traditions which continue to influence the fantasy genre,[1] and the European-American educational system that is increasingly present across the globe.[2] This selection of authors and texts is by no means representative of the diversity in the subgenre, and the Conclusion looks to works specifically by Black authors and about racialized protagonists as an area for further study of fantastic school stories. The analysis presented here is intended to provide a foundation for future analyses of texts which deviate from the white, Eurocentric tradition in one or more ways, opening up the possibility for examining more diverse texts and authors in context with the subgenre's origins.

Chapter 1 examines the seven core texts of Rowling's Harry Potter series (1997–2007), which follow the traditions of the school story genre very closely and are widely recognized as the first series in the fantastic school story subgenre to reach such widespread popularity (Galway; Manners Smith; Pesold; Pinsent "Education"; Steege). Here, I contribute to the substantial body of scholarship on the series through an analysis of the testing structures of Hogwarts, including the end of year exams and the standardized OWLs and NEWTs. Reading closely into the depictions of these tests and examinations through the lens of the key questions from the Introduction, I explicate the priorities of education in the wizarding world thus revealed and consider the ways in which these priorities inform the teaching practices of Hogwarts' staff. Looking then beyond the school itself, I demonstrate the societal gate-keeping function of the standardized exams, enacted through

Preface

the use of examination scores to determine career eligibility. The chapter concludes with a consideration of the failure to effectively use the carnivalesque structure of the individual texts and the series as a whole: as we shall see, the series fosters acceptance and complacency regarding the use of the OWLs and NEWTs as gate-keeping measures in part by situating Voldemort as anti-testing and therefore aligning the side of "good" with the tests and their traditional use, rather than utilizing the subversive potential of the carnivalesque structure to foster critical awareness of the issue.

Chapter 2 turns to Rothfuss's as-yet-unfinished *Kingkiller Chronicle*, currently comprised of *The Name of the Wind* (2007) and *The Wise Man's Fear* (2011), and once again brings to bear the key questions for interrogating the hidden curriculum of educational institutions in fantastic school stories, this time highlighting the role of capital in controlling access to education. Focusing on Kvothe's experiences learning "Sympathy" at the University, I analyze the ways in which Kvothe's access to the institution, the materials required, and time to learn and study are all constrained by his lack of economic capital, as well as the ways in which these constraints negatively impact his ability to gain social, cultural, or additional economic capital through his studies. I conclude the chapter with an examination of the series' consistent foregrounding of Kvothe's performances and general performativity, which I argue generates critical awareness of class identity as performative and contributes to the *Kingkiller Chronicle*'s critique of the role of capital and economic wealth.

The final two chapters take a half-step back and consider the ways in which deliberate play with genre can create, inform, and enhance the unique opportunities to foreground and challenge the hidden curriculum represented in fantastic school stories. Grossman's Magicians trilogy—*The Magicians* (2009), *The Magician King* (2011), and *The Magician's Land* (2014)—is the focus of Chapter 3. The foregrounding of the Fillory intratexts, which are a stand-in for C.S. Lewis' *Chronicles of Narnia*, as well as the consistent use of these stories to frame Quentin's experiences studying at Brakebills College for Magical Pedagogy, I argue, invite readers to approach *The Magicians*, in particular, as a portal fantasy. I explore the ways in which reading the series through this lens brings forward themes and legacies of colonialism and imperialism in the educational institution, encouraging an understanding of the school as an imperial center and the process of education as a process of colonization. Attending to the different experiences of various characters as they work within or outside the boundaries of Brakebills, I demonstrate the violence and trauma inherent in an imperial education process. Grossman's metatextual play with the Fillory novels and the portal fantasy genre facilitates a consideration of complex structures and inheritances in the education process, providing valuable opportunities for readers to question the ideology underlying educational institutions, particularly those as explicitly Anglophilic as Brakebills.

Finally, Chapter 4 analyzes the "Tiffany Aching" quintet, a sub-set of Pratchett's Discworld novels, which feature the protagonist Tiffany Aching: *The Wee Free Men* (2003), *A Hat Full of Sky* (2004), *Wintersmith* (2006), *I Shall Wear Midnight* (2010), and *The Shepherd's Crown* (2015). Where *The Magicians* plays deliberately with reader expectations through metatextual musings on the portal fantasy structure, *The Wee Free Men* flips this script and teases readers with promises of a school for witches and a traditional fantastic school story narrative. I consider the ways in which this genre play invites readers to understand the events of this first "Tiffany Aching" novel and the four which follow as school stories, despite the lack of a traditional brick-and-mortar educational institution and other common fantastic school story elements. Tiffany's education proceeds through a series of apprenticeships and experiential learning, analyzed in the chapter as exemplary of learning through peripheral participation in a community of practice. Rather than reading Tiffany's story as another fantasy *Bildungsroman*, the school story lens encourages us to consider the ways in which Tiffany engages with the educational structures of the witches' community, which are centered on care work and highly gendered. I demonstrate the ways in which Tiffany's rise through the witches' hierarchy challenges both the aetonormativity which commonly plagues children's and young adult literature and the gendered nature of witchcraft on the Discworld, which readers are better enabled to recognize through the series' foregrounding of the fantastic school story.

The melding of fantastic elements with the traditional school story in representing education foregrounds, critiques, and problematizes (or reinforces and supports) issues of power and control in education in ways not possible in purely realistic depictions of education and schooling, as demonstrated through each of the series examined; by focusing

Preface

on series, as opposed to stand-alone texts, we see the ways in which elements relating to education develop and change, further illuminating the issues explored in this subgenre. Moreover, the use of this interdisciplinary framework to analyze the fantastic school story genre allows us to develop the critique of hidden curricula and the ways in which these texts respond to current education practices and social values. The Conclusion considers the ways in which the analysis undertaken here—and further research inspired by it, particularly with texts by and about diverse individuals—is positioned within the projects of consciousness-raising from the field of education research and of emancipatory literary studies from the field of children's literature and Childhood Studies to further demonstrate the importance of work in this subgenre.

Introduction

A Framework for Analyzing Fantastic School Stories

> Departure from reality does not preclude comment upon it; indeed, this is one of fantasy's primary functions.
> —Kathryn Hume, *Fantasy and Mimesis*

> A story about school is a school.
> —Beverly Lyon Clark, *Regendering the School Story*

In this first chapter, I establish the essential three-part framework for holistically analyzing fantastic school stories as a unique subgenre. An illustrative analysis of Jane Yolen's novella *Wizard's Hall* begins and ends the chapter, demonstrating the necessity and value of approaching fantastic school story texts as a combination of the school story genre, the fantasy narrative, and representations of education which, together, bring forward societal structures and complex issues and make these available for reader critique and challenge, where they might otherwise risk blending into the mundane background of the familiar school setting and pass without critical consideration.

Introduction

Any time students at Wizard's Hall wish to travel anywhere within the school, they proceed according to their gender: boys go west with the sun's movement, and girls go east (or widdershins). Since the school is magic, they arrive almost instantly at their intended destinations, often going to the same places by travelling opposite ways; walking otherwise, students make no progress. Thornmallow, a new student (and

Introduction

the protagonist of Jane Yolen's 1991 novella *Wizard's Hall*), has not yet learned this rule, providing a narrative opportunity for another student to explain it both to Thornmallow and to readers:

> "Here, Thorny, you're going the wrong way," Will cried, grabbing him by the shoulder and turning him around. "Never go widdershins in anything."
> "Widdershins?"
> "That's going the opposite direction of the sun's movement, ninny. At Wizard's Hall, only girls can go that way. It's a rule. Number three, actually" [Yolen 53].

Thornmallow, now in the know about the rule, obeys it from this point forward, and it is never again a topic of conversation or inquiry, merely a reality of moving through the magic school obeyed by Thornmallow and his peers.

What do we make of this moment? How do we understand what is happening here, on both superficial and deeper levels of meaning? As scholars, as theorists, as critics, how do we approach an analysis of this scene—and of the text in which it occurs, and the subgenre in which the text is located? Do we treat it as fantasy, privileging the presence of magic and other impossibilities and rightfully recognizing the many generic tropes of fantasy within the novella? To do so, however, dismisses the fact that the story takes place within an educational institution and that, on at least one level, the process of education is the purpose of the narrative and is central to Thornmallow's development. Do we instead privilege the school setting and the focus on education in the narrative and base our analysis of the text on identifying it as a school story? Or do we let go of generic considerations entirely and instead direct our attention solely to the representation of education and the institution to examine issues of power, control, and ideology?

To approach this moment in the text with any one of these three frameworks—as fantasy, as a school story, or as a representation of education—is to look at its elements in isolation, to dismiss the whole and privilege the partial in our analysis. Examining this moment solely as fantasy denies its concurrent status as a school story and the tropes and themes inherent in this other tradition, while analyzing it as only a school story is to ignore the ways in which the introduction of fantastic elements exaggerates, embodies, and otherwise enhances the traditional aspects of the school story genre, offering something new.

Introduction

Removing this scene from the generic contexts which inform and influence the text, and interrogating it purely as a representation of education, is equally problematic, as both this moment and the ability of the text as a whole to comment on and work to (re)create or subvert structures of power in educational institutions and practices is inextricably connected to its generic status and conventions. Though it is possible to understand and explicate elements of this scene and others like it using any one of these frameworks, employing all three simultaneously acknowledges every element at work and also positions each element in relation to the others, illuminating the ways in which they interact to create a representation more nuanced and complex than may be immediately evident.

The way this scene and others like it must be approached to achieve a complete understanding and analysis, accounting for all influences and examining all possibilities, is as a fantastic school story: as part of a subgenre informed by both the fantasy and the school story traditions that concerns itself with representing the practice, process, and products of education, usually the protagonist's. Approaching this text and others like it in this way requires an awareness of the influence and inheritances of both its parent genres, as well as an understanding of the political and sociocultural ramifications of representing—and then either privileging or challenging—certain pedagogies and practices of education. Approaching a text with this three-part framework and analyzing it holistically, we are able to see the unique possibilities of this subgenre afforded by the introduction of the fantastic into representations of schooling and education. Furthermore, approaching this subgenre with such an interdisciplinary framework rightfully positions these texts and our analysis of them both within their greater generic contexts and within even broader contexts of education and school institutions.

This chapter first looks at the traditions of the school story genre; then at the conventions of fantastic literature; and, finally, at the political and sociocultural implications of schooling and textual representations of education. Returning at the end to an analysis of Yolen's novella and Thornmallow's education depicted within the text, the chapter concludes with a demonstration of the ways in which an interdisciplinary approach using the three-part framework introduced here illuminates the unique aspects of the fantastic school story genre and the possibilities and significance of these texts.

Introduction

The Traditions of the School Story Genre

Located under the broader umbrella of children's and young adult literature, school stories are already shaped by attitudes towards education and understandings of its methods and purposes, thanks to the field's inherent didacticism.[1] With education as the central focus of the school story genre, the underlying instructional affordances of children's and young adult literature are paired with a direct depiction of and commentary on the practices and purposes of education, amplifying both. As a result, scholars such as Beverly Lyon Clark assert that texts in the genre are not only about education, but are also an education in themselves:

> School stories lend themselves to didacticism because they are about schooling. ... Schooling is, in part, a metaphor for the effect that the book is supposed to have, whether it endorses traditional schooling or tries to school us in subversion. ... it is not just a product but a process to be undergone. ... A story about school is a school [*Regendering* 7].

As Clark explains, alongside and through depicting education, texts in this genre replicate, reinforce, and replace the lessons readers encounter elsewhere—inherently foregrounding education and schooling as topics deserving critical attention and analysis.

Which texts receive this attention or are considered in this vein, however, is limited by how the school story is defined. Ongoing debate regarding which texts can or should be considered as school stories, with different scholars applying different definitions in their work, means there is no definitive answer in existing scholarship to the question of what makes a school story a school story—of how to know when education is depicted as merely a common element in the lives of children and youth, as opposed to when it is of more central focus and is, therefore, deserving of more critical attention in the analysis of the text. One element of consistency across the various definitions employed, however, is that the parameters for inclusion consistently establish strict and narrow borders, particularly when scholars apply some variation of a content-based definition, which problematically excludes less-traditional texts in which an examination of education would be a productive—and necessary—undertaking.

This content-based definition is essentially a cataloguing of

Introduction

features, analyzing whether a given text includes such stock characteristics as, for example, a journey to the school, a wise headmaster, student rule-breaking, school spirit and loyalty, sports, and student codes of honor and conduct. For instance, though aware of the limitations of focusing on this inclusion of stock characteristics—noting that having or not having this content does not *automatically* define whether or not the text is part of the genre (Pinsent "Theories" 105)—Pat Pinsent is nevertheless preoccupied with outlining the characteristic content of girls' school stories, the differences of content in boys' school stories, and the ways in which the content of the genre as a whole changed with the introduction of the setting of day schools or with the inclusion of fantastic elements ("Theories" 109–118). Sue Sims, in introducing *The Encyclopedia of Girls' School Stories*, is equally concerned with the typical content of the genre from its beginning (2) to the "golden age" of the inter-war years (8–10); Robert Kirkpatrick, introducing the companion *The Encyclopedia of Boys' School Stories*, asserts that the genre has "a series of themes and motifs by which it identifies and limits itself" (5), focusing once again on stock characteristics as these are detailed and defined (5–7).

In addition to limiting the number of texts which can be considered school stories, the content-based definition struggles with delineating the genre's boundaries beyond the most traditional of texts, presenting a challenge whenever elements of the traditional school story are changed or new elements are introduced. Recognizing this limitation, scholars have begun to gesture towards other ways of defining the genre, but most have not begun to use alternate definitions, let alone explicitly articulate them. For instance, though Sims acknowledges as school stories some texts that introduce elements of other genres, such as the spy narrative or ballet narrative, most attempts to create cross-genre school stories, including fantasy cross-overs, are dismissed as failures (13). Sims does not consider most of the many modern books set in or featuring schools to be true school stories:

> they are in no way school stories of the traditional kind, and often include historical, fantasy and horror stories and 'problem' books dealing with modern concerns such as divorce, child abuse and racism. Certainly many of these books do not focus on the school in any way: it is part of the background, taken for granted [17].

Introduction

For Sims, the issue is not that other elements have been introduced, but rather that, in introducing these elements, the central focus on the school and its purposes and practices has been lost—gesturing towards an alternative focus-based definition for the genre, but remaining entrenched in the limited boundaries established by a content-based definition.

Kirkpatrick succinctly expresses these same ideas on the need for a text to focus primarily on school and the process of schooling in order to be considered a school story:

> when is a school story not a school story? One trend in recent children's fiction has been to examine modern day issues—racism, relationships, crime and drugs, for example—and when these are explored through the eyes of children school is often an integral part of the whole. Yet such fiction cannot be regarded as school fiction per se—while the school is in the background, and may provide the focal point for one or more aspects of the story, it does not provide the story's *raison d'être* [6, emphasis in original].

Kirkpatrick is willing to acknowledge the shared content characteristics between these modern stories and traditional school stories, but once again requires the *purpose* of the narrative to be school and education if the texts are to be considered true school stories, blurring the boundary lines but not quite opening up the definition of the genre.

Since the school story genre—where an analysis of the purposes, practices, and products of education is an obvious and productive undertaking—has so often been depicted with such strict borders (discouraging rather than inviting an investigation of education as represented in other texts), this content-based method of defining the school story presents an impediment to examining depictions of education across literature more broadly. Texts that detail the protagonist's education, but that do not meet the numerous criteria presented by content-based definitions, are excluded from the school story genre and are, therefore, often excluded from scholarly examinations of representations of education. Setting aside concerns with content and looking to the text's central focus—asking not "does this text have the characteristic content of school stories?" but rather, as Kirkpatrick suggests, "is education this text's *raison d'être*?"—provides a much more expansive definition of the genre and includes many more texts as potential school stories, inviting analyses of their depictions of education.

Introduction

I argue that the more expansive focus-based definition, in bringing more texts under the umbrella of the school story genre and shifting the focus of analysis to broader themes and issues, encourages an examination of elements inherent to the school story genre beyond stock characteristics of plot, setting, and characters and invites this analytical work in a wider selection of texts. These broader themes include the depiction of the protagonist's socialization into an ideal figure—a process the text is positioned to replicate with readers.[2] Scholars such as Ulrike Pesold, Mavis Reimer, David Steege, and Roberta Seelinger Trites have established that the socialization and personal development of the protagonist by the school is a central concern of the genre: as schools themselves serve to socialize students into particular structures and norms, the texts which present fictional accounts of schooling similarly serve to socialize readers. This second-hand socialization occurs through the texts' uncritical depiction of the protagonist's socialization and the suggestion that achieving this socialization is an unmitigated good and the ultimate goal. This potential is not limited to only traditional school stories, and is deserving of critical attention in a broader selection of texts.

In representing schools and schooling, the school story genre is also uniquely positioned to comment on educational institutions and the power they hold over individuals, which is another aspect to which a focus-based definition invites more consideration. Some texts unquestioningly and uncritically participate in the glorification of schools, furthering the second-hand socialization of readers, while others explore and exploit the possibility for challenge and critique in their representations. When protagonists eagerly adopt a belief in the wonders and benefits of their education, readers are vicariously encouraged to adopt a similarly positive and compliant attitude towards schooling, school institutions, and the values they propagate in the lives of readers.[3] The numerous positive portrayals of education, school institutions, and student experiences in these systems—as well as the complete indoctrination of protagonists and their peers into sharing these attitudes—result in an over-emphasis on the status and power of these institutions and practices, glorifying and romanticizing both education and its socializing function.

Resulting from this same position is another, directly opposed, tradition of critique and challenge: Reimer identifies "[c]riticism of schools

Introduction

as places of injustice, unhappiness and coercion" as a long-standing—though infrequent—theme in the genre (224), and some texts adopt a critical awareness of the socializing function of education, commenting on the process as it unfolds, with others directly challenging the methods and purposes of school institutions. Even these stories, however, carry with them the potential for socialization, albeit with different norms and values championed and, perhaps, a more critical understanding of the process and the results (Clark *Regendering* 10). Readers still engage vicariously in the process of alternative socialization undertaken by the protagonist, and the subversive messages of these texts are problematized, and often undermined, as the protagonist eventually adopts the role destined for them and becomes socialized into the community against which they have struggled—what Trites refers to as the paradox of "rebelling to conform" (34).[4] Looking not just at the fact of socialization for both reader and protagonist but also interrogating what attitudes towards education and schools are being presented, as well as the ways in which this socialization is potentially foregrounded or problematized, has been a productive undertaking in the school story genre which should rightfully be expanded to analyses of other texts depicting education, including fantastic school stories.

Employing the analytical and theoretical frameworks traditionally used with school stories to fantastic representations presents an invitation to examine the socialization of protagonist and reader and the attitudes towards school institutions, and education in general, present in fantasy variants, rightfully making these aspects topics of critical focus. It is imperative to extend the boundaries of the school story genre—operating, not with a content-based definition, but a focus-based one—to facilitate an examination of the representation and reproduction of the socializing elements of schools and school stories, which are heightened and modified through the inclusion of the fantastic in significant ways that must be addressed as part of understanding the subgenre.

The Traditions of Fantasy Literature

While opinions as to the precise method differ, the conclusion is categorically the same: though it is a literature of the impossible, the otherworldly, the unreal, fantasy is inherently and intricately bound

Introduction

up with reality, offering clarity, commentary, and critique upon what is possible and real within our own world. Two of the primary aspects of fantasy which enable this relationship, and imbue it with the ability to generate insight and critical analysis, are its allegorical re-presentation of issues and its juxtaposition of the real and the unreal. As scholars such as Brian Attebery have convincingly demonstrated, the simplification and exaggeration of complex issues through their imaginative re-presentation in fantasy parallels and metaphoric reworkings help readers reach a better understanding of their nuanced counterparts in reality, as well as provide readers with structures to use when engaging critically with the world. As Kathryn Hume corroborates, these mimetic presentations provide new perspectives, new interpretations, and new meanings to everyday lived experiences and the structures within which readers find themselves.

Combined with this re-presentation of real world issues is fantasy's juxtaposition of the possible with the impossible, which encourages an interrogation of familiar concepts. Ann Swinfen is among those scholars who have detailed the ways in which the defamiliarization inherent in fantasy serves to create a more critical and conscious awareness of what might otherwise pass unacknowledged. Swinfen claims that the "principal advantage" of fantasy "is that it engenders an extraordinarily enhanced perception of the nature of the primary world, which is so often only imperfectly grasped until a shock is given to the senses by the introduction of the marvellous" (234). Elaborating further, Rosemary Jackson sees the contrast as inviting a consideration of the real that might not otherwise occur, bringing attention to "the unsaid and the unseen of our culture: that which has been silenced, made invisible, covered over and made 'absent'" (4). Many more scholars have taken up this issue, convincingly demonstrating that fantasy literature, rather than offering only an escape from the world, helps us to better understand it. As David Sandner so succinctly says, fantasy provides readers tools to "think with" (278) in critically interrogating the issues and structures of their societies.

This unique relationship between fantasy literature and reality presents an opportunity for texts to act as a subversive force, an inspiration for change, and a model of what else could be. Hume refers to this potential as presenting plans for "revising reality"—though the declining popularity of overt didacticism has meant that this possibility is

Introduction

rarely explicitly addressed or fully developed, it nevertheless continues to exist in "brief sketches" or through implicit suggestion (56). In "present[ing] the reader with a new interpretation of reality," Hume argues, readers are invited by the texts "to acknowledge the possibility of a different reality" (xiii–xiv). As Jackson explains, fantasy is able to work in this way by foregrounding aspects of reality that do not often otherwise receive critical attention: "it is in the unconscious that social structures and 'norms' are reproduced and sustained within us," Jackson elaborates, "and only by redirecting attention to this area can we begin to perceive the ways in which the relations between society and the individual are fixed" (6), emphasizing the role fantasy can play in fostering subversion and critical awareness. In creating "space for a discourse other than a conscious one" (Jackson 62) and helping to bring these issues to critical consideration, fantasy literature carries the potential to be a subversive force and resource in the lives of readers.

The potential impact of this affordance can be profound. As Caroline Webb explicates, "engagement with fiction can be immensely powerful, as readers of story can not only learn about the world but can imagine new ways in which to grapple with that world, new possibilities" (3)—fantasy, in particular, "provide[s] opportunities for critique and speculation about alternative possibilities for living" (4). Furthermore, fantasy read by children and youth (whether or not these texts were intentionally or explicitly written for or marketed towards them) offers particular possibilities and benefits. For these young readers, Deborah O'Keefe sees fantasy literature as uniquely addressing a need for works which tackle the issues of our world without either despairing or remaining entrenched in unrealistic optimism, providing "a practice and example of making sense of a world" which readers can then employ in understanding their own experiences (18). Similarly, Webb sees fantasy as "an important way for readers to learn about the real world, to interpret and critique expectations within that world, to imagine new possibilities, and to develop the capacity for agency" (143), as fantasy works to "convey important lessons about the complexities and challenges of the real world—and how these may be faced and solved" (147). While fantasy presents tools for engaging with the world and a potential for subverting existing structures and norms to all readers, these offerings are particularly valuable for children and youth who are still establishing their understanding of the world and their relationship to

Introduction

its various structures—and the majority of whom are currently undergoing institutional educations ostensibly designed to prepare them for such engagement with society.

These offerings of fantasy are, essentially, the foundations of a critical reading practice; fantasy encourages and fosters the skills of critical examination and inquiry which are not always privileged in literacy practices in other contexts. As Jack Zipes explains, fantasy has a unique potential to develop these skills:

> the essential quality of all great fantasy works is linked to their capacity to subvert accepted standards and to provoke readers to re-think their state of being and the institutions that determine the nature of *existence*. ... Good literature for children provokes them to think seriously and critically for themselves, against the grain, and provides hope that they can find the moral and ethical vigor not simply to survive but to live happily with social codes and arrangements that they create themselves and enjoy to their heart's content [230–1, emphasis in original].

Zipes asserts that fantasy texts "play an extremely crucial role in furthering the critical consciousness of the young" by fostering the skills of critical literacy—which moves beyond simply knowing *how* to read and involves readers questioning and reflecting on what has been read and, by extension, themselves and the world (210). O'Keefe's understanding of fantasy as superior to realistic fiction for young readers reaches the same conclusions: as O'Keefe argues, in fantasy "everything is hypothetical, subject to examination" and, therefore, is inviting of critical reading and engagement (11), resulting in a natural capacity to address and develop critical literacy skills. Fantastic school stories, already favorably positioned to offer commentary and critique on education due to their status as school stories, further benefit from the introduction of fantasy elements that endorse and foster the development of critical reading and inquiry skills, offering examples and tools for engaging with reality through the texts' metaphorical re-presentations.

One of the ways to access the metaphoric meanings, the commentaries and critiques on reality, the alternative possibilities, and the implicit and overt plans for action present in fantasy fiction—including fantastic school stories—is through the method of thematic criticism. Farah Mendlesohn defines thematic criticism "as a deconstructionist route into a text's deeper meaning, finding it richer and more meaningful than it might otherwise be read," employing "a mode of reader

Introduction

response criticism" and acknowledging the reader's role in finding and assigning meaning ("Thematic" 125–26). In essence, thematic criticism is a "self-conscious filter, in which the reader-critic understands reading as an active experience"—moving away from questions of authorial intent, this method acknowledges the agency and responsibility of the reader in discovering and applying particular meanings based on their engagement with the text, which is influenced by their own experiences and position in sociocultural and political structures (Mendlesohn "Thematic" 127). Taking this methodology and these theoretical frameworks from the traditions of fantasy analysis and combining them with the critical focus on schooling of the school story genre, as outlined above, and theories of education, as outlined below, creates a comprehensive interdisciplinary method for approaching an analysis of fantastic school stories, considering them in their complete context and acknowledging the full extent of their potential.

Representing Education in Literature

As outlined above, to consider a fantastic school story within its two generic contexts is still to view it only in part, though admittedly in greater part than to limit its analysis to only one genre tradition. However, to fully comprehend, and so begin to analyze and explicate, the entirety of the text requires not just an awareness of *how* it makes its presentation—replicating or subverting traditions, juxtaposing impossibility with reality—or of *why* it makes its presentation—socialization, glorification, critique, challenge—but also *what* it presents: an education. It is not enough to look at the ways in which the incorporation of the fantastic alters the traditions of the school story genre; the implications and complications of the resulting education that is represented in the text must also be considered and interrogated. After all, one cannot understand the ways in which the incorporation of fantastic elements exaggerates or mitigates, emphasizes or hides, enforces or removes certain aspects or realities of education if one does not know how these changed aspects usually appear, or how these alterations will interact with the whole.

The most important element of education theory to understand for this purpose is the concept of a hidden curriculum. The interactions of

Introduction

school institutions and the larger societal contexts in which they are located create an important, powerful, but "often-ignored" relationship (Giroux and Penna 101): as a result, as Henry Giroux and Anthony Penna rightly claim, "[t]he belief that schooling can be defined as the sum of its official course offerings is a naïve one" (100). Simply stated, one of the purposes of schooling is indoctrination into the norms, values, structures, and beliefs of the dominant culture. This aspect of schooling plays out largely behind the scenes, in unspoken values and expectations that are not the content of lessons but nevertheless influence and inform them. This is the hidden curriculum.

The term "hidden curriculum" signifies a nuanced and complex set of social structures, practices, and expectations surrounding education which serve to (re)produce norms, including those related to gender, class, race, religion, and morality, with varying degrees of intentionality (Vallance 11). Here, the definitions primarily employed are those offered by Elizabeth Vallance and by Giroux and Penna: Giroux and Penna define a hidden curriculum as "the unstated norms, values, and beliefs that are transmitted to students through the underlying structure of meaning in both the formal content as well as the social relations of school and classroom life" (102), while Vallance adds a focus on the "non-academic but educationally significant consequences of schooling that occur systematically but are not made explicit" as well as "the social-control function of schooling" (11). It is important to note that "hidden curricula" and "non-academic learning" are not identical concepts, for non-academic topics can be part of explicitly-stated instructional goals, whereas hidden curricula are specifically focused on what is not overtly acknowledged as a goal or result of schooling (Martin 124). In other words, a hidden curriculum is "the systematic *side effects* of schooling" (Vallance 11, emphasis added) and not the explicitly-stated or primary effects.

This aspect of schooling has only become "hidden" relatively recently; historically, as Michael Apple and Nancy King demonstrate, it was the "overt function of schools" (87)—acquiring access to cultural capital was the explicit purpose behind attending school, reflected in early school stories such as Tom Hughes' *Tom Brown*.[5] As perceived sociocultural needs shifted, changing the accompanying perception of the purpose of schooling, what was once an explicit and accepted function of education became an unacknowledged reality as the structural

Introduction

institutions designed to support this agenda proceeded unchanged even as public attention moved to other explicit purposes (Apple and King 87–88). What and how schools decide to teach continues to be influenced and informed by—and, in turn, to influence and inform—cultural capital; schools continue, as Apple and King establish, to perform the role of "giving legitimacy to certain categories and forms of knowledge" and indoctrinating students into the traditions and norms of the dominant culture (83). Kathleen Lynch further explicates the relationship between controlling school knowledge and broader social control, explaining that:

> as schools are the principle institutions in our society, for both producing and reproducing cultural forms, those skills and knowledge forms which it fails to credentialize become marginalized in the wider sociocultural agenda. Schools only give accreditation to a limited range of mental labours; hence other labour ... is marginalized by the schooling process [xiii].

This privileging and reproducing of the dominant culture, and the pressure on all students to subscribe to the norms and values championed by the institution, results in what Pierre Bourdieu and Jean-Claude Passeron recognize as "symbolic violence" (5), subjugating all individuals to the dominant culture. As Apple and King note, asking "*Whose* meanings are collected and distributed through the overt and hidden curriculum in schools" is essential (84, emphasis in original), and reveals which specific social and cultural groups are dominant in influencing the institution at the time.

Though the dominant culture is the primary influence on what is taught in classrooms, and all students are thereby exposed to its norms, values, and traditions (and the aspirations and ambitions attendant with these), this is not to say that all students are, as a result, equally able to access and deploy cultural capital to achieve these ends and participate in these societal structures. Lisa Delpit outlines the inherent (dis)advantages attendant on a student's social position upon entering school: students from the dominant culture, already subconsciously aware of the "codes" or rules for participating in power that are established and enforced by their social group, enter school institutions better able to engage with these unspoken but influential rules. This preparation increases their odds of success as well as the amount of cultural capital they will accrue through the process of schooling.

Introduction

Conversely, students from outside the dominant culture, unfamiliar with the unstated requirements for engaging with power, struggle to participate in the educational institution and, later, in the society for which schooling is designed to prepare them—unless these rules are made explicit, which rarely happens. It is not easy to make these unspoken rules explicit: they are kept "veiled" and unaddressed both by a lack of awareness of the existence of such implicit structures and by the ways in which these structures influence behavior (Delpit 32, 35). The everyday interactions and choices of teachers and administrators, who act to protect their own status and power (Lynch xii), perpetuate a status quo which (re)creates and increases inequalities, such as those predicated on class, race, or gender (Lynch xi). Students who enter the institution with the privileges inherent in belonging to the dominant culture find greater success in school, while those from outside this specific group face additional barriers of needing to learn—and then obey—unspoken rules, reinforcing and often widening gaps in achievement and success between groups.

When a school or any deliberate process of education is represented in literature, a hidden curriculum—and the attendant distribution of cultural capital and perpetuation of inequalities—is represented as well. An awareness of this concept as it exists and operates in reality allows for an analysis of its literary recreation; knowing that hidden ideologies influence education practice and pedagogy prompts us to look for these elements in our reading practice. This active search is essential in analyzing this aspect of both real and fictional educations: "[a] hidden curriculum," Jane Martin asserts, "is not something one just finds; one must go hunting for it" (126). To engage in such a hunt, Martin explains, it is necessary to "find out what is learned as a result of the practices, procedures, rules, relationships, structures, and physical characteristics which constitute a given setting" (126)—interrogating what Apple and King refer to as the "'deep structure' of the school experience" (88). Apple and King offer a series of questions to help identify and explicate these deep structures and their consequences—which, applied to literary representations of education and schooling, illuminate the presence of implicit ideologies and sociocultural control and replication in texts:

> What underlying meanings are negotiated and transmitted in schools behind the actual formal "stuff" of curriculum content? What happens

Introduction

when knowledge is filtered through teachers? Through what categories of normality and deviance is knowledge filtered? What is the basic and organizing framework of normative conceptual knowledge that students actually get? In short, what is the curriculum in use? [88–89]

Apple and King add to this list one further question: "In whose interests do schools often function today?" (97). "Only by seeing the deeper structure," Apple and King claim, "does it become obvious that social norms, institutions, and ideological rules are ongoingly sustained by the day-to-day interaction of commonsense [sic] actors as they go about their normal practices," especially in classrooms (88–89). An awareness of the deeper structures inherent in literary representations is similarly necessary to understand what ideologies are at play in the text—with which readers are engaging, consciously or otherwise.

Fantasy literature, which is well-situated to draw attention to unspoken or unacknowledged aspects of sociocultural structures, and the method of thematic criticism are natural fits both for foregrounding the presence of hidden curricula and for engaging in an active "hunt" for them. Taking the questions posed by Apple and King and adapting them for the fantastic school story subgenre—What underlying meanings and ideologies are transmitted along with the formal content? How do teachers and administrators filter and distort knowledge? How do societal norms and expectations filter and distort knowledge? Whose interests shape and inform educational institutions, processes, and outcomes? How do schools distribute social, cultural, and economic capital in relation with one another?—we can then incorporate them as part of a thematic criticism approach to examining the ways in which fantastic school stories foreground the presence of hidden curricula for interrogation, rounding out the interdisciplinary framework for analyzing the subgenre of fantastic school stories.

Analyzing Fantastic School Stories

Analyzing fantastic school stories requires a framework which allows for a comprehensive analysis of these texts that is attendant to the generic and sociocultural contexts from which they arise and upon which they comment. Constructing this subgenre-specific framework is a matter of combining aspects from the analytical traditions of the

Introduction

fields which inform and underly fantastic school stories. From the analysis of the school story genre, we take the attention to broader themes of socialization and attitudes towards schools and schooling. To this we add the method of thematic criticism, foregrounding fantasy's commentary and critique on real world issues, from the field of fantasy literature. The final component is an awareness of hidden curricula and their impacts and implications from scholarship on schools and education, as well as a set of key questions for interrogating these deeper structures. It is this approach, using this comprehensive combined framework, that is most productive for interrogating fantastic school stories as texts in a unique subgenre, allowing us to attend to the ways in which the incorporation of fantastic elements impacts the representation of schooling and the ways in which the text might function to socialize readers into either complacency or critical inquiry.

Most existing scholarship on the fantastic school story subgenre has not approached the analysis of texts with this interdisciplinary three-part framework necessary to interrogate fully these aspects and their impact. Taking cues primarily from school story scholarship, most criticism that explicitly identifies this subgenre as its focus concerns itself primarily with content and stock characteristics. For instance, Pesold—identifying the "witch school story" at the intersection of school story and children's fantasy—is preoccupied with the characteristic content of the subgenre. Pesold's book details the difference in content between "escapist" and "metaphorical" witch school stories (135–136) and, in analyzing exemplary texts from the subgenre such as Jill Murphy's *The Worst Witch*, focuses on "features ... typical of the witch school story," cataloguing characteristics including a deemphasis on academics, Gothic settings, the prominence of black, the inclusion of subjects such as potions and chanting, and the presence of broomsticks and familiars (Pesold 138–141). For Pesold, defining a witch school story seems to require locating key characteristic content either in faithful recreation or "playful subversion" (241).

Similarly, when looking at individual texts or series in the subgenre, scholars such as Elizabeth A. Galway and Steege—undertaking separate analytical comparisons of J.K. Rowling's *Harry Potter* series to Hughes' foundational school story *Tom Brown's School Days*—also employ a definition of the school story genre based on its content. Both Galway and Steege focus their analysis of Rowling's fantasy series on the premise

Introduction

that it is, essentially, a school story and are preoccupied with detailing the shared characteristic content between these two texts and the school story tradition at large, from sports, headmasters, prefects, journeys to school, house systems and loyalty, a deemphasis on academics, and the paradoxical importance of both a code of conduct and frequent rule-breaking, devoting the majority of their analysis to such cataloguing (Galway 69–81; Steege 143–152).

These sorts of critical examinations, while they do serve to position individual fantasy texts within the school story genre and begin the work of expanding the borders for analysis of the genre's key themes into other works, nevertheless perpetuate the problematic content-based definition of the school story genre. As a result, such studies neglect significant themes of the school story genre beyond stock characteristics. More problematically, they also fail to apply analytical methods from fantasy scholarship to interrogate the texts as fantasy literature and illuminate the relationship to, and potential subversion or challenge of, the real world in which they are situated, and they do not attend to the underlying ideologies present in the representations of education through their hidden curricula or the ways in which the fantastic elements interact with these implicit ideologies.

Not all scholarship on fantastic school stories, however, has been limited to examinations of characteristic content; there is existing scholarship that does address the representation of education in children's and young adult fantasy texts with a broader purview, analyzing depictions of education and the commentaries and critiques presented. Elisabeth Rose Gruner's work, for instance, engages in this type of analysis, applying Clark's premise that school stories are themselves schools in an examination of fantastic school stories—as Gruner defines them, "the fantasy novel focused on the education of a witch or a wizard" ("Teach" 217). Gruner argues that these texts, through their depictions of education, "school [the reader] in how to learn" ("Teach" 217), concluding that "reading fantasy novels provides not only an insight into how children learn but a model of it," as the texts guide readers through an unfamiliar world, encouraging and helping them to reflect, ask questions, make connections, and come to conclusions about these new experiences based on evidence and evaluation (Gruner "Teach" 232). This study moves beyond examinations of characteristic content—emphasizing instead the central focus on education as the

Introduction

text's purpose—and explicates the commentaries, critiques, and messages related to education within these fantasy texts. However, though Gruner's analysis of fantastic school stories employs key elements of the three-part approach outlined above, it still does not attend to the hidden curricula of the texts or pay critical attention to the particular impact, for both characters and readers, of the inclusion of fantastic elements in the representation of education.

Whether they take these texts primarily as school stories or go further and attend to the representation of education in the text and its potential effect on readers, analyses such as these, in employing a partial approach, fail to consider fantastic school stories in all of their contexts. Undertaking analysis with the three-part framework attends to the inheritances, implications, and possibilities of the school story genre, fantastic literature, and the hidden curricula inherent in education and its representation. Doing so allows for a more nuanced and complex analysis of the impact of fantastic elements in these narratives, foregrounding the ways in which these elements exaggerate, embody, or enforce underlying ideologies and norms and offer encouragement to readers to interrogate these aspects of the text and their own schooling experiences.

Analyzing Wizard's Hall

Yolen's *Wizard's Hall*—and the scene highlighted at the beginning of this chapter, in which readers learn that students are not only expected, but required, to travel according to their gender—is most productively analyzed using the three-part interdisciplinary framework for interrogating fantastic school stories outlined above. This moment, in which the outsider protagonist is introduced to the rules of the school, is a common element in the school story genre, as is the mention of school rules in general: usually brought to the forefront through the related tradition of rule-breaking, school rules and the chance to disobey them play an important role in the protagonist's development into the ideal subject (Galway 69). Having rules of conduct based on gender is also common in schools, fictional or real, with rules around access to areas such as change rooms or dormitories almost always falling along binary-gender lines.

Introduction

The fact that Wizard's Hall is a magic school, however, changes the ways in which the protagonist is able to interact with this rule: where non-fantastic schools can create and manually enforce similar rules, these rules *can* be broken by students (who may or may not be caught and punished for their transgressions). This potential for misbehavior is an important element, as it allows the protagonist to develop their independence and teaches them to "distinguish between authority that is just and that which is abused" (Galway 81). At this fantastic school, however, it is *literally impossible* to disobey this edict and transgress. Students, such as the un-initiated Thornmallow, may be able to walk in the wrong direction, but the magical geography of the school means that they cannot access any of the school's resources—dormitories, libraries, meal halls, offices, classes—if they do not act in accordance with the gendered travel rule. Thornmallow may be able to break the rule on a superficial level, but this rule-breaking does not present the usual opportunities for growth and development and will prevent him from learning anything at all until and unless he behaves in accordance with this requirement.

In *Wizard's Hall*, magic is power: the power to change appearances or to change the actual fact or fabric of something. This is not an ability that everyone has or can have, and gaining this ability (and this power) is the promise of studying at Wizard's Hall. But to study at the school—to actually attend classes, research in the library, function as a student—individuals must obey the rule of gendered travel. This obedience requires all students to accept the underlying assumption the rule enforces: in physically dividing students along gender lines and forcing them to walk opposite directions, this rule (re)creates ideas of irreconcilable gender difference.[6] For individuals studying in a school where men and women must literally take different paths to access the same information and power, the everyday practice of travelling through the school becomes an assertion that there are two genders and that these are, somehow, fundamentally different. Every day they work and walk in Wizard's Hall, students are receiving and internalizing these messages about irreconcilable gender difference and binary gender.

It is possible, of course, that a student at Wizard's Hall could act in accordance with this rule and remain ideologically opposed to and avoid internalizing the implicit assumption informing movement through the school. The way in which the rule operates, however—as exemplified by the way it is explained to Thornmallow—does not encourage a critical

Introduction

awareness of the underlying beliefs, let alone a conscious consideration of, resistance to, or challenge towards them. The rule is explained, not as if it *were* a rule, but as if it were an unalterable fact, an unchangeable reality. There is no mention of the rule being put in place by the teachers nor any explanation behind its purpose; there is also no consideration of the fact that, with the power of magic at their disposal, the teachers could, potentially, change this requirement. It is also not explained as somehow inherent in the structure of the school itself, or any law of magic, which would shift responsibility for this rule from teachers, who might then have room to express disagreement or frustration. Rather, the rule is simply stated and then never considered again, an unchallenged reality supporting unspoken assumptions regarding gender.

To analyze this moment within the framework of the school story genre would be simply to see another example of the inclusion or exclusion of standard content, *with* rules or codes of student conduct included but *without* rule-breaking, while to analyze it simply as fantasy is to miss the ideological implications of the rule which is being unavoidably enforced by the fantastic nature of the school building in which Thornmallow and his peers study. Understanding the ways in which this fantastic element enforces and exaggerates an underlying belief—and the resulting (re)creation and internalization of problematic views towards gender—requires approaching this moment as a representation of education situated within the fantastic school story subgenre and actively looking for the ways in which the fantastic engages with a hidden curriculum.

Viewed within this three-part framework, there are other fantastic elements in Yolen's *Wizard's Hall* which interact in significant ways with the traditions of the school story and the inherent hidden curriculum of the education represented. The exciting climax of *Wizard's Hall*, for instance, sees young Thornmallow vanquish both the grotesque Beast and its evil Master using the text's theory of "correspondence": the idea that someone's name—even when it is not a True Name—relates to and reveals a fundamental aspect of their character (Yolen 93). Knowing that the Master's former wizard name was Nettle, and having researched nettles with his peers in preparation for this confrontation, Thornmallow employs the theory of correspondence to turn the Master's powers against him, defeating him by rhyming off and

Introduction

modifying types of nettles, including "false," "blind," "deaf," and finally, "dead" (Yolen 118–120).

Considering this is the method by which the antagonist is defeated, the theory of correspondence seems to hold considerable weight and power in the world of the narrative. What, then, do we make of the fact that the name given to our protagonist suggests he is of fundamentally flawed character, especially in combination with the text's suggestion that a person's character is immutable? This name is inextricable from his experience of schooling and the educational institution of Wizard's Hall, as the name is given to him upon his arrival at the school, replacing his former name of Henry. When Magister Oakbend renames him Thornmallow, he explains it as meaning "prickly on the outside, squishy within" (Yolen 11). From here on out, almost every time Thornmallow interacts with teachers at the school, they comment on one or the other of these presumed aspects of his character. Interpreting his words and behavior through these two potential traits, the teachers collectively establish "prickliness" and "squishiness" as flaws through the comments and associations they make.

Whenever Thornmallow is perceived as being disobedient or challenging—such as when he expresses reluctance to change his name (Yolen 10), doesn't agree with a teacher (Yolen 23), corrects a teacher on his new name (Yolen 27), or speaks up in the school assembly (Yolen 46)—he is called "prickly." Alternatively, whenever Thornmallow demonstrates excessive emotion or a lack of confidence and skill—such as when he hesitates in explaining himself (Yolen 13), gets emotional after unintentionally destroying a classroom wall and being chastised for it (Yolen 30), is caught unintentionally eavesdropping (Yolen 62), or feels "awful" and "unclean" and cries after killing the Master (Yolen 122)—he is called "squishy."

These consistent rebukes reveal an implied image of the ideal student: one who is obedient and does not ask questions or offer challenges; who is independent, skilled and competent without first requiring instruction. That this is the "ideal" is itself problematic, as it discourages engagement, critical inquiry, and actual teaching. As the protagonist fails to meet this ideal, and because of the power ascribed to names and the idea of correspondence, "Thornmallow" becomes a self-fulfilling prophecy, as his actions and character are continuously interpreted to confirm the bias suggested by his name.[7]

Introduction

Such constant criticism in any context would be damaging to a student, but the importance placed on names at Wizard's Hall through the fantastic element of "correspondence" makes this treatment even more problematic and potentially harmful for Thornmallow. In ascribing this much power and importance to names within the Institution, and behaving as if names are always an accurate reflection of a person's character and personality—and then connecting the aspects of Thornmallow's personality revealed by his name with various undesirable traits and behaviors—the teachers at the school are not simply rebuking Thornmallow's actions, but who he is on a fundamental level. If "Thornmallow" is an accurate representation of the protagonist's character, and it means prickly and squishy, and prickly and squishy are consistently and publicly connected with undesirable traits, then the message consistently given to the protagonist is that his character is undesirable and, to be better, he must fundamentally change who he is.

The potential for such a fundamental change is never discussed—rather, the possibility seems to be negated by the fact that the Master's wizard name still holds such power over him. Thornmallow, it seems, has no opportunity for change or growth. In fact, the last line of the novella reiterates the supposed accuracy of this name, emphasizing the fact that he cannot change and demonstrating Thornmallow's internalization of the evaluation of his character: "he waved his hands triumphantly, feeling nicely prickly on the outside and—if truth be known—fairly squishy within" (Yolen 133). Though there is some suggestion with this ending that Thornmallow may be able to redefine for himself what it means to be "prickly" and "squishy," the problematic public association of these characteristics with undesirable behaviors and attitudes throughout the rest of the text undermines Thornmallow's chances to redefine the public (or private) perception of his character.

While analyses of the rule of gendered travel and of Thornmallow's name in the context of correspondence reveal problematic underlying beliefs and values, the difference between Enchanters and Enhancers in this fictional society is perhaps the most troubling fantastic element of *Wizard's Hall*. The distinction between Enchanter and Enhancer is not mentioned until the final pages of the novella, when it is revealed as the explanation for why Thornmallow, who has demonstrated no aptitude for magic, was admitted to Wizard's Hall and was able to defeat the Beast and its Master: although he does not have magical abilities of his

Introduction

own, as an Enhancer, Thornmallow is able to "make any spell someone else works even greater simply by trying" (Yolen 131). The newly restored head of the school explains further to the assembled students and staff:

> "Alone he is only an ordinary boy, the kind who makes our farms run and our roads smooth, who builds our houses and fights our wars. But when he touches wizards he trusts and admires—or their staffs—he makes their magicks better. When he touches wizards he hates and fears, he turns their own evil magicks against them. ... My dear students, my colleagues, my friends: every community needs its enhancers. Even more than it needs its enchanters. They are the ones who appreciate us and understand us and even save us from ourselves" [Yolen 131–132].

Thornmallow, though he has saved the staff and students, as well as the very institution of Wizard's Hall, will not join the magic community as an Enchanter of equal status; rather, he is revealed as the ideal subordinate, the best possible kind of laborer. Classed somewhere between the wizards themselves and the average laborer who is only distantly connected to supporting the elite community of magic wielders, Thornmallow addresses the "need" of the magic community by contributing his effort and his labor to furthering the works of those in power—which will always cause him physical pain as a result of his struggle with the Master (Yolen 132). Despite the suggestion that Enhancers are able to overthrow or destroy corrupt individuals in power, the overall implication presented by the head of the institution is that the most glorious, most admirable position one could hold—the position with which the hero of the story is rewarded—is not a position of power itself, but rather the position immediately below in the social hierarchy that supports and enables those in power.

That Thornmallow's reward is to learn he will never access or wield power, but that he can, instead, serve a lifetime in pain to further and support the power of others, is even more damning than the idea of correspondence and the associations the text draws between undesirable traits and the meaning of "Thornmallow"—for, in the world of the narrative, personalities are immutable *and* those without power cannot ever access it. No one can change or grow, and the highest possible aspiration for those not born into power is to labor directly, as opposed to indirectly, in the service of powerful others. There is no room left for imagining a position in society which is not either oppressed or oppressor. An entire school operating on this premise and socializing students,

Introduction

as future oppressors, into this belief will perpetuate this social hierarchy, as students graduate believing they are deserving of their elite status and, furthermore, that it is an honor to serve them. Graduates will carry these beliefs with them into a wider society that, not having access to magic themselves, does not have the power to resist or challenge the behaviors of the elite predicated on this belief, and former students will return as teachers to perpetually replicate this hierarchy.

Analyzing *Wizard's Hall* as a fantastic school story and paying attention to the presence of a hidden curriculum in its literary representation of education illuminates these problematic attitudes, beliefs and behaviors Thornmallow encounters through his schooling. By nature of its position within both the field of children's literature and the specific genre of school stories, *Wizard's Hall* has the potential—and, on some level, the purpose—to socialize its readers into the beliefs it champions and presents; being simultaneously fantasy, the narrative is also uniquely applicable to the real lives of readers and carries within it the potential to expose this socialization. The fantastic elements of the text foreground the traditions inherited from the school story genre as well as the presence of a hidden curriculum inherent in any education, encouraging an examination of these elements through the process of exaggerating, embodying, and enforcing the underlying ideologies and the implied values. Attending to these possibilities in analyzing the text illuminates the ways in which the fantastic elements of Yolen's novella further the socialization of the protagonist into certain beliefs: about fundamental gender difference and binary gender, about desirable and undesirable behavior and the immutability of character, and about the privilege of a subservient role and the inescapable hierarchy of oppressor and oppressed. This approach also acknowledges that the novella, due to the ability of these same fantastic elements to draw critical attention to aspects such as these implicit ideologies, simultaneously holds the potential to subvert the replication of this socialization for readers and, instead, to foster a critical reading practice.

Conclusion

In each of the following chapters, the three-part framework introduced here is used to analyze a series of fantastic school stories

Introduction

simultaneously as a school story, a fantasy narrative, and as a representation of education, drawing out particular aspects of the schooling experience made visible by the combination of magic and the mundane. I consider both the ways in which the presentation of these elements is enhanced by the unique possibilities of the fantastic school story subgenre and how, if at all, their representation socializes readers into a critical awareness of the problems inherent in these structures, beginning in Chapter 1 with an analysis of testing practices in Rowling's *Harry Potter* series.

Chapter 1

Ordinary Wizarding Levels

High-Stakes Standardized Testing in J.K. Rowling's Harry Potter *Series*

> Their teachers were no longer setting them homework; lessons were devoted to revising those topics the teachers thought most likely to come up in the exams.
> —J.K. Rowling,
> *Harry Potter and the Order of the Phoenix*

> [J]ust how much faith should we put in the test and in procedures that use the scores as evidence to determine anything beyond whether a student did well or poorly on that specific test? Can we rely on the tests to actually and accurately measure knowledge and capability in a particular subject area?
> —Andrew K. Milton,
> *The Normal Accident Theory of Education*

In this chapter, the first of four dedicated examinations of fantastic school stories using the three-part framework from the Introduction, I use the questions for interrogating the "deep structure" of education to examine the representation of standardized and high-stakes testing in J.K. Rowling's *Harry Potter* series. The analysis is focused on the representation at the level of text, attending to the ways in which testing is presented, how various characters experience and react to the educational testing depicted, and what inferences about testing the text encourages readers to make as the usually mundane educational topic is brought to the forefront through the magical subjects in which the characters undertake their assessments.

Schools of Magic

Introduction

The *Harry Potter* series presents seven core texts in which to consider the institution of Hogwarts School for Witchcraft and Wizardry. With such a wealth and variety of material, examining the representation of education in Rowling's series is a fruitful endeavor, and one in which many scholars have engaged. Previous approaches to considering education and schooling in Rowling's series include: looking at representations of teachers and their pedagogies (Birch; Black and Eisenwine; de Vita; Dickinson; McDaniel; Stypczynski; Wong), occasionally drawing lessons for educators from the series (Beaton; Conn; Skulnick and Goodman; Zoller Booth and Booth); articulating practices such as self-teaching, inquiry-based learning, authentic learning,[1] and experiential learning beyond the classroom seen in the texts (Dickinson; Elster; Gruner "Teach"; Hopkins); examining the socializing function of and the implicit ideologies in a Hogwarts education (Alton; Battis; Black and Eisenwine; Chappell; Gutiérrez; Lacoss; Lavoie; Nikolajeva *Power*; Steege; Tribunella); interrogating Rowling's series as school stories, including their replication of the sexism and elitism inherent in the genre (Cockrell; Galway; Kirkpatrick; Mendlesohn "Crowning"; Pesold; Pinsent "Education" and "Theories"; Pugh and Wallace; Reimer; Sims; Steege; Tribunella; Webb; Westman); positioning Hogwarts as the "real protagonist" of the series (Gutiérrez); analyzing issues of curriculum control between the school and the Ministry (Helfenbein and Brown); and noting the ways in which it is the "sustained tension between the fantastic and the ordinary"—in large part through the representation of schooling—that gives the series its appeal (Sunderland 207; see also Eccleshare; Maier).

An analysis of the hidden curriculum writ large at Hogwarts would require much more than a single chapter—it would, perhaps, require even more than a single book. From the geographic location of the House dormitories and the inequality of access to the binary gender's rooms to the competitions for the Quidditch and House Cups and the five tables in the Great Hall, the quantity of material necessitating analysis even before we consider classroom practices and the actual teaching that occurs is prohibitive. To that end, this chapter will focus on a single element of the education experiences of Harry and his peers: testing. There are two categories of tests which Hogwarts students

1. Ordinary Wizarding Levels

take: the teacher-facilitated end-of-year exams in each subject, and the externally-created, administered, and evaluated Ordinary Wizarding Levels (OWLs) and Nastily Exhausting Wizarding Tests (NEWTs), assessing multiple years of learning and for which externally-recognized credentials are awarded. While an analysis of testing and examinations at Hogwarts is far from a comprehensive understanding of the institution's hidden curriculum, this narrow scope allows for the sort of in-depth investigation required to explicate fully the inherent ideology of any given component of teaching and learning.

As Jonathan Alexander and Rebecca Black note, with the current focus on high stakes educational testing in places including Britain and the United States, "it is not surprising that various manifestations of high stakes testing have made their way into popular fiction for young adults" (208). Alexander and Black limit their analysis of testing in Rowling's series to a brief examination of the Sorting Hat, which initially appears as a "relatively benign" representation of testing (208), but ultimately proves to be "extreme and consequential," with significant impact on future careers and sense of self (227). In this chapter, we will consider the representation of high stakes testing through both the end-of-year exams and the standardized examinations in the fifth and seventh years—which, while they may also initially appear benign, prove to have a detrimental effect on equality and inclusion in British wizarding society through their role in determining the career eligibility of Hogwarts graduates. As we ask critical questions about examination practices and discourses at Hogwarts, we reveal the ways in which the representation of testing, particularly the OWLs, establish rote performance as a key outcome of learning and privilege the associated credentials as being more valuable than the skills and aptitudes they are meant to represent, as well as the ways in which these tests function in wizarding society as gatekeeping measures perpetuating discriminatory ideologies. Ultimately, the representation of testing in the series uncritically reflects the current issues in the global testing culture and fails to challenge the false meritocracy upon which employment in British wizarding society is premised.

While the *Harry Potter* series are written in a British context—and so obviously speak to contemporary realities of secondary schooling in the United Kingdom, including the A Level exam system—the series' origins by no means preclude commentary on and reflection of the realities of testing beyond Britain's borders. Standardized and high-stakes testing is truly a global phenomenon: William Smith goes so far as to assert the existence of a "global testing culture," which he defines as "a culture in which high-stakes standardized testing is accepted as a foundational practice in education and shapes how education is understood in society and used by its stakeholders" ("Introduction" 10). Hogwarts and the OWLs, as fictional tests in an imaginary school teaching fantastic subjects, serve equally well as fodder for exploring issues related to testing in specific education contexts and at more general, abstracted levels. Focusing in this chapter on general issues with testing at Hogwarts, the conclusions drawn are globally applicable, whether considered in comparison to state testing or the SAT, LSAT, and ACT in the United States, provincial testing in Canada, A Levels in Britain, or one of the numerous other testing systems in countries around the world.

Before we move further into our analysis, it is worth understanding what precisely "high-stakes standardized testing" means and how the end-of-year exams and the OWLs and NEWTs of Hogwarts fit within this system. Tests can be subdivided into different categories depending upon their central purpose and the means of their implementation, as outlined by Ross Traub. *Achievement tests* evaluate how well an individual has mastered particular skills or knowledge within a subject (Traub 5); at a larger scale, *examinations* measure the comprehensive mastery of skills and knowledge for a subject or course, typically at the end of a course or the student's formal education (Traub 7). A *standardized achievement test* is always facilitated and scored in the same way each time and in each place it is given (Traub 5); standardized tests can be achievement tests or examinations. The final category is *assessments*, which measure something other than an individual student's mastery of the subject, such as the evaluations used in the name of accountability; these are typically standardized (Traub 7).

Considering the tests at Hogwarts—the end-of-year exams and the OWLs and NEWTs—we see two types of examinations, measuring students' learning in a subject in a single year or across multiple years. As there is no textual evidence comparing the end-of-year exams undertaken by Harry's cohort with those of other years, nor any discussion of these tests by their instructors, we cannot distinguish whether these exams are standardized or not. With the OWLs and NEWTs, however, the textual evidence suggests that they are, at least to some extent,

1. Ordinary Wizarding Levels

standardized: as discussed below, teachers feel confident that the same topics will be covered each year, and within each cohort we know that students sit the same written portions and undertake the same practical tasks. While the lack of secrecy around the exam papers once students have sat the examination suggests that, at least for the written portions, they are not identical across years (Order 566–8, 628), the tests given each year, as Andrew Milton has demonstrated, will nevertheless be nearly identical in terms of requirements, if not content, as test items can only differ so much while remaining within acceptable parameters and will therefore replicate consistent patterns, which students can learn to predict and master (87–88). Focused as the narration is on Harry and his friends, there is no indication in the texts of how OWL or NEWT results may be used by the Hogwarts instructors or administration or by the Wizarding Examinations Authority beyond evaluating student mastery, nor is there any sense of whether the results are reported to the Ministry and to what use they may be put there; while we can certainly speculate on the other ways in which the OWLs and NEWTs may be used, there is no definitive textual evidence that suggests they are assessments.

In addition to being standardized examinations, the OWLs and NEWTs—and, to a lesser extent, the end-of-year exams—are also high-stakes. As Diane Meaghan and François Casas explain, *high-stakes tests* are those that do not take into consideration previous performance or comparative improvement and use only the test results to determine the future courses for which a student is eligible, whether they may advance, or whether they may graduate or be awarded a credential (47, note 3). Whether or not the end-of-year exams are truly high-stakes is debatable: the exams are cancelled for the whole school twice during Harry's academic career, and Harry is personally exempted for an additional third year, and this seems to have no impact on any student's progress into the next year, nor is there mention of any student (even the most incompetent) who is prevented from moving into the next year of study as a result of their end-of-year exam performance. In contrast, the high-stakes nature of the OWLs and NEWTs is undeniable, as students' work in the previous years is given no consideration and it is their performance on these tests alone which determine their OWL and NEWT scores, in turn dictating what further courses they may take and the careers for which they are eligible, as discussed below.

So what is happening with these high-stakes standardized tests at Hogwarts? What is the hidden curriculum of the OWLs, and what values and structures are being reinforced for both Hogwarts pupils and readers through the examinations? Drawing on the questions for interrogating the "deep structure" of education presented in the Introduction, this remainder of this chapter examines the representation of high-stakes educational testing in the *Harry Potter* series. The first section explicates the social and political purposes the exams at Hogwarts serve beyond their explicitly-stated goal of evaluating student achievement, including the ways in which they frame the purpose and value of education, influence the instructional practice of Hogwarts teachers, and function as gatekeeping measures. The following section then analyzes the ways in which the representation of testing in the texts socializes both pupils and readers into an acceptance of testing as an unproblematic norm, as the carnivalesque structure of the series fails to achieve its subversive potential and instead functions to re-confirm the role of high-stakes testing in the fictional society. The unrealized carnivalesque in the series presents the OWLs and NEWTs, and their function in wizarding society, without prompting critique and awareness of these norms as arbitrary or of the damaging repercussions of using test scores to perpetuate a false meritocracy.

The Hidden Curriculum of Testing

Decontextualized Skills and Facts

In answering the first of the questions for interrogating the "deep structure" of education—what underlying meanings and ideologies are transmitted along with the formal content?—we must consider what knowledge is tested and how this knowledge is assessed. As we develop these answers, we see the ways in which both the end-of-year exams and the OWLs participate in framing the purpose of education as receiving credentials, rather than mastering subject knowledge and skills. Through this prioritization of credentials, Hogwarts functions as the gatekeeper to future employment, informing which students are eligible for which positions in the guise of a meritocracy based on academic achievement.

1. Ordinary Wizarding Levels

Since Harry, the focalizing protagonist, is exempt from the exams in his fourth year as Triwizard Champion, and the exams are cancelled in his second and sixth years in recognition of the extracurricular events within the institution, readers only see two end-of-year exam periods in detail. Nevertheless, the information given on these culminating tests in Harry's first and third years is enough to establish a general sense of what knowledge is evaluated. In studying for the first-year exams, Harry, Ron, and Hermione focus on abstracted facts, such as the uses of dragon blood, the ingredients for various potions, or the dates of historic discoveries and rebellions (Stone 167–8, 179), as well as the performance of memorized wand movements and incantations, including memorizing which spell produces which effect (Stone 167–8, 179).

What constitutes a typical end-of-year exam is established in the first book, where written papers are completed in a large, hot classroom with "special, new quills ... bewitched with an Anti-Cheating spell" (Stone 191) and followed by practical demonstrations, showing us how student learning is assessed:

> Professor Flitwick called them one by one into his class to see if they could make a pineapple tap dance across a desk. Professor McGonagall watched them turn a mouse into a snuff-box—points were given for how pretty the snuff-box was, but taken away if it had whiskers. Snape made them all nervous, breathing down their necks while they tried to remember how to make a Forgetfulness potion [Stone 191].

The exception to this pattern is History of Magic, which constitutes only a written paper, described as "[o]ne hour of answering questions about batty old wizards who'd invented self-stirring cauldrons" (Stone 192). The end-of-year exams in third year mostly maintain this structure: turning teapots into tortoises for Transfiguration; casting Cheering Charms in Charms; tending a Flobberworm in Care of Magical Creatures; brewing Confusing Concoctions in Potions; writing essays on the medieval witch hunts in History of Magic; working in the greenhouses for Herbology; and reading portents in crystal-balls for Divination (Prisoner 233–4, 236–8). With the exception of History of Magic, which is still described as a written exam (Prisoner 234), there is notably no mention of written portions for any other subject, potentially putting even greater weight on the practical tasks students are asked to perform in exams after the first year.

Schools of Magic

Standing out from all the other end-of-year exams—emphasized by the descriptor of "unusual"—is Harry's third-year Defense Against the Dark Arts exam set by Professor Lupin:

> Professor Lupin had compiled the most unusual exam any of them had ever taken; a sort of obstacle course outside in the sun, where they had to wade across a deep paddling pool containing a Grindylow, cross a series of potholes full of Red Caps, squish their way across a patch of marsh, ignoring the misleading directions from a Hinkypunk, then climb into an old trunk and battle with a new Boggart [Prisoner 234].

Where the other end-of-year exams decontextualize the performance of various skills and the recall of facts, Lupin's exam attempts to re-contextualize the abilities and knowledge being assessed. Rather than asking students to explain how to perform these tasks or the dangers represented by the various creatures, or having students identify and cast spells in the typical classroom context, this exam asks students to actively apply what they have learned throughout the year. Lupin's exam is a performance-based assessment, requiring students to use what they have learned in an authentic task, the successful performance of which indicates a deeper understanding of the subject and an ability to connect their knowledge to real-world situations, providing a better measure of students' actual learning in a subject (Firestone and Schorr 3). We know that each of the creatures included on this exam has been covered in Lupin's classes: we see in detail their lessons on Boggarts (Prisoner 99–106), hear of their time on Red Caps (Prisoner 107), know that their lessons involve a Grindylow (Prisoner 116), and see them address Hinkypunks (Prisoner 139). Despite this, Lupin's exam proves more challenging than those in other subjects. Ron struggles with the Hinkypunk, Hermione is unable to best the Boggart, and all students are required to demonstrate their subject mastery in an unfamiliar way (Prisoner 234). While this third-year Defense Against the Dark Arts exam ultimately generates a more accurate evaluation of students' abilities than the typical end-of-year exam, we can see it is a structure with which students are unfamiliar and for which they are therefore unprepared.

Lupin's exam seems to be the proverbial exception that proves the rule, and the typical end-of-year exam at Hogwarts is established as the decontextualized recall of facts and rote performance of skills. These

1. Ordinary Wizarding Levels

typical exams are limited, as one task is understood to represent an entire year's learning in the subject; furthermore, this single representative task requires students to perform a routine (cast a spell) or engage in purely factual recall, rather than engaging in higher-order application or analysis. As Derek Copp demonstrates, it is impossible for even a test with multiple tasks to effectively and comprehensively evaluate all of the intended learning for any subject (471); furthermore, having students recite basic facts and perform basic skills does not indicate readiness for or ability in higher-level thinking (Milton 91), nor does it facilitate or draw on authentic learning (Volante n.p.). These end-of-year exams, as tests most often do, prioritize declarative knowledge and decontextualized skills (Volante n.p.), particularly the single skills selected as test items, implying that facility with these single tasks adequately represents mastery of an entire subject—priorities and implications that we see magnified with the OWLs.

Overall, the purpose and internal value of the end-of-year exams are difficult to determine, as both the implementation of these tests and the institutional discourse surrounding them are inconsistent and unclear regarding their importance and their function in determining student advancement. While it is established through Hermione in Harry's first year that passing the exams is a requirement to advance to the next year (Stone 167), the actual events throughout the series suggests this is not true. Take, for instance, official communications from staff regarding the examinations in Harry's second year: insisting at first that the end-of-year exams are of such importance that the school must remain open and exams must be written despite the mortal peril to all present (Chamber 210), the exams are then cancelled "as a school treat" when staff and students are no longer in danger (Chamber 210). Harry's exemption from the exams in his fourth year further complicates the claims of their centrality to students' education, as does Harry's speculation that Dumbledore intervened to prevent Snape from failing Harry in Potions following Harry's personal altercation with Professor Snape at the end of the third year (Prisoner 313). Even Hermione, by far the most academically-driven of the main trio, prioritizes extracurricular activities over exam revision in their fourth year (Goblet 528, 533), a marked change from her original insistence on their absolutely essential role in her education. In practice, end-of-year exams seem to be hurdles over which each student must jump when asked, but whether or not

Schools of Magic

they leave the hurdles standing is of less consequence than having run the course at all.

Turning now to the OWLs, we can see that what knowledge is assessed and how it is evaluated is not substantially different from the end-of-year exams. Given the inconsistent rhetoric surrounding the importance and purpose of the end-of-year exams in their own right, it would not be unfounded to conclude that the primary function of these yearly tests is to provide students with practice in this type of test-taking so that, when credentials are at stake, students are familiar with the process of testing. Over the two weeks of the OWLs, the fifth-year students write theory papers in the mornings and perform practical examinations in the afternoons (Order 625). As with the end-of-year exams, the OWLs ask students to recite and perform memorized routines without engaging higher-order skills or deeper understanding. For instance, the first question on Harry's Charms exam asks for recall of basic facts: *"(a) Give the incantation and (b) describe the wand movement required to make objects fly"* (Order 628, emphasis in original). Other questions in the written portions include defining a Switching Spell (Order 629), describing the effects of Polyjuice Potion (Order 631), and naming Jupiter's moons (Order 632), which similarly ask for recall and recitation.

Surprisingly, it is History of Magic—the least engaging of the classes—which demonstrates the greatest requirement for analysis and application in the written portions. While the majority of the questions fall into the same category of basic recall as seen with other subjects, such as *"How was the Statute of Secrecy breached in 1749 and what measures were introduced to prevent a recurrence?"* or the question which asks for a description of the circumstances of the formation of the International Confederation of Wizards and Liechtenstein's refusal to join (Order 639, emphasis in original), there is one notable exception to these usual requirements. The question *"In your opinion, did wand legislation contribute to, or lead to better control of, goblin riots of the eighteenth century?"* requires students to put facts into their broader context and present an argument on the topic, which demands inference and a deeper level of understanding. It is possible that the way in which this topic was taught in class assumed an answer, in which case the question again requires only recall of how the information was presented; however, without knowing how the topic was covered, it is at least somewhat plausible to assume this question is asking students to

1. Ordinary Wizarding Levels

formulate an independent argument, in which case it is the first and only of the questions we see to do so.

The practical portions of the OWLs, with each student tested individually by one of the examiners, also evaluate isolated skills without requiring higher levels of thinking or application. In his Charms practical, we learn that Harry is asked to make an egg cup cartwheel and to perform Levitation and Colour Change Charms (Order 629); with Transfiguration, students Vanish iguanas (Order 629); for Potions, they brew an unspecified concoction (Order 631–2); Divination requires students to read crystal balls, tea leaves, and palms (Order 632–3); and the night-time Astronomy practical has them fill in a star chart (Order 633). In Defense Against the Dark Arts, Harry and his peers are required to perform counter-jinxes and defensive spells, and the fact that there is no mention of a Boggart present when Harry demonstrates a "perfect Boggart banishing spell" suggests that these demonstrations—unlike their third-year exam—are completely decontextualized and are an artificial performance rather than practical application (Order 630).

The Care of Magical Creatures exam, while filled with practical tasks, nevertheless has similar problems:

> students were required to correctly identify the Knarl hidden among a dozen hedgehogs (the trick was to offer them all milk in turn …); then demonstrate correct handling of a Bowtruckle; feed and clean out a Fire Crab without sustaining serious burns; and choose, from a wide selection of food, the diet they would give a sick unicorn [Order 632].

While this practical portion initially seems to include high-level tasks, such as problem-solving to identify the Knarl or the application of knowledge to select the unicorn's diet, the way in which these tasks are reported does not suggest that the exam was challenging or stimulating in this way. Harry does not *discover* or *deduce* a means of identifying the Knarl; rather, he employs a "trick" that he has seemingly memorized for exactly this purpose. Selecting the unicorn's diet, since it does not seem to have been accompanied by any sort of explanation of the choice or particular details they must take into consideration when making their selection, is actually more like a physical multiple-choice question than one requiring higher-level thinking. Handling the Bowtruckle and caring for the Fire Crab are similar demonstrations of performing a memorized routine; though the Fire Crab, at least, does seem to promise an element of the unpredictable which may, at last, require some problem-solving and quick-thinking, we know that students' lessons at the start of their fifth year on Bowtruckles have prepared them to demonstrate this particular skill if they can remember and replicate the proper technique they were shown (Order 233–5).

As with the end-of-year exams, the OWLs consist of low-level questions which ask for factual recall and memorized performance, prioritizing declarative knowledge and decontextualized skills; while many subject exams consist of multiple tasks or written questions, Potions, Transfiguration, and Astronomy are all reported as single-task tests, and even the multiple tasks of the other subjects cannot possibly be a comprehensive representation of five years of subject content. The OWLs not only maintain the implication that mastery of a subject means the ability to perform certain individual skills or recall a handful of "important" facts, but exacerbate this perception, since the successful performance of these representative skills is all that is required to earn the OWL credential in each subject, and these credentials are understood to be adequate career preparation, as discussed below.

Teaching to the Test

What impact do these tests and what they measure have on teaching? Turning to the next question for examining the "deep structure" of education—how do teachers and administrators filter and distort knowledge?—helps us see their effect. The answer, as we shall see, is that teachers adapt their practice to the high-stakes OWLs and NEWTs, engaging in what is called "teaching to the test." This approach reinforces the prioritization of decontextualized and representative facts and skills and positions the achievement of external credentials as the ultimate goal and purpose of education, valuing the attainment of the qualification over the learning and mastery the credential is meant to represent.

When tests require students to recall factual information or replicate a memorized routine rather than requiring higher-order application or analysis, as we see with the end-of-year exams and OWLs at Hogwarts, teachers are indirectly rewarded for employing teaching methods which position students as passive receivers of information and that drill facts over fostering interest, creativity, or even

1. Ordinary Wizarding Levels

understanding (Firestone and Schorr 2; Meaghan and Casas 37). In the global testing culture, teachers feel pressure from multiple sources to ensure that their students perform well (Firestone et al., viii), with a pervasive perception that teachers who do not do everything possible to prepare their students and help them excel on high-stakes tests are "bad" (Smith "Introduction" 14–15). This is particularly the case with exams that are high-stakes for students, directly informing their academic standing or their ability to advance or graduate, but which are not similarly high-stakes for the instructors; research suggests that this is the most common context for problematic test-focused instructional practices (Copp 478–9).

As a result, instructional time and effort is spent developing isolated skills related to the specific test content and which are not likely to be transferable, while more general—and critically important—skills related to analysis, inference, comparison, and evaluation see little to no development as teachers aim to maximize test-preparedness in their students (Meaghan and Casas, 37; Volante n.p.). To prepare their students, teachers spend more time on the subjects that are to be tested that year and replicate the examinations in their instruction, classroom tasks, and evaluations (Firestone and Schorr 11; Milton 78), employing similar tasks and grading schemes to help students "get a feel" for the expectations and standards of the tests (Monfils et al., 48). This preparation lends itself to didactic teaching, specifically by "providing students with routines to follow and plenty of opportunity to practice" through demonstrations followed by student repetition and rote memorization of the facts and skills most likely to be tested (Schorr and Firestone, 162).

This trend in practice is referred to as teaching to the test, which William Firestone and Roberta Schorr acknowledge is an ambiguous term with many possible and overlapping meanings, though the general implication is that "teachers are doing something special to help students do well on a test, often without helping them to better understand the underlying subject matter," consequently reducing the "quality and quantity" of students' learning and privileging didactic teaching practices which render students passive (2). Teaching to the test practices can be divided into two broad categories: embedded preparation, which sees teachers work throughout the year to incorporate preparation and to reflect test content in their everyday practices, and decontextualized preparation, which sees an "intensification" of didactic, teacher-centered practice as students are drilled in facts or taught methods for taking the test through a "special activity" that may or may not be related to regular lessons and course content (Firestone et al., viii; Firestone and Schorr 2). This distinction is also made as curriculum-teaching, which focuses on the knowledge and skills test items are intended to represent, versus item-teaching, which centers on and uses actual test items or very close replicas (Popham 16), and as teaching (to) the curriculum versus teaching to the test (Copp 469).

With the end-of-year exams, which are set by each individual subject teacher, it is generally impossible to tell from the textual evidence provided whether Hogwarts professors are structuring their classroom activities throughout the year to prepare students for pre-determined test tasks or whether teachers are selecting their end-of-year test items on the basis of what was covered throughout the year. In Harry's third year, there is some indication that Professor Flitwick matches his class content to a pre-determined test, as he is able to hint during lessons that Cheering Charms will be evaluated at the end of the year (Prisoner 217–8), though this is not conclusive; with other instructors, including Hagrid and Lupin, there is no concrete evidence from which to infer how they are aligning their lessons and their evaluations. Combined with the general lack of detail on lessons in Harry's first and third years, it is not possible to assess what, if any, test preparation practices Hogwarts instructors engage in around the end-of-year exams.

With the OWLs, however, it is definitively apparent that all of the Hogwarts instructors are engaging in teaching to the test practices, using the upcoming examinations to dictate their instruction. While the instructors do not know precisely what skills and knowledge will be evaluated, since the OWLs are externally set and administered by the Wizarding Examination Authority, this does not prevent the instructors from making every attempt to prepare their students for the particulars of the examinations. Extrapolating the content of the year's exam from what has been asked in previous years,[2] the second-hand, conjectural, and incomplete information instructors are able to glean has a significant influence on their curriculum decisions for the year as they replicate the tendencies of real-world teachers in prioritizing the likely content of the upcoming tests (Meaghan and Casas, 36; Volante n.p.).

We can see the emphasis on test preparation in almost every

1. Ordinary Wizarding Levels

subject from the very first classes of Harry's fifth year, when the OWLs are administered. Examining the subjects for which Harry has had a consistent teacher and which have been represented in substantial detail throughout the core texts of the series in order to compare teacher's instructional practices in the OWL year to their normal methods,[3] as well comparing Care of Magical Creatures as taught by Hagrid and Professor Grubbly-Plank, we can see the ways in which Hogwarts instructors employ teaching to the test practices as they work to prepare students for their OWLs.

Transfiguration and Charms are two subjects in which we see explicit and sustained test preparation practices informing classroom activities and instructional methods in the OWL year. Professors McGonagall and Flitwick both preface their fifth-year instruction with this explicit focus, spending "the first fifteen minutes of their lessons lecturing the class on the importance of OWLs" (Order 231). Flitwick reminds his students of the influence of these qualifications on their future career prospects and ambitions, then dedicates the remainder of the first class to test preparation: "They then spent over an hour revising Summoning Charms, which according to Professor Flitwick were bound to come up in their OWL" (Order 232). From the very first, Flitwick privileges reviewing likely test topics and skills over new content, and has students preparing at the level of rote memorization and repetition rather than seeking to foster greater understanding or expanding their facility.

McGonagall takes a slightly different approach in Transfiguration, also beginning test preparation immediately but having students begin with Vanishing Spells, which she explains are "among the most difficult magic you will be tested on in your OWL" (Order 233). Considering only Hermione is successful with the spell in this first class, we see McGonagall's assessment is accurate, and we can perhaps appreciate her strategy of giving students as much time as possible to master the most difficult of the likely test items—an extension of her approach in the previous year, when she pre-emptively increased their workloads to help them begin preparing for their OWLs well in advance (Goblet 205). While McGonagall does teach something new, the choice is also dictated by likely test topics and by a desire to see students well-prepared for the OWLs. We see in later classes that McGonagall's plan for helping students master the Vanishing Spell includes gradually increasing the complexity of their practice, beginning with snails and then moving to more complicated animals like mice (Order 286–7), working on this spell for at least two weeks, at which point Hermione alone has progressed to Vanishing kittens (Order 295). McGonagall mentions that the complexity of the animal influences the difficulty of the spell, but we do not see her elaborate on the theory behind this or provide any further explanation (Order 287), situating her instructional practices alongside Flitwick's as skill-drilling rather than increasing genuine understanding.

In Divination, Professor Trelawney claims to reject the importance of the OWL exam and the associated qualification thereby earned, prefacing her first lecture of the year with the caveat that she does not believe "'examination passes or failures are of the remotest importance when it comes to the sacred art of divination'" (Order 214). Nevertheless, Trelawney explicitly sets her curriculum to help prepare students for the test, introducing their initial focus on dream interpretation as a skill "that may very probably be tested in your OWL" (Order 214). While Trelawney does not seem to feel any pressure to help her students succeed, she cannot ignore the pressure from administration, acknowledging that it is Dumbledore's belief in the importance of the OWLs that has led to her consideration of them for this year's curriculum (Order 214). Even this pressure, however, is not enough to make Trelawney desire anything more than to have students "sit the examination" as Dumbledore "likes" (Order 214), and so we see no further explicit mention of the OWLs or further framing of their coursework as test preparation, as we do with other instructors. Luckily, when the OWLs arrive, we see that the tested skills (crystal balls, tea leaves, and palm-reading) were all covered in their classes in third year (Prisoner 80), with crystal balls having been the focus of that year's final exams, as well (Prisoner 236–8). Were we feeling generous, we might conclude that Professor Trelawney is engaging in embedded preparation practices across multiple years of instruction, but the combination of her dismissive discourse surrounding the exams and her general failure to foster her students' skill in the subject in any year makes it unlikely that this has been a deliberate pedagogical decision.

Care of Magical Creatures is an interesting case, allowing us to compare the test preparation practices of two different instructors for the same subject. At the start of the year, with Hagrid's unexplained

1. Ordinary Wizarding Levels

absence, Professor Grubbly-Plank covers his classes. She makes no mention of the OWLs during their first class, but she begins with Bowtruckles, a creature we later see on the OWL exam. The implication that Grubbly-Plank is, in fact, deliberately working to prepare students for their test is made explicit during Umbridge's inspection: Grubbly-Plank explains that her planned curriculum for the year, should she stay for that long, is to "take them through the creatures that most often come up in OWL"—they've done unicorns and Nifflers, so she plans to "cover Porlocks and Kneazles, make sure they can recognise Crups and Knarls" (Order 289). Knarls, as we know, also show up on the exam. The fact that Grubbly-Plank has deliberately chosen to cover the material that is most likely to be tested but has not made this focus explicit to the students suggests that she may be the most successful in embedding her test preparation practices and teaching to the curriculum, rather than exclusively to the test. Unfortunately, with Hagrid's return, we do not see more of Grubbly-Plank's lessons, and so we do not know what she might have covered beyond these testable topics or whether she would have maintained an embedded approach through the entire course or switched to more didactic preparation as the exams neared. We do know, however, that when Grubbly-Plank covered classes for Hagrid in the previous year, she taught students about unicorns (Goblet 379), which also show up in the OWL, suggesting that Grubbly-Plank may focus on an embedded curriculum across multiple years, potentially beginning deliberate test preparation before the fifth year.

Hagrid, in contrast, has planned his curriculum around the creatures he considers interesting, assuring the trio that the creatures he has saved for their OWL year are "'somethin' really special'" (Order 388). Hagrid selects the topics for his curriculum based on his own personal standards of interest, with seemingly no consideration for either the OWLs or for general best practices in teaching. When Hermione urges Hagrid to focus his lessons on "how to look after Porlocks, how to tell the difference between Knarls and hedgehogs, stuff like that"—in short, Grubbly-Plank's planned curriculum of likely OWL topics—Hagrid dismisses this as "not very interestin'" compared to his "impressive" choices (Order 388, 391). Hermione continues to plead "for something dull that's bound to come up in our OWL," and while she does so seemingly out of concern for Umbridge's vendetta against Hagrid (Order 388–9), we can also see in this exchange the expectations of both students and administrators for what will be covered in classes this year: Hermione, an exemplary student, desires test-material coverage, which would be in line with the administrations' expectations for the course. Under the combined threat of Umbridge's constant supervision and his exhausting extra-curricular efforts with his hidden half-brother, Hagrid eventually seems to take Hermione's advice (Order 487); while we receive no further details of Care of Magical Creatures lessons, either under the rest of Hagrid's tenure that year or after his dismissal, we do know that all of the most likely test material must eventually have been covered, for Harry and his classmates do, in fact, learn the "trick" behind distinguishing Knarls from hedgehogs that we see employed during their exam.

Due to the antagonistic relationship between Harry and Professor Snape, Potions is one subject in which we see detailed classes across the years; this, combined with Snape's consistent tenure, allows us to compare his usual pedagogical practice with his teaching in Harry's OWL year. In Harry's first year, Snape's instructional methods include asking students to recite facts, having them take notes while he lectures, and brewing various potions, with Snape highlighting the exemplary efforts of students during these brewing sessions for others to observe (Stone 102–4). In the second year, we learn that these brewing sessions continue to be "the usual way" of Snape's lessons, with Snape supervising students' practice and providing immediate feedback (Chamber 140); these practices continue in the third- and fourth-year classes we see represented (Prisoner 94–8; Goblet 444, 447–50). Readers rarely get the name of the potion students are brewing and have no indication how many times prior to the exams students have practiced preparing a given potion, but we have every indication that the vast majority of class time in Potions is dedicated to these practical brewing sessions.

In the cohort's OWL year, Snape begins the first class with a lengthy speech, during which he emphasizes the importance of the upcoming exam, outlines his high expectations for all of his students, and informs them of the requirement to excel in the exam if they wish to continue Potions at the NEWT level (Order 209–10). Snape does not frame the OWLs as being of personal importance to the students in terms of their potential career aspirations, as other instructors do, but rather considers their importance as it relates to his own reputation and standards as an instructor. Explicating the purpose of the OWLs

1. Ordinary Wizarding Levels

as being a chance to "prove how much you have learned about the composition and use of magical potions," furthermore, Snape emphasizes the importance of the learning the material over the credential of the OWL itself, the only teacher to explicitly do so (Order 209). His opening speech concluded, however, Snape—as with Flitwick, McGonagall, Grubbly-Plank, and even Trelawney—begins his curriculum for the year with a likely OWL topic and is explicit with his students about this decision: "'Today we will be mixing a potion that comes up often at Ordinary Wizarding Level: the Draught of Peace, a potion to calm anxiety and soothe agitation'" (Order 209–10). This proves to be a "difficult, fiddly potion" requiring precision and exactness with which Harry and the other students, save Hermione, struggle (Order 210-2), suggesting that, like McGonagall, Snape may have deliberately begun with some of the hardest material.

At the end of the class, Snape assigns students an essay on moonstone's properties and uses (Order 211); when Harry receives a D for "Dreadful" on this homework, we learn Snape will be grading everything this year to OWL standards with OWL grading schemes. In explaining this practice, Snape parallels the approach of teachers who introduce students to test standards well in advance to help students "get a feel" for the requirements (Monfils et al. 48): "'I have awarded you the grades you would have received if you presented this work in your OWL,' said Snape with a smirk, [...]. 'This should give you a realistic idea of what to expect in the examination'" (Order 277). While it may seem cruel that Snape banishes Harry's botched potion in a subsequent lesson, the supplementary homework Snape sets him "on the correct composition of the potion, indicating how and why you went wrong" (Order 324) serves as remedial instruction and encourages Harry to learn from his mistake and improve his understanding of the potion, substituting but also supplementing his practice with brewing it. While Snape is far from a nurturing figure, his instructional methods throughout the year—brewing practice, grading to OWL standards, and supplementary theoretical homework—are not only effective test preparation, but potentially are achieving something that the instructors in other classes do not even seem to be attempting by encouraging theoretical learning and deeper understanding rather than simply drilling facts and skills. During her class inspection, Umbridge's comment that the cohort "'seem fairly advanced for their level'" (Order 323) can, despite the admitted bias of the speaker, be taken as an indication that Snape's methods, while harsh, are effective in helping students achieve the high standards he demands.

Hogwarts' administration explicitly condones these teaching to the test practices, through both Dumbledore's leadership of the school and Umbridge's more tyrannical oversight. As discussed above, Dumbledore reportedly demonstrates his own belief in the importance of the OWLs and the associated credentials through Trelawney, who claims it is his desire to have all students sit the examinations (Order 214), while Umbridge's commitment to the exams—and, through her, the Ministry of Magic's understanding of their value—is implied through Hermione's plea that Hagrid focus on a likely OWL topic in order to pass Umbridge's observation of his teaching (Order 388–9). This implicit approval of the instructors focusing on test preparation sends a clear message about the institution's priorities, regardless of individual instructor's personal pedagogical beliefs: it is more important that students receive the externally-assessed credentials than that they achieve real understanding and facility; the OWL itself is worth more than the learning it is meant to represent, given the importance of OWL and NEWT credentials for students' futures. This prioritization both creates and derives from Hogwarts' position as gatekeeper in British wizarding society and the role it serves to control access to future careers through these credentials.

Taken alongside the content and structure of the examinations themselves, the test preparation practices of the Hogwarts instructors all serve to reiterate the perception that the OWLs are a valid test of students' knowledge and ability and that the associated credential students earn is important, perhaps even the most important outcome of their education alongside their subsequent NEWT scores. As students memorize surface-level facts and rehearse decontextualized spells and skills in their classes, they internalize the implication that this is genuine and worthwhile knowledge in the subject—failing to value, let alone develop, a deeper understanding of the subject or an ability to apply the skills they are drilling beyond artificial classroom and test contexts. The Hogwarts instructors and administration, rather than challenging this implication, reinforce this perception through their teaching practices as well as their discourse surrounding the importance of the OWLs; as we will analyze below, with the career prospects and trajectories of

1. Ordinary Wizarding Levels

British wizards informed by the OWLs and NEWTs scores they receive, Hogwarts' fundamental purpose in this society is to assign these scores to students, supporting and perpetuating a system which presents itself as a meritocracy based on academic achievement, but which in reality functions to concentrate wealth and power in Pureblood families.

Political Interests and Economic Ramifications

The role of the OWLs as a gatekeeping measure in wizarding society becomes clear as we consider the final three questions for interrogating the "deep structure" of education: How do societal norms and expectations filter and distort knowledge? Whose interests shape and inform educational institutions, processes, and outcomes? How do schools distribute social, cultural, and economic capital in relation with one another? Connected as they are with the future career prospects of students, the OWLs and NEWTs are direct and significant influences on the distribution of cultural and economic capital in wizarding society; in combination with the categories of normalcy and deviance associated with these examinations, the OWLs and NEWTs function in favor of Pureblood ideology as they help perpetuate a myth of meritocracy (not unlike legacy admissions in some real-world institutions).

Considering first the question of normality and deviance, we can see that "normal" is earning an OWL after five years of study for core subjects or three years of study for electives, going on to earn a NEWT two years later; "deviance," meanwhile, is failing to achieve passing scores and not earning these credentials. This idea of normal is highly flawed: underlying the expectation that all students should be able to achieve a passing score on the examinations in their fifth and seventh years is the assumption that all students have had equal opportunities for learning and skill development, and that the tests themselves are administered in an equitable manner. Research on standardized high-stakes testing in the real world shows us that this assumption is far from the reality. Rather than equality of opportunity, students from low socioeconomic backgrounds, minority students, disabled students, students taking the test in a language other than their first, and female-identifying students are all disadvantaged in the global testing culture, lacking the same privileged access to education opportunities but held to the same standards on the same timelines as students with significant advantages resulting from their privileged positions in these structures (Meaghan and Casas 38). The use of high-stakes testing to determine student placement and progression compounds the "harmful effects" of these inequalities, as disadvantaged students are offered only reduced learning opportunities or denied further opportunities altogether based on their low test scores (Meaghan and Casas 42). This compounding serves to widen—rather than close—gaps in achievement and to exacerbate differences in access and attainment (Camilli and Monfils 143; Meagan and Casas 42). These systemic inequalities of high-stakes testing systems and the use of test results to determine student advancement, credentials, and employment opportunities inscribe and reinforce what Meagan and Casas term "a gender and ethnic/racial caste system" that sees students from the dominant groups in society accrue more education opportunities and achievements, preparing them for greater career and financial success, while those from minority or marginalized groups are denied this access (40).

The divided system which the OWLs and NEWTs serve to perpetuate is that of blood status: the hierarchy of Purebloods, Halfbloods, and Muggleborn. As other scholars have remarked, there is shockingly little diversity at Hogwarts, with only a small handful of racially diverse students and little evidence of varying socioeconomic status, save for the Weasley's romanticized poverty and the Malfoy's extreme wealth (Park; Waetjen and Gibson); what discourse around diversity there is in the *Harry Potter* series rests on the issue of blood status. As is so often and so problematically the case in fantasy texts, this fantastic distinction between Pureblood, Halfblood, and Muggleborn wizards replaces and subsumes almost all consideration of difference along racial and cultural lines, perpetuating what Helen Young labels as fantasy's "habits of Whiteness" by centering Whiteness as the unquestioned "default" in the text and eliding issues of race through the metaphor of blood status.[4] To be a Pureblood, one must have two magical parents; often, this concept of "purity" stretches across multiple generations, including uniformly magical grandparents, great-grandparents, and so on. Halfbloods have one magical and one non-magical, or Muggle, parent, and may be raised in either wizarding or Muggle society, while Muggleborns have two non-magical parents and are raised entirely outside of wizarding society and unable to explain their bursts of accidental magic until the arrival of their Hogwarts letter. Blood status in wizarding society

1. Ordinary Wizarding Levels

influences the cultural, social, political, and economic capital of individuals: Pureblood families, such as the Malfoys, have significant privileges in terms of social, cultural, and economic access and resources, and even the Weasleys, in their relative poverty, have inherent social and cultural capital as a result of their Pureblood status.

Raised within the structures of wizarding society, Pureblood students enter Hogwarts with an innate understanding of its norms and traditions, the expectations for their behavior, and what advantages are available to them and how to secure access to these. Their families, also knowledgeable about the intricacies of wizarding culture, politics, and the magic economy, can advocate for and advise their children as they progress through their education, helping them adequately prepare for desirable careers and future positions of power. In contrast, Muggleborn students have none of these advantages: they know nothing of wizarding society before learning of their admission to Hogwarts, have no familial support or guidance, must be their own advocates, and bring with them very little, if any, cultural capital. Furthermore, in social circles like those of the Death Eaters, what cultural capital Muggleborns bring is to their detriment. As Chantel Lavoie notes, the eleven-year-old students beginning their studies at Hogwarts "have obviously mastered the basic skills not only of reading and math in order to carry on with their complicated history lessons, spells, summarizing of chapters, mixing of potions, and later Arithmancy; they also arrive capable of writing research essays, some of which are assigned over the summer" (46, note 4). These implicit expectations for students entering Hogwarts are substantially higher than we would typically see for students of this age. It is, therefore, not unreasonable to assume that students whose parents are aware of these expectations and can specifically prepare their children to meet them will fare better scholastically than those students whose parents—unaware of the *existence* of Hogwarts, let alone its first-year curriculum—have provided them with only a typical education up to age ten.

When we look at the range of educational opportunity and support available to Hogwarts students, those from Pureblood and even Halfblood families have significant advantages compared to Muggleborn students. Even if we could conclude that all Hogwarts students have received perfectly equal educations—which is demonstratively false, as we see multiple instances where a student's House affiliation impacts the educational opportunities and supports they receive, as just one example—the cultural and economic capital with which Pureblood students begin their education would still result in greater achievements for these students in comparison to Muggleborns, already behind before the race has begun. Pureblood students are better positioned to attain "normal" achievements and earn their OWL credentials, while Muggleborn students are at greater risk for "deviance" and failure in these examinations.

Since the underlying assumption is that all students *have* had equal opportunity and access, and that the tests themselves are equitable, should Muggleborn students fail to attain a passing OWL grade, this deviance would be understood as a personal failing of the individual and not a consequence of a structure which we can conclude systemically disadvantages Muggleborn students. This perception, in turn, then reinscribes and reinforces the social hierarchy of wizarding society that sees Muggleborns as inferior, all while framing this prejudice as predicated on the ability of individuals and not their blood status. The OWL and NEWT examination structures of Hogwarts, in which Muggleborn students are at greater risk for "deviance," assist in maintaining the sociocultural structures of wizarding society, specifically reinforcing the ideology of blood purity, and replicate an economic caste system, as Pureblood graduates are more likely to be formally qualified for positions of political and economic power. The OWLs and NEWTs are likely to distribute cultural and economic capital to already-advantaged Pureblood graduates at a disproportionate rate, and in doing so perpetuate an illusion of individual merit that justifies and conceals an ideology of blood purity. The fact that exceptional Muggleborn students like Hermione are able to succeed in these structures despite their systemic disadvantages serves to further reinforce this false meritocracy, since these token successes can be held up as proof that the system is not biased and individuals with merit will receive their due rewards.

Rather than challenging the centrality of these credentials in wizarding society, the series insists on their importance, positioning the examination structure as an essential component of a just society, such as in a scene where Harry eavesdrops on a conversation between Draco Malfoy and his Slytherin peers. Draco asserts that the OWL and NEWT qualifications, and the education they are meant to represent, would

1. Ordinary Wizarding Levels

be meaningless under Lord Voldemort's rule: an individual's position then would be based on "service" and "devotion" to Lord Voldemort, and the tasks set to his followers would not be "something that you need to be qualified for" in terms of academic credentials (Half-Blood 145). What we know of Hogwarts under Death Eater administration corroborates Draco's speculations: students in attendance that year, like Neville, report almost nothing of their classes or academic pursuits, speaking instead of the emphasis on enforced compliance through extreme corporal punishment and coercion and the explicit privileging of Pureblood students (Deathly 461–4).

The little we do hear of classes in this year presents a corruption of the usual curriculum, with Defense Against the Dark Arts becoming a course in the Dark Arts themselves, where students are required to practice the Unforgivable Cruciatus Curse, and Muggle Studies becoming a course in Pureblood ideology and propaganda (Deathly 462). In teaching the wrong content, students' chances at passing the externally-set OWLs and NEWTs in these subjects this year are substantially harmed, demonstrating that—for these subjects, at least—the Death Eaters do not prioritize the earning of credentials in the same way as Hogwarts' usual administration. In fact, where these two subjects in particular are concerned, Voldemort has a vested interest in actively undermining them and preventing students from receiving these particular OWL and NEWT credentials. Undermining the Muggle Studies curriculum will see fewer future graduates who are qualified to work in positions which would support Muggles and Muggleborn individuals in wizarding society, participating in the erosion of these careers and their related ideological stances, and changing the focus of Defense Against the Dark Arts to simply the Dark Arts simultaneously prepares students to join Voldemort's ranks of enforcers within the Death Eaters and disqualifies them for traditional Auror positions opposing the Death Eaters. Voldemort is interested in controlling Hogwarts not only because it allows him to infuse the curriculum of the nation's only wizarding school with his explicitly Pureblood-supremacist ideology, but also because it is an important means of controlling access to political power and financial wealth for Hogwarts graduates by eroding or warping the standardized testing system which provides the credentials for careers in government and law enforcement.

Draco's speculations and the actions of the Death Eaters in power at

Hogwarts equate tyranny, terrorism, and despotism with the dismissal of the importance of these educational tests and the credentials earned through the OWLs and NEWTs, conversely equating democracy, peace, and a just society with valuing education and its testing structures. In asserting and demonstrating that Lord Voldemort's reign would see no value in these credentials, Draco and the Death Eater instructors also imply the opposite: that a free, just society must then see the value in OWLs and NEWTs and use these credentials as the basis for determining qualifications for roles in a democratic society. A meritocracy which relies on OWL and NEWT credentials is positioned as the ideal alternative, but the risk that Muggleborn students will be systemically disadvantaged in these exams means that this foundation for an ideal society is inherently flawed, as it is premised on a system which reinscribes the ideology of blood purity and would perpetuate the same social hierarchies by relying on OWL and NEWT scores in this way, all while claiming to be truly equitable and unbiased.

The reason the OWLs and NEWTs are so heavily implicated in the maintenance of the social and economic hierarchies in wizarding society is their direct impact on the career prospects and eventual employment of students, and the connection between career and both social standing and economic wealth seen in the series. As Jarrod Waetjen and Timothy Gibson demonstrate, socioeconomic disparities are exacerbated through employment, as groundskeepers like Hagrid and low-status bureaucrats such as Arthur Weasley find themselves "stuck in dead-end jobs, with the constant demands of work yielding little more than the bare necessities," sharply contrasted by the concentration of wealth, power, and influence with families like the Malfoys (Waetjen and Gibson 11). The inextricable relationship between these high-stakes examinations and students' future careers—and their future wealth, power, and influence—is emphasized from the first introduction of the OWLs and NEWTs. When we, as readers, first learn about these standardized examinations, we do so partly in relation to Percy Weasley's career ambitions:

> Even Fred and George Weasley had been spotted working; they were about to take their OWLs (Ordinary Wizarding Levels). Percy was getting ready to sit his NEWTs (Nastily Exhausting Wizarding Tests), the highest qualification Hogwarts offered. As Percy hoped to enter the Ministry of Magic, he needed top grades [Prisoner 231].

1. Ordinary Wizarding Levels

This connection is again foregrounded on the first day of classes in Harry's OWL year with Ron's comment on the exams: "'OWLs are really important, affect the jobs you can apply for and everything. We get career advice, too, later this year, Bill told me. So you can choose what NEWTs you want to do next year'" (Order 206). Compounding these informal mentions, the official discourse surrounding the OWLs also consistently emphasizes the relationship between the exams and students' future career prospects, and how closely connected a student's NEWT-level course choices are with their career ambitions is evident when Professor Snape, who to our knowledge has no prior information regarding Harry's career ambitions, deduces that Harry aspires to be an Auror based on the subjects in which he is enrolled in his sixth year (Half-Blood 299). From the first day of classes with Flitwick's reiteration of this point—"'What you must remember ... is that these examinations may influence your futures for many years to come! If you have not already given serious thought to your careers, now is the time to do so'" (Order 231-2)—to the start of the exams themselves with McGonagall's final reminder that "'You have your own futures to think about'" (Order 625), the official discourse of Hogwarts repeats and reinforces the connection between the OWLs and students' career prospects, demonstrating precisely how high the stakes are for this high-stakes testing.

Further foregrounding the influence of their OWL scores on their careers, as Ron indicates, each student receives individual career counselling and guidance for the first time during their fifth year, the timing of which can hardly be taken as a coincidence:

> As though to underline the importance of their upcoming examinations, a batch of pamphlets, leaflets and notices concerning various wizarding careers appeared on the tables in Gryffindor Tower shortly before the end of the holidays, along with yet another notice on the board, which read:
> CAREERS ADVICE [Order 578]

If we take these pamphlets and Harry's one-on-one meeting with McGonagall as representative, Hogwarts' career counselling is as much about informing students what NEWTs they will need—and, therefore, indirectly dictating the OWLs towards which they should put the most effort, in order to achieve the requisite scores—as it is about discussing their interests and aptitudes and where they might find personal fulfillment in line with their life goals and values.

Schools of Magic

As they look over the pamphlets in preparation for their scheduled one-on-one sessions with their Head of House, whether it is what the materials themselves emphasize or what Harry and his friends notice, the focus is on the credential requirements for the various careers advertised: healing requires "at least an 'E' at NEWT level" for Potions, Herbology, Transfiguration, Charms and Defence Against the Dark Arts; Muggle Relations is only "an OWL in Muggle Studies"; Curse-Breaking with Gringotts requires Arithmancy (Order 578–579). Over and above descriptions of the work involved, what personality types are well-suited, information on the working culture or standards, or anything else that might be communicated about these potential careers, these pamphlets are presented as primarily communicating information on the test scores and subsequent credentials required for eligibility.

In Harry's one-on-one counselling, McGonagall frames the meeting's purpose in terms of Harry's career ambitions, continuing to emphasize the connection between the examinations and students' job futures in official discourse, telling Harry that "'this meeting is to talk over any career ideas you might have, and to help you decide which subjects you should continue into sixth and seventh years'" (Order 583). When Harry mentions his desire to be an Auror, though McGonagall does eventually note the difficulty of the career and the stringency of the recruitment process, her first response is to outline the necessary coursework and examination scores: "You'd need top grades for that.... They ask for a minimum of five NEWTs, and nothing under 'Exceeds Expectations' grade, I see" (Order 583). McGonagall and Harry discuss the five NEWTs she would recommend he take and the minimum OWL level he will need to continue in each subject, as well as how he is currently faring in those courses (Order 584–5). Specifically informing Harry that he will need to put significant effort into achieving the needed Transfiguration mark, urging him to "put in some good hard work before the exams" to improve his current "Acceptable" performance and achieve the necessary "Exceeds Expectations" OWL score (Order 584), McGonagall explicitly connects their meeting with Harry's exam preparation and ties his exam outcomes to his future aspirations.

Through Harry, we see the ways in which the relationship between exam performance and future career opportunities is internalized by students. As Harry takes his OWLs, his worries are centered on his Auror ambitions, wishing that he had "expressed a more achievable

1. Ordinary Wizarding Levels

ambition" in his consultation with McGonagall (Order 627) and despairing that his Potions exam "would be the downfall of his ambitions to become an Auror" (Order 631). When Harry receives his results, his reaction to the scores he received is similarly colored by his career ambitions: while he managed a passing OWL in Potions, it is not the "Outstanding" Snape has set as the prerequisite to continue in the subject at NEWT level, and so Harry understands a job as an Auror to be now unattainable, since he cannot earn the suggested NEWT credential in Potions (Half-Blood 102).

While not the explicit purpose of examinations, this gatekeeping function—where a test "determines who is granted a privilege such as admission or graduation" (Nagy 262)—is a common end to which test scores are used. Gatekeeping with tests can happen at two stages: entrance exams control who is able to access education and exit exams control who is able to claim mastery of particular knowledge, ostensibly by proving their attainment of a minimum standard of competency (Nagy 264). OWL results control access to NEWT-level study, and both OWL and NEWT scores serve as prerequisite qualifications for wizarding careers, positioning NEWTs as exit exams while OWLs function as both exit and entrance exams. Considered alongside the risk for Muggleborn students to experience systemic disadvantages in these test structures, the ways in which the exam scores are used in gatekeeping may disproportionately place Pureblood and even Halfblood students into prestigious careers while keeping Muggleborns out of high-level study and these powerful positions in wizarding society.

In using OWL and NEWT scores as gatekeeping measures, the underlying assumption is that a student's achievement on the exams is indicative of their ability both to advance to NEWT-level standards and to perform the duties of a given career or position. This assumption is, predictably, flawed; there is no evidence that the scores of high-stakes tests are effective predictors of future success (Meaghan and Casas 40). Understanding the OWL and NEWT exams in this way, however, contributes to their role in perpetuating blood-purist ideologies, as those best positioned to demonstrate potential aptitude are Pureblood students, while Muggleborns disadvantaged by the testing structures will be perceived as incapable or incompetent, using their exam scores as a (falsely) objective basis for continuing prejudice and discrimination.

Schools of Magic

Socializing Acceptance

In their analysis of representations of testing in young adult literature, Alexander and Black interrogate how these texts may both reflect and shape readers' perception of high-stakes testing, asking whether the "hyperbolic" representations may nevertheless "resonate with young people's experiences today" and what the prominence of high-stakes testing in the genre says about "current cultural values and norms around testing" (209). Dystopic young adult fiction, at least, seems to offer a critique against many of the features of high stakes testing, including the privileging of certain types of skills and knowledge, the link between testing and access to further education and resources, and the focus on job-readiness over personal aptitude and passion (Alexander and Black).

The final question which we must ask is whether the *Harry Potter* series similarly invites readers to critique and challenge these examinations and the uses to which they are put; as we consider the failed subversion of the series' carnival structure and the post–OWL careers of the main trio, we shall see that the answer is no. The series serves to encourage an acceptance of testing structures as the norm, and potentially even as beneficial, more than it serves to subvert or interrogate the global testing culture.

The *Harry Potter* series has ample opportunity to develop a critique of testing and the use of test results in wizarding society, particularly through its carnival structure. As scholars such as Maria Nikolajeva have asserted, the *Harry Potter* series is classically carnivalesque; it exemplifies the "temporary reversal of the established order" outlined by Mikhail Bakhtin and seen so frequently in children's literature ("Harry" 226).[5] Throughout Harry's tenure as a student at Hogwarts, we see the regular testing systems break down, temporarily changing the usual procedures and requirements: end-of-year exams are frequently cancelled or missed, Harry's performance in the OWLs is compromised by Lord Voldemort's return, and his cohort misses their NEWTs entirely when Hogwarts becomes the site of the final battle between good and evil. These elements in Rowling's series do not, however, achieve the subversive and critical potential of the carnivalesque. Harry as protagonist fails to achieve the level of self-awareness and critical consciousness that generates a subversive critique through the

1. Ordinary Wizarding Levels

carnivalesque experience (Nikolajeva "Harry"), and so the series fails to foreground the arbitrary foundation of norms and hierarchies through their temporary reversal.[6]

Nikolajeva convincingly demonstrates the ways in which Rowling's series fails to realize the subversive potential of their carnival structure in regard to their portrayal of adult normativity and absolute authority over children and youth, concluding that "Harry emerges from his carnival without the wisdom that carnivalesque subversity usually presupposes" ("Harry" 237). There is no overt or implied critique of the return to previous norms and hierarchies in the wizarding society seen after the final battle and in the concluding epilogue, and so the series "confirm[s] the social order based on conventional Western values, on solid beliefs in indisputable dogmas, and on unquestionable authorities" (Nikolajeva "Harry" 239–40). In a series where power hierarchies are both numerous and "unequivocal"—wizards over non-wizards, Purebloods over Muggleborns, rich over poor, and so on—Harry as protagonist is the "bearer of normativity" (Nikolajeva "Harry" 228); rather than making inferences from his carnivalesque experience, thereby exposing the existing norms and hierarchies as arbitrary and changeable and encouraging readers to recognize the same, Harry embodies and perpetuates these norms. The potential of carnival to present subversive critiques is squandered as power structures are reproduced and the oppressed become the oppressors with no change in the operation of the hierarchies—and without even an implied critique of this lack of change (Nikolajeva "Harry" 229).

The series fails to realize its subversive potential in regard to representations of educational testing, as well. Throughout the seven core books, testing procedures and the educational structures in which they are located become increasingly interrupted and corrupted. Beginning with the cancelled and missed exams under Dumbledore's reign as Headmaster, we see the structures of Hogwarts modified by Dolores Umbridge, on behalf of the Ministry, who embodies and exacerbates the focus on decontextualized skills and knowledge that informs testing through the policies she enforces and her own purely-theoretical teaching practice in Defense Against the Dark Arts. When Snape becomes Headmaster and Hogwarts falls under the control of Voldemort and the Death Eaters, the testing structures are changed so dramatically as to be absent entirely: the NEWTs and, presumably, the OWLs and end-of-year exams are not held that year, as the castle is in disrepair when the tests would normally be held and the student population is in hiding, in recovery, or in jail awaiting trial.

As these testing structures are modified and eventually lost, there is ample opportunity to generate awareness of the arbitrariness of their importance and role in society. As we see with the triumph of Harry and his friends at the end of each year in increasingly challenging and dangerous tasks, they are learning and progressing with their skills and knowledge; there is no formal test required to demonstrate this reality, and in three of Harry's six years of schooling, the cancellation of the end-of-year examinations implicitly support this understanding. The learning and ability the trio demonstrate in extra-curricular events and pursuits, including both school-sanctioned events like Quidditch and the Triwizard Tournament as well as the trio's encounters with Voldemort and his supporters, far exceed the decontextualized recitation they perform in any of the academic tests they undertake. And yet, there is no commentary presented on the fact that students are demonstrating their learning without and outside of the formal testing structures: the closest we come is with Harry's exemption from the end-of-year exams in his fourth year (Goblet 533), which implies that his performance in the Triwizard Tournament is an acceptable alternative to demonstrate his learning for the year, or is, at the very least, the more important focus for his efforts. The reasons for the school-wide cancellations of exams, however, and the times Harry participates in these tests *despite* the extracurricular events in which he participates undermines this brief implication and fails to present a unified argument about the false value placed on testing.

The epilogue of the seventh book leaves unanswered the question of what happens to Harry and his friends after the end of what should have been their final year of schooling: Do they return to school? Do they write their NEWTs? Are they able to get any job at all, let alone those they had hoped for, without these official credentials? The only information about any character's employment that we receive is Neville, who is now the Herbology Professor at Hogwarts. If we look beyond these core texts, however—to interviews with Rowling and to the play *The Cursed Child*—we receive details of the career trajectories of Harry, Ron, and Hermione. Having missed sitting their entire last year of schooling and, therefore, their NEWTs, neither Harry nor Ron have any official

1. Ordinary Wizarding Levels

NEWT credentials (Rowling "PotterCast"); both Harry and Ron nevertheless become Aurors, and Harry is promoted to Head of the Auror Office and then to Head of the Department of Magical Law Enforcement itself (Rowling, Thorne, and Tiffany). Rowling explains their ability to work as Aurors as a consequence of their participation in the battle "on the right side," with Kingsley specifically recruiting Harry, Ron, Neville, and other of-age fighters to serve in Magical Law Enforcement at the close of the wizarding war (Rowling "PotterCast"). Here, we have yet another missed opportunity for commentary on the arbitrariness of the norm in using NEWTs (and OWLs) to determine career eligibility, as it is being modified in recognition of the unique circumstances of these students; by not including these details in the final novel of the core series, another chance to potentially foster readers' critical curiosity about these norms is missed. Had these details been included, however, we would see that, once again, the series fails to present even an implied critique of the role testing serves in British wizarding society, instead confirming the original norms and structures of the society. Leaving school early and skipping both the seventh year of study and the NEWT exams, which supposedly provide the prerequisite credentials for wizarding careers, has no significant effect on the ability of Harry or Ron to secure their dream jobs and, in Harry's case, to advance within the profession; we see similar exceptions in the core series with Fred and George, who also experience immediate career success without taking their NEWTs, leaving school early and opening Weasley's Wizard Wheezes. These deviations from the norm, however, fail to translate into any character expressing a critical awareness of the arbitrariness of the usual role OWL and NEWT credentials play in wizarding society, particularly in relation to careers, which might thereby prompt critical consideration by the reader. Furthermore, Hermione's choice to write her NEWTs and receive her credentials after the war (Rowling "PotterCast"), abiding by the normative trajectory even when she is not being asked to do so, further confirms this as the accepted and necessary norm and reinscribes the role and understood value of the NEWTs and OWLs.

"What has then changed in the power hierarchy of the Harry Potter universe as the saga has been concluded?" Nikolajeva asks; "What has been interrogated and what has been confirmed?" ("Harry" 237). In regard to high stakes and standardized educational testing, nothing has changed, nothing has been interrogated in the reinstatement of the previous norms, and the previous false meritocracy which uses the OWLs and NEWTs results as its foundation has been confirmed and reinscribed, continuing to operate in ways that privilege Pureblood graduates and systemically disadvantage Muggleborn individuals. The failure to achieve the potential for subversive and critical commentary within the carnival structure of the series serves to foster acceptance of testing and the use of test scores as gatekeeping, since they are positioned as part of the peaceful and fair society to which the wizarding world has returned and there is no critical awareness within the text to foreground these as arbitrary norms or a false meritocracy. The representation of testing in the series reinforces the elitist ideology represented in the books—which, as Elizabeth Galway asserts, is no accidental depiction, but is rather "fundamental to its appeal" (77). While Alexander and Black lament that the dystopic texts they consider offer "only the most extreme kinds of solutions to the problems of sorting and testing that dominate characters'—and increasingly readers'—time" (232), at least these texts offer a critique and a potential, though problematic, solution, something we find lacking in Rowling's *Harry Potter* series.

Conclusion

The testing structures of Hogwarts and Rowling's wizarding society are deeply flawed. The tests themselves prioritize the recitation and performance of decontextualized facts and memorized routines, presenting subject mastery as something that can be demonstrated through individual tasks; the relationship between the OWL and NEWT exams and career eligibility further makes attaining the necessary credentials the ultimate purpose of education. This, in turn, encourages instructors to engage in practices which prepare students for these recitations and performances, drilling them in decontextualized skills and facts to help them excel on the tests while leaving significant gaps in their knowledge and failing to develop any deep understanding or true aptitude. The results of the tests are used as gatekeeping measures to control access to higher levels of study and to careers in the wizarding world post–Hogwarts; Muggleborn students, at significant risk of disadvantage in these structures, are least likely to achieve the high scores

1. Ordinary Wizarding Levels

necessary for further study and prestigious careers and most likely to be "deviant" and fail their exams, keeping them out of the upper levels of society while providing an acceptable explanation for continued prejudice and discrimination against them, reinforcing ideologies of blood purity. This problematic credential-based meritocracy is, furthermore, positioned as a central component of a just and free society through contrast with Lord Voldemort's predicted dismissal of the exam scores as qualifications of importance and the actions of the Death Eaters while in control of Hogwarts, paradoxically presenting a structure that is complicit in the creation and maintenance of a blood-purity hierarchy as the ideal alternative to Voldemort's tyranny. The failure to generate critical awareness through the series' carnival structure, with no commentary provided on the exceptional experience of characters like Harry and Ron or Hermione's choice to abide by the normative route despite the alternative available to her, squanders carnival's subversive potential; rather than encourage readers to consider the issues with testing by foregrounding these norms as arbitrary, the series instead fosters acceptance and complacency by unquestioningly presenting educational testing and credentials as an inherent and important feature in a just society.

In the next chapter, I turn to Patrick Rothfuss's *Kingkiller Chronicle* and, once again using the questions for interrogating the "deep structure" of education, analyze the role capital plays in the series' representation of higher education, as the protagonist Kvothe's abilities to access an education in magic throughout the narrative are informed by his access to social, cultural, and economic capital.

Chapter 2

Not a Bent Penny More
Capital in Patrick Rothfuss's Kingkiller Chronicle

> My poverty hung around my neck like a heavy stone. Never before had I been more aware of the difference between myself and the other students. Everyone attending the University had a safety net to fall back on. ... If things got rough for them, they could borrow against their families' credit or write a letter home.
>
> I, on the other hand, couldn't afford shoes. I only owned one shirt. How could I hope to stay in the University for the years it would take me to become a full arcanist?
> —Patrick Rothfuss, *The Name of the Wind*

> A college education has been seen as a means of escape and a pathway of social mobility since colonial times ... a sentiment that became ingrained in the American dream. Promoting an opportunity structure through educational attainment is a critical piece of our social policy, yet several scholars believe that opportunity structure is more fictive than real.
> —MaryBeth Walpole, "Socioeconomic Status and College: How SES Affects College Experiences and Outcomes"

In this chapter, I examine the representation of educational institutions and schooling in Patrick Rothfuss's *Kingkiller Chronicle* and the ways in which access to capital informs the protagonist's access to education.[1] Once again, I use the key questions for analyzing the "deep structure" of education—What underlying meanings and ideologies are transmitted along with the formal content? How do teachers and administrators filter and distort knowledge? How do societal norms

2. Not a Bent Penny More

and expectations filter and distort knowledge? Whose interests shape and inform educational institutions, processes, and outcomes? How do schools distribute social, cultural, and economic capital in relation with one another?—focusing particularly on issues of normality and deviance and on the distribution of capital. As with the previous chapter on *Harry Potter*, the analysis is focused on the representation at the level of the text, attending to the ways in which capital is understood and employed, how characters experience and react to the role of capital in higher education, and what inferences about the relationship between education and capital the text encourages readers to make as the usually mundane educational topic is brought to the forefront through the magical institution in which the protagonist is enrolled.

Introduction

Rothfuss's as-yet-unfinished trilogy *The Kingkiller Chronicle*—composed of *The Name of the Wind* (2007) and *The Wise Man's Fear* (2011), with *The Doors of Stone* slated for future release—presents the adventures and exploits of Kvothe, with a framing narrative in which the protagonist is recounting his own life story. The series has recently begun to receive scholarly attention, focused primarily on analyzing its construction as a not-quite-conventional fantasy text: in addition to interrogations of the series through the lens of structuralism (Schroer), scholars have examined its use of narrative techniques (Al Ghoraibi), character archetypes (Tikkanen), methods of characterization (Reams), spatial and temporal motifs (Giebert), and modifications to the traditions of the medieval romance (Watral) in order to understand the ways in which Rothfuss creates a compelling fantasy text which feels both familiar and excitingly new, to expand on Breeanna Watral's concept of "comfortable alienation" within the texts. Others have looked to the representation of music in the series (Schmitz) or the implications of character names in the series (Tomková). Of greatest interest here, Katherine E. Bishop touches on *The Kingkiller Chronicle* as an example of what she terms "pedagogical fantasy," examining Rothfuss's texts alongside those by J.K. Rowling and Lev Grossman.

Kvothe undergoes a number of formal and informal educations, including his early tutelage under the arcanist Abenthy, his studies at the

Schools of Magic

Arcanum within the University, his instruction under Felurian, and his training with the Adem. Each of these instructional periods and systems has a deep structure to analyze, and each of these deep structures have many and varied components and could be productively examined from numerous angles to explicate their hidden curriculum. One of these educational experiences looms large, however, receiving a far more thorough and lengthy representation than the others: Kvothe's formal education at the University, which is the focus of the bulk of the first book and a substantial portion of the second. Within the educational experience represented in the narrative, the issue which arises again and again is money—namely, the money Kvothe does not have. Kvothe's choice to emphasize the impact of his financial status in the retelling of his life experiences reveals economic capital as an influential force within the University and invites readers to analyze its function within the deep structures and hidden curriculum of the institution. To this end, this chapter focuses on the role of capital in the University and the hidden curriculum in operation, which requires certain amounts and forms of capital from its students as a prerequisite for accessing an education.

There are multiple forms and types of capital students bring to, activate in, and acquire through their educational experiences, and while this chapter will focus primarily on economic capital—an individual's financial assets, the money to which they have access—we will also consider social and cultural capital, as these three are inherently connected to one another, with access to and activation of one type facilitating and enabling the acquirement of others (Rios-Aguilar and Kiyama 11). While there have been multiple definitions of both social and cultural capital presented in various scholarly fields,[2] in this chapter, we will use the definitions articulated by Cecilia Rios-Aguilar and Judy Marquez Kiyama, which are formulated specifically for use in analyzing the experiences of under-represented students within educational institutions. In this chapter, social capital refers to "the resources that individuals ... can access, which both result in, and are the result of, collective and socially negotiated ties and relationships" (8), while cultural capital is "the different sets of linguistic and cultural competencies, knowledge, and dispositions that are passed from one generation to another by way of the class-located boundaries of [an individual's] family," recognizing that cultural capital can also be objectified through the purchase and possession of valued cultural goods and institutionalized to

2. Not a Bent Penny More

pre-determine the value of these objects and knowledge (11). Throughout this chapter, we will consider economic, social, and cultural capital in relation to one another, since foregrounding the connection between these forms of capital is important for seeing the ways in which reproduction works and, specifically, how economic capital enables other forms of capital (Rios-Aguilar and Kiyama 12).

Capital, however, can be understood only in relation to a field, the space in which particular resources and knowledge have value and can be acquired and activated. The field is a "social universe," a space in which individuals' positions are defined by the amount and value of their capital; they are also "contested hierarchies" within which individuals compete to acquire the most and the most highly valued capital, as well as attempting to increase the relative value of the capital they hold (Rowlands and Gale, citing Grenfell). In Rothfuss's series, where the entire universe has been invented whole-cloth, we have the opportunity to examine which elements in relation to capital have been deliberately changed and which have been kept, perhaps unconsciously. Here, the three forms of capital are considered in relation to the field of higher education, specifically the field of the fictional elite University, in order to examine the hidden curriculum of capital's operation in education. Educational institutions as fields reflect the dominant cultures in which they are located (Stuber 10), thereby participating in the maintenance of inequality through reinforcing and recreating social class structures (Rios-Aguilar and Kiyama 10). The University is no exception, reflecting the dominant culture and reinforcing its norms and social structures through its requirement for particular amounts and forms of capital for its students.

This replicating function of educational institutions and the role of capital in maintaining inequality creates an understanding of the normative student as being from the dominant culture and privileged class; students with different identities or from other social locations, here referred to collectively as under-represented students, experience barriers to access and significant hardships throughout their engagement with these institutions as a result of their non-normative status. At Rothfuss's fictional University, the implied normative student has access to substantial amounts of each form of capital and usually comes from an upper- or middle-class background within the Commonwealth or its geographical and cultural cousins. This normative model is a stark contrast to Kvothe's own background,[3] as Kvothe falls within the under-represented student category many times over: his background as a trouper and travelling performer positions him as working- or lower-class; his time living in poverty on the streets of Tarbean locates him as low socioeconomic status; his identity as Edema Ruh makes him a racialized minority; and his lack of (known) family history with formal education categorizes him as a first-generation student.[4]

For under-represented students like Kvothe, accessing the required capital to participate in an educational institution is "incredibly difficult," perpetuating inequality (Rios-Aguilar and Kiyama 11), and research in the field of higher education tends to conceptualize a binary relationship that equates having capital with achieving desirable educational outcomes, while not having capital results in negative or under-realized educational outcomes (Rios-Aguilar et al. 170, 174). As Rios-Aguilar and Kiyama demonstrate, students' "social class and position within the field of education provide them with unique opportunities to access, to possess, and to activate certain forms of social (and cultural) capital" (Rios-Aguilar and Kiyama 11)—Jenny Stuber reiterates this claim, asserting that "students, then, will be advantaged to the extent that the social and cultural world of their campus resembles the social and cultural world they were socialized to inhabit while growing up" (Stuber 15). Educational institutions reward those students who possess valued capital with access and opportunities to acquire more capital, and the University is no exception, reflecting the dominant culture and further privileging middle- and upper-class individuals as normative students who are able to engage with the University and benefit fully from the education and related opportunities it offers.

While Kvothe's complex identity as an under-represented student cannot be understood as determinative of his experience at the University,[5] it undeniably influences his choices and his available resources in undertaking an education at an elite institution. What students like Kvothe do not know about postsecondary education—the social and cultural capital they lack, or are unable to activate—compounds with their lack of economic capital to create barriers and prevent access to all that a higher education promises to provide: namely, social mobility and improved life outcomes, measured in a variety of ways.[6]

How does Kvothe's access to capital influence his educational experiences and attainment at the University? What is the hidden curriculum of capital at the institution, and what values and structures are being reinforced for both aspiring arcanists and readers through the representation of Kvothe's studies? From the outset, Kvothe's experiences at the University are informed by what he does not know and what he does not have: without inherited knowledge of the institution, or earned or inherited wealth, Kvothe does not have the capital usually required to attend the University, and his attempts to pursue an education regardless foreground the role that capital plays in educational attainment and the hidden curriculum of gatekeeping it enables. Kvothe's experiences learning magic at the University are shown to be drastically different from those of his peers, who better fit the model of the University's normative student. This contrast is emphasized and brought to the foreground by Kvothe's challenges while studying sympathy and sygaldry within the Arcanum and by his conscious cross-class performance of the normative student, illuminating for readers the hidden curriculum of capital in operation at the University and the consequent barriers to access for those from the lower class.

Drawing on the key questions for interrogating the "deep structure" of education from the Introduction and used in Chapter 1 to examine the *Harry Potter* series, the following sections first explicate the ways in which the University controls access to an education and the opportunities to acquire capital it affords. By requiring students to have and activate certain forms and amounts of capital in order to access the institution, the University creates significant barriers for under-represented students, using capital as a gatekeeping measure. The following section then analyzes the ways in which the depiction of Kvothe's cross-class performance, which readers are enabled to understand and interrogate as both class-passing and reverse slumming, encourages readers to engage with a critique of the gatekeeping function capital performs in educational institutions and the ways in which the requirements for capital preclude the University from functioning as a force for social mobility or change.

The Hidden Curriculum of Capital

Access to Education

To analyze the deep structures and hidden curriculum of capital within the University, and see the ways in which these preclude social mobility through education, we must consider the ways in which access to an education at the University is predicated on access to and activation of economic, social, and cultural capital, which act as the foundation for the institution's conceptualization of normality and deviance (Apple and King 88)—asking, in essence, how do societal norms and expectations filter and distort knowledge? And how do schools distribute social, cultural, and economic capital in relation with one another? The typical or normative student of the University has certain amounts and types of capital; Kvothe's limited means position him as a non-normative student, evident in both the expected capital Kvothe does *not* have and in the unexpected or unsought capital he *does* have. The capital Kvothe has obtained through his lived experiences in a travelling troupe, surviving in the wilderness, and living unhomed in a major city, while valuable to him, are shown to have little worth in the field of the University and the dominant culture it reflects, in both Kvothe's perception of how this capital is received and through the explicit comments and actions of others. Kvothe's non-normative student status results not just from the atypical capital he possesses but also from the unusual paths and actions Kvothe takes in activating his atypical capital to achieve his goals within the institution. Throughout, the gatekeeping function of capital within the University is evident, as it is capital—rather than academic potential or skill—which Kvothe lacks, and it is his inability to meet the institution's demands for capital that causes Kvothe's issues with access, persistence, and educational attainment.

Before Kvothe can begin his education in sympathy (the magic of this fictional world), he must be admitted to the University. Admittance is a daunting prospect for an individual with limited capital such as Kvothe, as there are multiple barriers to entry which require students have access to very particular types and forms of capital. First, prospective students require social capital in the form of a letter of recommendation and formal sponsorship from a previous instructor, a "customary" piece of the admissions process (Name 249), which also implies possession of specific cultural capital. The letter demonstrates two things about a prospective student: one, that they have existing ties to the University's network through studying under an arcanist alum, who are the masters' preferred sponsors (Name 249); and two, that they have participated in a formal foundational education (Name 250).

2. *Not a Bent Penny More*

Underlying this "customary" component is the requirement for prospective students to already have certain valued social capital through existing connections with the University, as well as the cultural capital gained from participating in the foundational education structures of the dominant culture.

Without a letter from Abenthy, who served informally as Kvothe's tutor, Kvothe must find and offer an equivalent demonstration of social and cultural capital to be allowed to continue in the admissions process: before they will even agree to assess his intelligence or aptitude, Kvothe must produce a letter or an acceptable equivalent. What Kvothe is able to offer is an inscription Abenthy wrote in the copy of *Rhetoric and Logic* he gifted to Kvothe, currently located in a pawn shop in Tarbean (Name 249–50). This is a barely acceptable equivalent, especially given its physical absence, but the lesser social capital it represents as indirect proof of tutelage is supported by the cultural capital of the object itself, as a text with inherent value in the field of the University. In combination with Kvothe's recital of his prior educational attainment, which is an implicit claim of the cultural capital Kvothe has acquired (Name 250), it is enough to earn Kvothe the chance to demonstrate his skill and potential.

Kvothe's subsequent exceptional performance in his admissions interview challenges the implied institutional belief that only students who have prepared in the anticipated fashion, and therefore accrued the desired social and cultural capital, will be able to perform satisfactorily and earn admittance. Kvothe's life experiences, which have taught him to seek any advantage he can find, and which have *not* ingrained in him norms around cheating or plagiarism, make spying on an hour's worth of admissions interviews a logical choice (Name 251–2), informed and enabled by the mismatched habitus he developed through his prior experiences.[7] This spying, in addition to his previous study under Abenthy and his lived experiences, prove more than adequate preparation as he performs exceptionally well in answering the masters' questions. Kvothe's demonstration of skill and knowledge definitively refute the implication that those without the "customary" letter cannot possibly be viable candidates for entry; limiting admissions interviews to only those who can prove they have taken this specific route by producing the required letter, then, serves primarily to deny the possibility of entrance to potential students from more diverse and varied backgrounds.

Schools of Magic

In addition to a presumed and required access to social and cultural capital, admittance to the University demands access to economic capital. In retelling his experiences, Kvothe emphasizes the barrier to entry that his lack of economic capital presents, wryly noting that he has a better chance "to get a piece of the moon than that much money" (Name 252). However, Kvothe is aware of the University's meritocratic promise that students with exceptional aptitude will be admitted for a lower tuition: as Kvothe recounts, "'I knew from my previous discussions with [Abenthy] that you needed money or brains to get into the University. The more of one you had, the less of the other you needed'" (Name 251). This binary between intelligence and capital—which informs the hidden curriculum of the institution—provides further insight into the normative student and the values of the University, as it implies that economic capital is of greater importance than academic skill and ability, since students may enter the University without academic skill if they have abundant coin, but even highly-skilled students are still set a tuition. As Lorren affirms, no student can enter without economic capital, regardless of their academic merit: "'You had to have a tuition. Everyone does.'" (Name 260). As with the letter of introduction outlining a student's prior education, which prioritizes social and cultural capital over actual potential, the arbitrary tuition structures of the University value wealth over knowledge and are deliberately used to control who has access to the University.

The variability of tuition enables its use as an explicit gatekeeping tool. In the interviews on which Kvothe spies, he sees tuitions range from four talents and six jots to as much as thirty talents, a significant sum (Name 252); throughout his time at the University, Kvothe himself is set tuitions of negative three talents (Name 258), three talents, nine jots, and seven pennies (Name 353), six talents (Name 436), nine talents and five jots (Wise 97), twenty-four talents (Wise 1041), and fifty talents (Wise 1092).[8] Kvothe's experiences and comments emphasize the many non-academic influences which determine these amounts: while absences from class are a factor in raising tuition (Name 653), as is promotion through the ranks (Name 264), the greatest influence is an individual student's relationship with each of the masters and what the masters know of the student's reputation. Students who are known to be wealthy, and who can therefore afford a bit of a "squeeze," are charged more (Wise 42). The same is true for students, like Kvothe, who

2. Not a Bent Penny More

are known to cause trouble and face disciplinary measures, both within the University (Wise 42) and, more damagingly, in the public eye (Wise 385–7). Kvothe's tuition rises in the second term because he has earned the disapproval of Master Lorren and the outright hostility of Masters Hemme and Brandeur (Name 353), and these personal relationships continue to explicitly influence the behavior of the masters and Kvothe's tuition amounts in subsequent interviews, with Kvothe eventually set a fifty talent tuition by Master Hemme, using the influence of his role as acting Chancellor to weaponize his grudge against Kvothe (Wise 1092).

While Kvothe's friend Simmon has not, apparently, "even considered the possibility of personal grudges or politics entering into the equation" of determining tuition—naively believing it to be based solely on academic performance in the admissions interview alone (Wise 42)—the system is well-designed to allow such influence and misuse. As another friend, Manet, explains, "the masters pick their own questions, and they each get their say" (Wise 42). Kvothe himself rants against this potential for abuse while drugged with an inhibition-removing alchemical substance: "'The whole admissions process is flawed to the point of blinding idiocy,'" he tells Simmon. "'Master Kilvin knows what I'm capable of. So does Elxa Dal. Brandeur doesn't know me from a hole in the ground. Why should he get an equal say in my tuition?'" (Wise 71). As Kvothe laments, regardless of his relationship with each of the masters or whether or not he studies their subject, they each get an approximately equal say in his tuition for the next term. The masters can and do use these opportunities to control and limit Kvothe's access to the institution; while it begins as a more passive constraint with their choice not to consistently account for Kvothe's circumstances in setting his tuition, it later becomes a deliberate act of exclusion and hostility.

When advocating for himself during his first admissions interview, Kvothe eloquently explains the ways in which tuition controls access to the University:

> "Admit me for more than two jots and I will not be able to attend. Admit me for less and I will be here every day, while every night I will do what it takes to stay alive while I study here. I will sleep in alleys and stables, wash dishes for kitchen scraps, beg pennies to buy pens. I will do whatever it takes."....
>
> "But admit me free, and give me three talents so I can live and buy what I need to learn properly, and I will be a student the likes of which you have never seen before" [Name 257].

Schools of Magic

Kvothe's self-advocacy speaks to the challenges faced by students with no financial resources or available supports as they pursue an education, emphasizing the way in which the University's structures effectively prevent students with limited capital from accessing an education.[9] Kvothe emphasizes the need for sufficient economic capital to access both these supporting necessities and, implicitly, the luxury of time to dedicate to studying and schoolwork, which must otherwise be spent securing these basics. By requiring that students spend economic capital on tuition in addition to their own support and provision, the University ensures that only those with a certain amount of wealth are able to attend at all, let alone attend *and* thrive academically.

Kvothe's plea, however, also demonstrates the disconnect between a student's ability and their access to capital: nothing changes about Kvothe's skill and dedication in the three scenarios he presents, only the University's relative demand for or provision of economic capital. If Kvothe cannot access higher education, or if he cannot fully participate and benefit from his studies because he is simultaneously working to support himself, Kvothe implies that this will be the fault of the institution for requiring more economic capital than he can provide, rather than any failing of his. The decision of the masters to grant him an unprecedented negative tuition to serve as a scholarship (Name 258–60), as he requested, corroborates this disconnect, as it acknowledges that a student does not strictly need access to economic capital to demonstrate their potential and simultaneously brings into question the need to charge a tuition at all, if they can choose to forgo it for Kvothe (though we do not know the details of how, exactly, the University is funded).

Kvothe is not so lucky in subsequent terms, however, as the University reverts to its usual practices and begins requiring steadily increasing amounts of economic capital from Kvothe, which he must pay to preserve his access to the institution and the education it offers. Beginning in his second term, Kvothe must rely on a predatory loan to secure this access, and the requirement that Kvothe acquire and provide economic capital to pay for both loan interest and each tuition constrains Kvothe's ability to access and benefit from his education, as he predicted in his first admissions interview. The normative student has access to cultural and social capital which they can convert to economic capital when necessary, making the University's requirement for

2. Not a Bent Penny More

tuition at worst an inconvenience or embarrassment: they can activate non-economic capital through a letter home requesting more funds or a visit to the moneychangers for a loan (Name 353–4). Without this access to social, cultural, or economic capital, Kvothe faces the very real possibility of losing access to the University, ruminating on his difficult position after he has been refused by the moneychangers on which other students rely:

> While I wasn't surprised, the experience was sobering, reminding me again of how different I was from the other students. They had families paying their tuition, granting them allowances to cover their living expenses. They had reputable names they could borrow against in a pinch. They had possessions they could pawn or sell. If worse came to worst, they had homes to return to.
> I had none of these things. If I couldn't come up with eight more jots for tuition, I had nowhere in the world I could go [Name 353–4].

Without the economic capital of his peers, and without social or cultural capital to activate and convert,[10] Kvothe must seek other means of affording tuition if he is to maintain access to the institution—which, while costing him a great deal, is also his best opportunity to earn an income moving forwards through the promised upward social mobility and positions of status for those who graduate as arcanists.

Driven by the need to access economic capital to preserve his access to an education, Kvothe twice takes on a loan from Devi, a partially-trained arcanist who can visit serious harm upon those who cannot pay, and who insists Kvothe take on loans much higher than the minimum amounts he requires (Name 357–9; Wise 107–8). Despite the cost and the risk, Kvothe understands that, fundamentally, what he is borrowing from Devi is continued (if potentially limited) access to an education and its benefits: "That's what I was really borrowing: time. One more term" (Name 361). The dangerous measures which Kvothe is forced to take in order to secure the required capital further emphasize the gatekeeping role of capital in the University, as the non-merit-based tuitions Kvothe is set jeopardize his ability to access the institution and persist in his studies. And, while Kvothe manages to secure the needed capital to purchase continued access, his educational attainment is constrained by his need to generate an income to cover the loan interest *and* tuition moving forward.

Schools of Magic

    Kvothe's need to prioritize earning an income negatively impacts his educational attainment by limiting the time he has available for his studies, dictating which projects he pursues, and jeopardizing his physical and mental health and well-being. Selecting artificing as his primary academic focus,[11] Kvothe makes a strategic choice to access its immediate earning potential and to leverage his developing relationship with Master Kilvin as the fastest means to convert social capital into advancement through the University.[12] From here, Kvothe finds himself caught in a vicious cycle: he sacrifices his learning and his opportunities to acquire social and cultural capital, because he must prioritize earning an income, which is necessary if he is to continue accessing these opportunities for learning and capital acquisition; the continued access and attendant opportunities he has attained at so dear a cost, however, must then also be compromised in the pursuit of further earnings. He frequently faces the displeasure of Master Kilvin, who views Kvothe's focus on quick-but-lucrative projects as evidence that Kvothe lacks academic curiosity and ambition; Kvothe also faces the displeasure of his friends, as his inability to spend time socializing leaves them feeling neglected.[13] As Stuber demonstrates, "The model of the highly involved, sociable college student is not class neutral"—students who do not need to work and, therefore, have more time available are more likely to be involved in social and extracurricular pursuits within the institution (Stuber 65).[14] Kvothe, whose need to work is based upon both a desire to continue his education and the risk of very real harm through failing to pay his loan interest, has neither the time nor the agency to perform within these ideal models.

    In addition to presenting these substantial barriers to educational persistence and attainment, the requirement to have economic capital in order to access an education can also be deliberately weaponized by the institution to exclude undesirable students, as we see at the end of Kvothe's fourth term. Having been publicly accused of malicious magic as part of his ongoing feud with fellow student Ambrose, and having defended himself in court with all the flair his entertainer background can lend (Wise 361–3), Kvothe unwittingly brings scandal and undesirable attention to the University. It is widely understood within the University community that Kvothe will be punished for this: he will be set a tuition so high in the next admissions interview that he will not be able to afford to continue in his studies. Master Elxa Dal, with whom Kvothe has a good working relationship, takes Kvothe for a casual lunch following the trial to warn him of this coming punishment; while the superficial purpose seems to be curiosity about Kvothe's plans post–University (Wise 381–5), Manet helps Kvothe recognize this as a warning from the master to take the term off to avoid a punitive and exclusionary tuition (Wise 385–7). As Manet explains: "'The trial has given the University a great shining black eye. It's reminded folk that while *you* might not deserve burning, some arcanists might. ... You can be certain the masters are uniformly wet-cat mad about that'" (Wise 386, emphasis in original). Willem predicts the consequence of the masters' collective anger will be a tuition of "'at least thirty-five talents'" (Wise 387). Kvothe's public trial, only the most recent scandal with which Kvothe and Ambrose have been connected during their ongoing feud, makes Kvothe an undesirable student, and the masters are able to leverage the institution's structures to deny him continued access. The threat, however, accomplishes the same purpose as actually being set such a high tuition, and Kvothe is successfully excluded from the University as he makes the non-choice to take some time away, leaving him entirely at loose ends without access to his studies or his artificing work (Wise 387–8).

Changed Circumstances

When Kvothe returns from this reluctant time away, his changed situation—as he brings back with him additional social, cultural, and principally economic capital—emphasizes the ways in which the University uses requirements for capital to control access to the institution and limit the educational attainment of particular groups of students.[15] With an unlimited sponsorship agreement from a wealthy and powerful foreign noble, Kvothe no longer needs to prioritize income-earning over everything else, and his ability to fully dedicate himself to his studies and subjects of interest, as well as socialize with his friends and participate in the social networks of the University, are in stark and explicit contrast with his previous experiences.

As part of securing this financial stability, Kvothe manipulates the biased tuition structures that give the masters significant control over institutional access. Through an off-the-books agreement with the bursar, Kvothe arranges to receive a reimbursement from any tuition he

Schools of Magic

is set over ten talents (Wise 1039–40). Kvothe then proceeds to deliberately drive up his tuition by incorrectly answering the questions of those masters who hold a grudge against him—though he is careful to preserve his reputation with some, such as Masters Kilvin and Elxa Dal, aware of the value of the social capital he has earned with each of them. Finishing his admissions interview by outrageously insulting Hemme,[16] Kvothe leverages his knowledge of the hidden curriculum of capital to earn a tuition of twenty-four talents, from which he receives back seven talents (Wise 1040–1). With Hemme as acting Chancellor going into Kvothe's sixth term, we see the outsized influence the Chancellor has on deciding a student's tuition when Kvothe's repeated deliberately-lackluster performance this time earns him a tuition of fifty talents; Hemme's unpleasant smiling suggests that he understands this will be a significant hardship for Kvothe, presumably looking to drive him out of the University again (Wise 1092). While Hemme outright remarks that he had assumed the threat of a high tuition would keep Kvothe away permanently (Wise 1040), now that Kvothe has access to far more than the minimum economic capital the University requires of its students, he cannot be kept out in this way, and we see the truth of Kvothe's comment in his very first admissions interview that having ample wealth meant someone could attend the University with very little brain at all. Cultural, economic, and social capital are all distributed through the University primarily to students who already have substantial amounts and established avenues for activating their stocks; now that Kvothe has secured these things through his external exploits, the structures of the University work to his advantage in helping him acquire more, rather than serving to keep him out. Kvothe has worked hard to earn peripheral membership in the group in whose interests the institution functions, and now he gets to reap those rewards.

As a result of his increased stocks of capital, Kvothe is able to prioritize his educational attainment and his personal academic interests for the first time. In addition to returning to his work in the Fishery because he misses it and not out of financial necessity or desperation (Wise 1043), Kvothe finds himself able to pursue new studies in the time previously dedicated to earning an income, a change upon which Kvothe remarks explicitly: "Since poverty no longer forced me to work long hours in the Fishery, I was free to study more broadly than ever before" (Wise 1052). He continues to study sympathy, medicine, artificing, and

2. Not a Bent Penny More

naming, and adds new classes in chemistry, herbology, and mathematics (Wise 1052, 1059). Kvothe also undertakes independent studies in his newly-spare time, including in the medicinal properties of arrowroot (Wise 1059), and in Yllish story knots, which results in an offer of private tutoring in Yllish with Chancellor Herma, an opportunity to gain both learning and valuable social capital (Wise 1052). To support these studies, Kvothe is able to purchase reference books for the first time: he acquires a Yllish dictum, a herbology text, and a reference for artificing schema (Wise 1054–5). And when these studies go poorly—as they do with Yllish, which he struggles to pick up; in artificing, with many false starts on a new invention; and in chemistry and mathematics, which he chooses to abandon (Wise 1058–9)—Kvothe is able to take these "failures" in stride. Rather than representing lost income or a potentially devastating setback in rapid promotion, as Kvothe's mixed success with his artificing journeyman project represented (Name 470–4), these are simply the everyday failures of a student figuring out his strengths and interests in postsecondary education. Kvothe has the luxury of time to learn the subjects which hold his interests and no external pressures to master everything he undertakes; furthermore, he is able to fully engage in and enjoy the process of tinkering and experimenting to create something new in the Fishery (Wise 1060–1), rather than rushing the process while plagued by fears of lost financial investment should he fail.

While this access to economic capital does not turn Kvothe into a normative student, it does allow him to better play the part and meet expectations that he has previously been unable to achieve due to a lack of time, access, or funds. Kvothe's lived experiences and the attitudes and values they inform will always set him apart from the normative student, but he can at least now perform the role as expected when it is required of him or otherwise beneficial to do so. His changed amounts of and access to capital make Kvothe's winter term "carefree as a walk in the garden" (Wise 1049), which proves to be extremely unfamiliar:

> It was strange not having to live like a miser. I had clothes that fit me and could afford to have them laundered. I could have coffee or chocolate whenever I wanted. I no longer needed to toil endlessly in the Fishery and could spend time tinkering simply to satisfy my curiosity or pursue projects simply for the joy of it [Wise 1049].

Kvothe is able to secure supporting necessities as well as luxuries, including six sets of well-fitting clothes, ample paper, fine ink, his own engraving tools, dinners for his friends, presents and necessities for Auri, and "two pairs of shoes. *Two*" (Wise 1054–5, emphasis in original)—and still with money left in his purse (Wise 1055). He is also finally able to accept Count Threpe's invitation to dine (Wise 1053), allowing Kvothe to convert economic capital into social and cultural capital in the networks beyond the University, successfully adopting new roles within the various social networks and fields surrounding the institution.

Frustratingly, it is having access to this economic capital and not *needing* to earn more that finally allows Kvothe to earn significant sums of money through his labors, and which provide opportunities to secure cultural and social capital at long last. The facts of Kvothe's changed circumstances, and that they result from his exploits beyond the University, rather than the institution's promise of social mobility through education, demonstrates that the institution is not designed to help students rise in this way, and would have kept Kvothe grinding and disadvantaged if he had continued to pursue the faulty promise of rising through study at the University alone. Seeing these stark changes in Kvothe's experiences—and having the second book's recounting of Kvothe's time at school end on a moment of success, celebration, and optimism for the future—effectively foregrounds the role that capital, and most notably economic capital, plays in an individual's experiences in higher education as a gatekeeping measure to prevent just such a rise in status.

Socializing Critique

So what does the *Kingkiller Chronicle* have to say about the ways in which the University's requirement for capital functions to control access to the institution and constrain the possibilities for social mobility and change through education for under-represented students like Kvothe? Through demonstrating the false foundations which underlie the conceptualization of education as a meritocracy and foregrounding the requirement to *have* capital in order to access more through the opportunities afforded by the institution, the series also challenges the validity of higher education's promise of social mobility. Researchers studying the field of higher education have questioned "whether real

2. Not a Bent Penny More

upward social mobility by education is possible, or whether the educational system in fact serves to reproduce social inequity" (Ostrove and Long 366), a question which Kvothe's experiences urge readers to consider. While postsecondary institutions are understood to be meritocracies, what Stuber refers to as the "great equalizers," scholarship shows that they "contribute to—rather than ameliorate—social inequalities" through who is able to attend which school and who then persists to graduation (5), reinforcing social stratification through controlling access to cultural and social capital based on prior levels of capital and class background (6). The way in which capital functions as a gatekeeping measure in institutions like the University, and the myth of meritocracy which accompanies these practices, means that postsecondary education can promise social mobility and change for underrepresented students while simultaneously denying them access based on the capital they lack, undermining the fulfillment of these promises and often outright precluding it.

With prerequisites for capital functioning to keep those without it from obtaining an education, how are those in the lower- and middleclasses supposed to access the capital that such an education provides and, in doing so, attempt to realize the elusive promise of social mobility? Beyond simply demonstrating that possession of and access to capital function as a gatekeeping measure in higher education, *The Kingkiller Chronicle* shows us that this requirement means education is only available to the middle and upper classes and that these institutions are not, in fact, designed to facilitate the upward social mobility of those from the lower class. This consequence of the prerequisites for capital is made evident to readers through Kvothe's conscious performance of—or, in some less-than-successful cases, his attempt to perform—a class status other than his own lower-class identity. To gain access to the University, Kvothe must "fake" the capital he does not have, which means engaging in a sustained performance of a middle-class identity; this performance is foregrounded for readers through both Kvothe's meditation on his performance through the series' narration and by his established background as a trouper and actor, with which accounting the trilogy opens. While we cannot yet know whether the *Kingkiller Chronicle* as a whole will invite readers to critique and challenge the role of capital in education, the first two volumes certainly invite critique far more than they foster complacency.

Schools of Magic

John Kucich reminds us that "class mediates behavior ... [with] many variables that induce individuals to either accommodate themselves to social classifications or to transform them," which makes it possible for individuals to "deploy dualistic conceptions of class self-consciously to understand or modify their own social positions" through cross-class performance (471).[17] Such cross-class performance involves a self-conscious self-presentation of class identity, accomplished through repeated clothing and accessory choices and through an individual's actions and speech, deliberately selected and enacted to locate them within an established frame for evaluating and understanding class identity (Forsberg 1215–1216). As Bast notes during his late-night conversation with the Chronicler in the framing narrative, recalling stories where goose-girls dress like nobility and display stunning poise and eloquence, "there's a fundamental connection between *seeming* and *being*.... We all become what we pretend to be" (Name 716, emphasis in original). Dress and appearance are an important part of this performance, as tangible and visible markers of class status (Foster *Class-Passing*; Hitchcock; Varholy),[18] but speech, social manners and etiquette, specific subject knowledge, and other elements of social and cultural capital also become part of the performance of class.

There are a number of ways to categorize and understand Kvothe's cross-class performance, including as both class-passing and reverse slumming. Gwendolyn Audrey Foster compares class-passing to "race-passing, gender-passing, or straight/gay-passing" as a conscious performance which attempts to disguise or elide its artificiality, so that the performance is taken as genuine or "natural" (*Performing* 102). Kucich offers another term for a similar type of performance, defining reverse slumming as "a mode of middle- or lower-middle-class performance that mimics upper-class behaviors": as Kucich elaborates, "Such performers 'slum' because they adopt the speech, manners, and cultural reference points of a class remote from their own to assume some degree of mastery over what they simultaneously distance as socially other. They 'reverse slum' because the gradient of impersonation is upward" (472). While both class-passing and reverse slumming reveal the constructedness of the categorical boundaries of class (Foster *Class-Passing* 5), serving to "reaffirm the social hierarchy in the very process of denaturalizing it" (Kucich 472), passing is not intended to draw attention to itself as performance and seeks to conceal its own artificiality. Kucich remarks upon this difference, asserting that reverse slumming "flaunts its artificiality—it attempts to fool no one"; where class-passing seeks to change the social location of the individual, if only in the perception of others, reverse slumming "claims no radical shift in the social identities of cross-class actors" (472).

From the perspective of those within the narrative, Kvothe's cross-class performance is best understood as class-passing: he does not want to draw attention to his performance, actively working to hide his lower-class identity and the means he takes to be perceived otherwise. Comments by his friends foreground Kvothe's desire to have his performance taken as natural—or, at the very least, not to have it examined too closely—including Willem's observation that "you do not make any loud announcements that you're Edema Ruh"(Wise 320). To understand the significance of this comment, we must understand the social location of the Edema Ruh: they are a nomadic cultural group, not tied to any specific geographic region within the Four Corners, who travel by wagon train in troupes and work as entertainers. It is stated explicitly in the text that the Edema Ruh are mistrusted among and frequently persecuted by other groups, and this is evident in many of Kvothe's interactions throughout the series: for instance, Hemme uses an ethnic slur in calling Kvothe a "ravel bastard" in an admissions interview, which Kvothe explains derives from the historic systemic purge and slaughter of the *"travelling rabble"* (Wise 95–6, emphasis in original).[19] To draw attention to his Edema Ruh identity would, rightfully or not, locate Kvothe as lower class, potentially even below it; while recognizably displaying markers of his Edema Ruh identity would not prevent Kvothe from continuing to perform a middle-class identity, it would draw inescapable attention to the artificiality of this performance, shifting it into reverse slumming. While Kvothe rightfully refutes the implication that he is ashamed of his ethnic identity, Willem's observation is nevertheless true: as part of the middle-class identity Kvothe is enacting, he does downplay the elements of his appearance, speech, and behavior that would mark him as Edema Ruh in the eyes of others and, in so doing, draw attention to the artificiality of his class performance. Where the other characters in the narrative moment of Kvothe's education are concerned, Kvothe seeks to "pass" as middle-class through his deliberate performance.[20]

Readers, however, have a different vantage point than the characters with whom Kvothe interacts; there is no hiding Kvothe's class identity, and we recognize the artificiality of his performance even—and perhaps especially—when other characters do not. The framing narrative in which Kvothe recounts his life story presents Kvothe engaged in a different class performance, this time of a lower-middle-class identity as the innkeeper Kote: while the class-status Kvothe performs in this role may be genuine, Kote's ignorance of the arcane and his apparent powerlessness are, at least in part, a role Kvothe consciously adopts from unknown motives. As Bast laments,[21] this performance has become so encompassing that he fears Kvothe has lost himself to it and has altered his class status in his own eyes and not merely in the eyes of others, becoming Kvothe's felt identity and no longer a performed disguise (Name 716). But readers are also given moments that remind them of the artificiality of the Kote persona and draw our attention to the aspects of Kvothe's appearance and behavior that are incongruent with this performed role, including his numerous scars and his strongly muscled arms, which "weren't the doughy arms of an innkeeper" (Wise 11). While Kvothe is deeply embedded within his performance as Kote, the construction of the framing narrative and the commentary of Bast ensure readers recognize its artificiality by juxtaposing Kvothe's performance as an innkeeper with his performances of other identities throughout his past.

The framing narrative chapters, occurring at the start and end of each volume and interspersed at random throughout each, juxtapose Kote's present and Kvothe's past; consequently, Kvothe's two sustained class performances are also placed in direct contrast with one another, with the explicit commentary in the framing narrative encouraging reader consideration of the same type of performance in Kvothe's autobiographic retelling. In these chapters, while we receive some explicit commentary by other characters and through the narration, such as with Kvothe's deliberate social-climber performance at the Golden Pony (Wise 281), attention is primarily drawn to Kvothe's class performance through references to his theater and entertainment background. Reader awareness of the performance is heightened by our knowledge of Kvothe's background as an Edema Ruh trouper, which he uses to construct and employ these performances, and by the attention Kvothe himself draws to moments where he employs these specific skills in acting and performance to present a middle-class identity to others. As

2. Not a Bent Penny More

Cristine M. Varholy demonstrates, cross-class dressing onstage speaks to the use of the same self-presentation strategies off stage. Even more directly, Foster asserts the connections between these two realms of performance: "The very nature of acting itself is about *passing*; passing oneself off as an/other and, in the process, throwing off the shackles of any natural or normal identity markers" (*Class-Passing* 8, emphasis in original). Through this lens, we can see the ways in which Kvothe's on-stage background draws for readers this same parallel between the two modes of performance within the text.

As the very first step to entering the University, for instance, Kvothe enacts a deliberate performance of a young nobleman in order to procure clothes decent enough to wear for his admissions interview: walking naked through the streets after his first bath in years, Kvothe adopts the mannerisms of an upper-class noble, explicitly drawing on the role of an entitled young page with an important father that he'd previously played with his troupe. Through this brief performance, Kvothe uses his acting skills and a concocted story about stolen clothes in order to procure clothing appropriate for a middle-class man (Name 220–3). With this new costume, Kvothe is unrecognizable to the innkeeper who saw him dirty and dressed in an urchin's clothes only hours before, and Kvothe notes that what had before felt like a hostile environment now felt welcoming and comfortable by virtue of the innkeeper's changed perception and reception (Name 223–5). Temporarily performing an upper-class status in order to secure the required middle-class clothing at an affordable price—and linking this cross-class performance with his past performances on stage, drawing readers' attention to the artificiality of his posturing—Kvothe settles into the middle-class role he must play as an aspiring University student.

These clothes are the foundational component of the middle-class identity Kvothe must perform to gain admittance to the University; from there, earning admittance into the Arcanum proper is a matter of performing a specific variation of this role, that of the confident student with substantial prior education. As we've discussed above, the social, cultural, and economic capital required to *actually be* a confident student with substantial prior education makes this a performance of a middle-class, if not upper-middle-class, identity. In retelling the events of the demonstration Master Hemme arrogantly invites Kvothe to give, Kvothe explicitly names the performance skills he uses to successfully portray this identity: a "good stage voice" so he can be clearly heard (Name 280), "one of the tricks of the stage" to prompt applause from the students, and the "stage training" that allows him to calmly offer a handshake to Hemme in the face of the master's anger (Name 284). Kvothe continues this performance, though slightly modified to be humble as well as confident, when he is brought up before the masters for discipline following this demonstration: using his "best distraught voice" and wringing his hands, Kvothe notes that it is a "good performance" which would have made his father proud (Name 292).[22] At the conclusion of this two-act play, Kvothe earns access to an education at the preeminent institution of the Four Corners world and continues to perform his middle-class student status throughout his subsequent studies.[23]

Readers see Kvothe perform two different class identities in two different times and places and are privy to both the moments in which Kvothe is not performing at all and those in which he remarks upon his performance. As a result, readers recognize the artificiality of Kvothe's middle-class performance, situating it as closer to reverse slumming in the eyes of readers. This dual and simultaneous understanding of his performance as both overt and hidden, transparent and successful, creates space for readers to critically interrogate both the means and the ends of Kvothe's cross-class performance and what commentary this makes on the necessity of his performance within the University. While Kvothe's lower-class identity is obvious to readers, who know of his origins and how he came to be admitted into the University, we see Kvothe work to hide his class status from his friends, teachers, and colleagues within the University wherever possible, inviting consideration of his motives for engaging in these class-passing acts. An exceptionally potent example is Kvothe's decision to take on a punitive and inhibiting loan rather than asking to borrow money from one of his friends, as analyzed above: Kvothe is too proud to reveal his "desperate poverty" (Name 354), reflecting the common actions under-represented students take to conceal their differences from other students, particularly differences related to socioeconomic status and financial capital (Aries and Seider; Granfield; Ostrove and Long). While some students may choose to advertise their identity as working-class, low socioeconomic status, or first-generation (Granfield 339–40), with Kvothe, we see the frequent concern of under-represented students about their self-presentation and the perception of their status in comparison to others (Aries and Seider 426–7; Granfield 336; Ostrove and Long 376). Readers understand both Kvothe's motivations for rejecting the possibility to borrow from his peers, sympathizing with his desire to fit in and his fear of poisoning his friendships, and the hardship and danger Kvothe is accepting in making this choice. While these loans, for a time, allow Kvothe to continue a successful class-passing performance, readers are consistently privy to the artificiality of the act and the costs to Kvothe of maintaining this façade.

Kvothe adopts a common strategy of concealing his difference to facilitate his integration into the academic and social life of the Arcanum, which is accomplished through mimicking and assimilating with his peers as much as possible and working to conceal any remaining differences and discrepancies. To this end, Kvothe's experience at the University parallels those of under-represented students at elite institutions: their experiences are marked by changes in speech, dress, and behavior to align and conform with those of their peers and the expectations and norms of the school (Aries and Seider 431), performances which provide these students access to the cultural capital of their affluent peers as well as disguise their own divergent background (Aries and Seider 421). Successful concealment, such as through a change of dress or avoiding social contact that would reveal their true class status, confers benefits which encourage further concealment, helping to minimize the discrimination students like Kvothe encounter and allowing for greater participation in "the culture of eminence" at elite institutions to thereby "reap available rewards" (Granfield 338–40).[24]

When he reluctantly pauses his studies and travels abroad, Kvothe's ability to shift his performance to an upper-class identity while among Maer Alveron's court earns him the favor of—and a line of credit from—this powerful nobleman that allows Kvothe to return and continue his studies in newfound comfort and security: but here, the artificiality of Kvothe's performance is damagingly revealed with Kvothe's acknowledgment of his Edema Ruh identity. The performance of an alternate class identity, whether it is meant to be perceived as genuine or deliberately artificial, draws attention to the essential performative nature of all class identity, which is an uncomfortable and often undesirable reminder for those who benefit from the established class hierarchy (Foster *Class-Passing*; Varholy).[25] While Lady Meluan's prejudiced hatred of the Edema Ruh primarily informs her response to this revelation, the unavoidable acknowledgment of the artificiality of Kvothe's performance, both present and prior, makes him an uncomfortable presence in the Maer's court who is almost immediately dispatched. These moments of revealed artificiality, where characters within the narrative acknowledge and react to what is consistently obvious for readers, indirectly prove the success of Kvothe's cross-class performance in other moments where he is able to disguise the artificiality of his performance.

With what critique are readers presented through Kvothe's cross-class performance? What commentary is made on the gatekeeping function of capital? Kucich claims that reverse slumming, unlike satire or caricature, "upholds distinctions of rank even while mimicking them, thus suspending social critique," serving primarily, perhaps, to emphasize the "skills and privilege of those able to cross class lines through performance" (472). Conversely, Peter Hitchcock claims that slumming "enables social protest and critique" (166), that it serves as a "contact zone in which class gets rearticulated and disarticulated in surprising ways" (183); here, we see the same can be true of reverse slumming. Cross-class performance, in "blurring the boundaries between that which is 'real' and that which is performed" (Varholy 11), carries the inherent risk, or possibility, of destabilizing social hierarchies and bringing into question the means by which we interpret the identities of others. Through Kvothe's cross-class performance—and the ways in which readers are enabled to understand this performance as class-passing, alongside the other characters in the narrative, and simultaneously as the more deliberately artificial and subversive reverse slumming—the series draws attention to the arbitrariness and mutability of class structures and, by connecting Kvothe's performance with his access to an education, to the injustice of limiting access to those in the middle- and upper-classes through the implicit requirements for economic, cultural, and social capital.

Though the answer cannot be definitive without knowing the ending of Kvothe's story, what is represented for readers of Kvothe's experiences studying at the University in the first two volumes of the trilogy, and the ways in which this is related as Kvothe's own retelling, consistently and explicitly invites readers to critique the role of capital in higher education. Through Kvothe's example, we see that both the meritocratic assumptions of higher education and its promise of social mobility and change are false, as access to an education and the opportunities to acquire social, cultural, and economic capital it presents are predicated on already having and being able to activate certain forms and amounts of capital, preventing under-represented students like Kvothe from attending or from finding success within the University.

Conclusion

While postsecondary institutions are understood as spaces to acquire capital—and, therefore, achieve social mobility—the University distributes capital almost exclusively to those who already have it, with prerequisite levels of capital that preclude the institution's function as a force for social mobility or change. The hidden curriculum of the University in *The Kingkiller Chronicle* includes a requirement for capital, primarily economic, that makes access, persistence, and academic attainment unobtainable or extremely difficult to achieve for under-represented students with limited access to capital, as seen through Kvothe's recounting of his experiences. Throughout this representation of Kvothe's education, the series invites readers to critique this gatekeeping function of capital through the framing device, which positions the narrative as Kvothe's autobiographic retelling, and through comments on and references to Kvothe's performance background, both of which foreground his cross-class performances. The awareness of Kvothe's cross-class performance translates to awareness of the institutional structures which mandate such concealment, drawing readers' attention to the ways in which Kvothe's struggles and limitations are caused by the University's structures, with very little blame for these hardships located with Kvothe, bolstered by Kvothe's explicit comments challenging the validity and equity of the institution's practices.

As the magical nature of the education depicted in Rowling's *Harry Potter* brings the issues with high-stakes standardized testing to the foreground, so too does the fantastic institution of Rothfuss's *Kingkiller Chronicle* illuminate the role of capital and gatekeeping in educational institutions. Where Rowling's series fails to realize the potential of its carnivalesque structure, fostering in readers complacency rather than subversion, Rothfuss's series explicitly engages with the issues of capital

Schools of Magic

in the text and invite readers into a conscious critique of these structures through the emphasis of Kvothe's performance of class status and associated capital, made all the more visible to readers through the fantastic nature of the institution and Kvothe's learning and exploits within and beyond its walls. In these first two chapters, I have considered representation at the level of the text, looking to what is presented within the series and how; the next chapter begins a new section, where I take a step back and consider the representation at the level of genre, looking first at what happens to depictions of hidden curriculum when a school story is presented through the framework of a portal fantasy with Lev Grossman's *Magicians* trilogy in Chapter 3 and then at the presentation of a fantasy narrative through the frame of a school story with the "Tiffany Aching" books of Terry Pratchett's *Discworld* saga in Chapter 4.

CHAPTER 3

Imperial Institutes
Portal Fantasies and Education in Lev Grossman's Magicians *Trilogy*

> He felt like an overdressed English explorer trying to impress a skeptical tropical native. But there was something he had to ask.
> "Is this–?" Quentin cleared his throat. "So is this Fillory?"
> —Lev Grossman, *The Magicians*

> The notion that education has been (and currently is) colonization cannot be denied. Historic reasoning and contemporary practice illustrate the intrinsic tendency for education to be conceptualized as control of the "other" (whether physically, socially, intellectually, or in the construction of desire), especially regarding those who are younger.
> —Gaile S. Cannella and Radhika Viruru, "(Euro-American Constructions of) Education of Children (and Adults) Around the World: A Postcolonial Critique"

In the first two chapters, I have considered the hidden curriculum in operation within the fictional institution and its program of education as represented in two fantasy school story series. Now, our consideration turns to the representation of education and the hidden curriculum that exists in the text itself: for not only does a story about school contain a hidden curriculum through the education represented, but also through the representation itself, the way in which the protagonist's educational experience is framed and delivered through the text. As Beverly Lyon Clark reminds us, "[a] story about school *is* a school"

(*Regendering* 7, emphasis added). To this end, this chapter examines the ways in which the metatextual elements of *The Magicians*, particularly the Fillory intratexts, encourage readers to apply the lens of the portal fantasy to their reading of the texts and the ways in which this deliberate play with the inheritances of fantasy literature within the fantastic school story subgenre brings forward issues of imperialism and colonialism within institutional education structures.

The key questions for examining the "deep structures" of educational institutions still apply, though here we must consider also: What underlying meanings and ideologies are transmitted by the expectations and structures of genre along with the formal content of the narrative? How do authors and readers filter and distort knowledge, as teachers and administrators do? How do generic norms and expectations filter and distort knowledge alongside societal norms? Whose interests shape and inform narratives as well as educational institutions, processes, and outcomes? How do texts represent the distribution of social, cultural, and economic capital that occurs through the process of education?

Introduction

While Lev Grossman's *Magicians* trilogy has been popular with the public, seeing a successful television adaptation and launching a spin-off of graphic novels, it has received relatively little scholarly attention to date. What scholarship there is often attends to the relationship between Grossman's series and C.S. Lewis's *Chronicles of Narnia* (Cecire; A. Himes; Kramer; Nester). Tony M. Vinci has twice applied a posthumanist lens to analyzing the series, looking at Julia's trauma and subsequent multiple embodiments ("Mourning") and the series' demonstration of fantasy's transformative potential through posthumanist engagement ("Posthumanist"). Reeba Sara Koshy has analyzed the system of magic in the series, positioning it as a way for women to seize power; others have looked to themes of ennui or depression (Kramer; Nester), issues of spirituality and faith (A. Himes; J.B. Himes), or have used the series to help develop the "campus clique crime novel" subgenre (McGovern). This chapter extends my own prior work on the banking and unschooling, or autonomous, pedagogies represented in

3. Imperial Institutes

the text, analyzing this time not how content is taught, but rather what implicit ideologies are imparted alongside the official curriculum.

To understand the hidden curriculum in operation in Grossman's *The Magicians*, we must consider not just what is taught at Brakebills College for Magical Pedagogy, by whom, and for what purpose, but also how this education is framed within the text. Through its metatextual focus on portal fantasies and its use of the Fillory intratexts as a lens for Quentin's educational experiences, the *Magicians* series operates with a two-fold hidden curriculum, as both the school represented and the means of representation itself engage with an ideology of colonialism and imperialism inherent in the portal fantasy structure.

Revealing the hidden curriculum in operation at Brakebills is a matter of repeating the process from the previous two chapters, interrogating the education represented in the series and its processes of teaching and learning. Attending to the ideology through which knowledge is filtered at Brakebills—both on an institutional level through the staff and the official curriculum, and on an individual level through Quentin as the protagonist, who filters his experiences through the *Fillory and Further* intratexts—we can recognize the imperialist attitudes and structures which provide foundational support to the institution, and see the ways in which the educational experiences of individuals are enabled or constrained as a result of their relationship to Brakebills as an imperial center. Where Quentin can successfully embody the institution's ideal student, a position which provides him with privileged access to the education Brakebills offers, the failure of students like Josh and Penny to achieve key elements of this ideal see them marginalized within the institution; meanwhile, individuals such as Julia who too strongly embody the opposite of this ideal are excluded entirely, and must resist the institution's efforts to deny them an education as they struggle to access knowledge and power. Understanding where characters are located in relation to Brakebills as an imperial center, and identifying the particulars of conformity or deviance that inform these positions, allows us to see the ways in which an individual's education is influenced by their status within the imperial structure of the educational institution.

To explicate the twofold hidden curricula operating in the texts and identify the ideology underlying the means of representation itself, however, we must ask slightly different versions of our founding questions.

Seeing the underlying meanings which are negotiated and transmitted to readers through the text requires asking what happens when a school story is filtered through a portal fantasy, what categories of normality and deviance this establishes, what organizing framework this creates, and in whose interest this frame functions. To properly frame its consideration of the hidden curriculum of colonialism in operation at Brakebills, this chapter first explicates the ways in which the trilogy uses the *Fillory* intratexts as a framework for the fantastic in the text, particularly Quentin's use of them to process his own educational experiences. These intratexts, in foregrounding and thematizing the portal fantasy mode, filter the school story narrative of *The Magicians* through a portal fantasy structure, emphasizing the imperialism inherent in education and presenting readers with a unique opportunity to analyze and critique this aspect of Brakebill's hidden curriculum.

The Hidden Curriculum of Portal Fantasies

Foregrounding Fillory

The education represented in the *Magicians* series is filtered on two levels: Quentin filters his own school experience at Brakebills by means of his reading of the *Fillory and Further* books, an intratextual fantasy series deliberately reminiscent of C.S. Lewis's *Chronicles of Narnia*, which contributes to the series' general filtering of a school story plot through the lens of a portal fantasy structure. This filter provides the framework with which Quentin *and* readers approach the education represented and contributes the categories of normality and deviance against which experiences and individuals are measured.

The portal fantasy, defined by Farah Mendlesohn as the portal-quest,[1] is one of four rhetorical modes or structures common in the fantasy genre, each denoting a different way in which the fantastic interacts with the narrative and the resulting relationship between reader-author-text (*Rhetorics* xiv). Drawing on John Clute's definition of "portals" from *The Encyclopedia of Fantasy*—which exist whenever a movement between two distinct places or states "is dramatized or put in ritual form" (Clute "Portals" 776)—Mendlesohn defines the portal fantasy as "a fantastic world entered through a portal" in which

3. Imperial Institutes

the fantastic remains in that other space and does not cross back into the mundane world, though characters can and do make this transition (*Rhetorics* xix). Typically employing a descriptive narrative mode, the two key movements of this mode are transition and exploration; the reader accompanies the protagonist as, together, they gain understanding and mastery of the new space through their cumulative experiences (Mendlesohn *Rhetorics* 1–2).

From the outset, the *Magicians* trilogy thematizes the portal fantasy through its meta-textual elements: this is accomplished primarily through the inclusion of the *Fillory and Further* intratexts, a series of portal fantasies upon which the characters and the narration frequently comment, but also through moments of self-referentiality when the text uses these references to the Fillory books to comment upon its own status as a portal fantasy story. The *Fillory and Further* intratexts are, definitively, portal fantasies. In these intratexts, the secondary world of Fillory is accessed through various portals,[2] including a grandfather clock (Magicians 7): this movement is heavily ritualized, with Quentin musing that "half of the fun of the books was waiting for the Chatwins to find their way into Fillory, for the magic door that opens for them and them only to appear. You always knew it would, and it always surprised you when it did" (Magicians 169). The magic and fantasy of Fillory definitively does *not* pass back through the portal, as Martin Chatwin angrily laments in one of the Fillory novels (Magicians 75); each of the Chatwin siblings have the same experience of accessing and benefiting from the fantastic within Fillory when they pass through the portal, but they are sent back beyond its borders without any possibility of retaining or transporting the fantastic elements and their attendant powers. The Fillory narratives also satisfy other key characteristics for "portals" set out by Clute and used by Mendlesohn to define the portal fantasy mode: the portals to Fillory are "warded" through "conditions and prohibitions" (Clute "Portals" 776), as the ram gods Ember and Umber guard access to Fillory and enforce limits on the arrival and departure of the Chatwin children; furthermore, the Fillory portals "represent acts of selection and election" (Clute "Portals" 776), seen very clearly in the special status of the Chatwin children and Quentin's idolization and jealousy of their privilege in being the "chosen ones" who have this unique access and connection to Fillory, which Plum inherits as her Chatwin birthright.

These details of the *Fillory and Further* novels, as well as the details of the world of Fillory and their author Christopher Plover, may well sound familiar: the parallels with Narnia, C.S. Lewis, and *The Chronicles of Narnia* are explicit and intentional. Grossman's adaptation of Narnia in his trilogy is a common topic in interviews,[3] and the references and parody are frequently noted in the small body of scholarship on the series.[4] Grossman has catalogued many of the allusions to Lewis's series, alongside other works, in a post for *Tor.com* ("Brief") and has answered questions about his Narnian allusions on *Goodreads* (Response). These paratextual confirmations are not necessary to see the adaptation, however: any reader with even a basic familiarity with Lewis' series would be able to grasp the allusion. The two series are more alike than not,[5] with a family of British children out in the country on their summer holidays entering a fantastic secondary world through various portals, where they rule temporarily as kings and queens over talking beasts and under an animal god, returning home at the end of each book.

The remarkably frequent mentions of Fillory throughout Book I of *The Magicians* (the section detailing Quentin's education at Brakebills) and the general thematizing of the mode demonstrate the importance of the portal fantasy narrative as a framework for understanding Quentin's schooling experiences and the text as a whole. Readers' expectations are shaped by the protagonist's, and Quentin's are informed by his obsession with the *Fillory* series. From the beginning, Quentin processes his educational experiences through the lens of this mode: the narrative opens with Quentin's Princeton alumni interview, which he processes through a Fillory filter.

> If this were a Fillory novel—Quentin thought, just for the record—the house would contain a secret gateway to another world. The old man who lived there would be kindly and eccentric and drop cryptic remarks, and then when his back was turned Quentin would stumble on a mysterious cabinet or an enchanted dumbwaiter or whatever, through which he would gaze with wild surmise on the clean breast of another world.
> But this wasn't a Fillory novel [Magicians 7–8].

Quentin's understanding that his life is not a Fillory novel does nothing to prevent him from using these narratives as a framework for his own experiences or from wishing that he *were* living a Fillory story, and his use of this frame encourages readers to apply a similar lens in their

3. Imperial Institutes

reading of *The Magicians*. While Quentin is understandably confused by the events which unfold during and immediately after this interview, leading to his discovery of Brakebills College for Magical Pedagogy, readers—primed through the meta-textual references and commentary, as discussed further below—are prepared to recognize and enter Brakebills as a secondary world and read through the portal fantasy mode.

Through Quentin's eyes, readers discover a secret world where those with the right potential study magic and learn to wield immense powers, a world where time runs two months behind and everything is emblazoned with the bee-and-key crest of Brakebills. Readers progress with Quentin as he slowly masters the rules and customs of this new world, transitioning from ignorance and awestruck naivety through mastery to eventual boredom and disengagement, as the fantastically new becomes numbingly normal. But where Quentin expects the rolling pastoral landscape of a kingdom to rule, he and readers are instead given the confines of a college campus and a curriculum to follow. What happens when the portal fantasy meets the school story? What do we find when we approach a school as a secondary world and interrogate Brakebills within the framework of the portal fantasy?

Imperialist Educations

Processing Quentin's education at Brakebills—and *The Magicians* as a whole—through the portal fantasy mode foregrounds the imperialism inherent in Brakebills as an institution, as the imperialist ideology, structures, and violence of the portal fantasy mode illuminate these same aspects in the education of Quentin and his peers.[6] Portal fantasies are inherently imperialist; Lewis's *Chronicles of Narnia*, which the Fillory novels parallel and adapt, are particularly so. The invitation presented through the foregrounding of the portal fantasy structure to interrogate Brakebills as a secondary world explicates the imperialism that is also always present in school stories and in any education, real or fictional.

Portal fantasies are about "entry, transition, and exploration" (*Rhetorics* 2), all key facets of imperial expansion. Mendlesohn sketches out the imperialist underpinnings of the portal fantasy: as the protagonist *"moves through"* the secondary world, growing and changing as a result of their experiences, the indigenous populations of these fantastic worlds are "orientalised" into the "unchanging past" (*Rhetorics* 6, emphasis in original). As Aishwarya Subramanian elaborates, it is the European observer/reader whose worldview is privileged in this process when the portal is entered from our own world (375), a phenomenon by no means unique to this series. As the archetypal and foundational portal fantasy (Mendlesohn *Rhetorics* 1), Lewis's *The Chronicles of Narnia* exemplify the imperialism of this mode, generated by their sociocultural and historical context.

The imperialism of Lewis's *Narnia* series is further entrenched by virtue of its status as children's literature: as demonstrated by scholars including Clare Bradford, Donnarae MacCann, Perry Nodelman, Jacqueline Rose, Peter Hunt and Karen Sands, and Jo-Ann Wallace, the connection between imperialism and children's literature is inherent and long-standing (and shows little signs of abating).[7] Wallace examines the ways in which children's literature influenced empire, arguing that the figure of "the child" as created largely through children's literature was a *"necessary precondition* of imperialism" (176, emphasis in original) as an ideological model for conceptualizing the "savage Other." MacCann notes the "special connection" between children's literature and imperialist policies, "since the ideal imperialist strategy is to impel the young to colonize and marginalize themselves" (185), and positions children's literature as "agents of art that help produce a colonial-based socialization" (186). In "The Other: Orientalism, Colonialism, and Children's Literature," Nodelman draws on Rose's demonstration that children's literature represents a form of colonization and uses Edward Said's *Orientalism* as an evaluative framework, similarly concluding that children's literature is "a form of colonization" (29) and an "imperialist activity" (33). In recognition of the imperialism inherent in children's literature, Hunt and Sands argue for increased attention to imperialism specifically in British children's literature, where it is so obvious as to go unexamined; in particular, they demonstrate the continued role of children's literature in sustaining imperial ideologies, particularly through fantasy texts.

Recognizing the doubled imperialism of Lewis's series as both children's literature and portal fantasies, scholarship in recent years has approached the Narnia texts with the explicit intention of analyzing them as imperialist texts. The publication of the Narnia texts in the 1950s coincided with the final decline of British empire, influencing

3. Imperial Institutes

the development of the portal fantasy structure (Cecire; Subramanian). Subramanian convincingly demonstrates that the secondary worlds of this mode are uniquely positioned to support colonial fantasies, as they are entirely accessible to the protagonist and, as is the case with Narnia, "bounded by human, British subjectivity" (375), functioning to reaffirm Britain as the center of empire. Indeed, Subramanian locates this ability to re-create and perfect the processes of imperialism as the primary attraction of secondary world fantasy in a postimperial context, noting that the timing of their emergence situated them as "a repository for colonial desire, as well as a space for the working out of postimperial anxieties" (371), ultimately providing a space in which to present "fantasies of British imperial innocence" and continue imperial projects (379). In this way, Lewis's fantasy series is a distinctly imperial fantasy for those living in postimperial Britain, where the secondary world of Narnia presents a space for the continued enactment of British colonialism (Subramanian 374).

While Nicole M. DuPlessis asserts that "there is no sanctioned 'colonization' of Narnia" (117), and that what colonization we do see enacted in the text is performed by humans other than the "legitimate" British child monarchs through their "benign monarchy" and is thoroughly condemned in the narrative (123), other critics have challenged this assertion. Clare Echterling directly counters DuPlessis' claim (102), arguing that Lewis's series "implicitly encourages imperial exploration and control of distant lands" (100), demonstrating the ways in which selected texts from the series perpetuate the idea of the "fantasy of the white man's burden," as the (White, British) children *must* assume positions of authority (102, 107–108), as well as the ways in which this fantasy privileges the British reader (109). Subramanian also troubles the perception of the series as ostensibly anticolonial narratives, arguing that Narnia is presented as "a colonizable space" (372) and develops "a peculiarly specific colonial fantasy" of destined, welcome colonial rule (373). Subramanian draws on Maria Sachiko Cecire's analysis of *The Voyage of the Dawn Treader*, in which Cecire demonstrates that the text presents to both its child protagonists and its child readers "new opportunities for English exploration, imperial expansion, and colonial governance" (112) at a time when British children and youth no longer had access to real-world opportunities for the same (124), creating a space where imperialism could be "unproblematically celebrated" (126).

Schools of Magic

Deliberately positioning themselves as parallel to the Narnia texts, the *Magicians* trilogy participates in the imperialist traditions and replicates the colonial structures of portal fantasies written for children, drawing on and merging these inheritances with the imperialist ideology of the school story genre, which has its own inextricable ties to British imperialism.[8] The "echoes of Empire" (Cecire 119) throughout *The Chronicles of Narnia* are also heard in Grossman's depiction of Fillory, and are acknowledged by Cecire through a very brief discussion of the ways in which *The Magician King* reworks *The Voyage of the Dawn Treader* and shapes the ways in which Anglophone readers relate to the world by sustaining an imperialist ideology (126). Fillory, however, is not the only secondary world of Grossman's series, nor is it the first: before Quentin explores Fillory, he passes through the protected borders and enters the "secret, exclusive magical enclave" of Brakebills College (Magicians 122). To understand Fillory as a secondary world participating in the imperialist structures of the portal fantasy but not to consider the ways in which Brakebills is also positioned in the same ways (engaging with the same traditions) misses the opportunity to interrogate imperialism as a significant force at Brakebills, in the ways that this force influences the education received by various characters.

Moments in *The Magicians* encourage readers to make this connection and to look specifically at Brakebills through the lens of imperialism, such as the moment of Quentin's official entry into the institution. The entrance paperwork—"a fat sheaf of closely handwritten paper that looked like a treaty between two eighteenth-century nation-states" (Magicians 40)—metaphorically locates the relationship between Quentin and Brakebills during the height of British Empire. While the term "treaty" might imply potentially equal status between the two parties, the fact of Brakebills' absolute monopoly on and control over knowledge of and ability in magic negates any possibility that this treaty *can* be between equals, positioning Brakebills as the dominant colonizing power over Quentin and his peers.[9] Through this comparison, readers are not only prompted to examine the imperialism of the institution, but also reminded of the close relationships between the figures of the child and adolescent and that of the savage, the uneducated Other,[10] and the ways in which education is understood as the salvation for each group through the remedy of their ignorant condition.[11] Readers are positioned from the outset to understand Quentin's education as

3. Imperial Institutes

a process of colonization and Brakebills as an imperial power, amplifying the innate imperialism present in the narrative as a portal fantasy and encouraging a recognition of Brakebills' structures as imperialist.

Other features of Brakebills participate in establishing the school as an imperial institution, such as the explicit references to Brakebills as being situated in the past and out of step with the world outside its borders. Time at Brakebills is literally two months behind everywhere else, as a result of the slow but accumulative temporal misalignment caused by the protective spells keeping it hidden. Eliot reports that time began to diverge in the 1950s, growing steadily apart each year since and putting them "a little behind the mainstream" (Magicians 43–44).[12] The position of Brakebills as literally "behind the times" invites consideration of the ways in which it is also figuratively regressive, drawing further attention to its imperial ideology and its colonial practices.

Using the portal fantasy mode as a frame for interrogating Brakebills as an institution, we draw our categories of normality and deviance from imperial ideologies: specifically, the traditions of the British boarding school are brought to the colonies and perpetuated at Brakebills. One of the most explicit examples of this is the use of the prefect system, identified in the narrative as "yet another absurd, infantilizing idea borrowed from the English public school system, a symptom of the Anglophilia that was embedded so deeply in the institutional DNA of Brakebills" (Magicians 197). Another striking aspect—or symptom—is the unique accent of Brakebills students, who come to embody the institution's Anglophilia over the course of their studies as they develop "an affected, overly precise, quasi–British diction that came from all those vocal exercises, like they were just back from a Rhodes scholarship and wanted everybody to know it" (Magicians 209). Even Dean Fogg has this Brakebills accent, as Quentin notes upon meeting him that he speaks "as if he wished he had an English accent but wasn't quite pretentious enough to affect one" (Magicians 20), suggesting the Anglophilia of Brakebills infects both staff and students alike.

The performative exoticism of the faculty is yet another contributing element of its imperialism: readers learn that "'multicultural' spellcasting" had become fashionable in the 1930s and 1940s and, as a result, exoticized Others were brought in to perform stereotypical representations of diversity:

Schools of Magic

> Professors were imported at huge expense from around the world, the more remote the better: skirt-wearing shamans from Micronesian dot-islands; hunch-shouldered, hookah-puffing wizards from inner-city Cairo coffeehouses; blue-faced Tuareg necromancers from southern Morocco [*Magicians* 146–147].

Those members of the faculty who are not "multicultural" (and thereby participating in the creation of an imperialist environment through their presence as colonized Others) tend to enact a performatively Anglophilic identity, as Dean Fogg does. Quentin's eventual colleague Professor Hamish Bax, for instance, deliberately and conspicuously performs an Anglophilic identity: "he was unbelievably affected: he was black and from Cleveland but dressed in Scottish tweeds and smoked a fat Turk's-head pipe. He was the first person Quentin had ever seen in real life wearing plus fours" (*Land* 40). Quentin recognizes that his colleague's affected appearance may be a deliberate act, a conscious choice by Hamish to perform a particular version of Professor Bax within the structures and values of the Brakebills institution that makes him "hard to read" (*Land* 40), acknowledging the performative nature of the collectively Anglophilic identity of the faculty working within the imperial structures of Brakebills.[13]

The physical space of Brakebills also demonstrates the institution's imperial roots in a number of ways, with certain places on campus registering a particular significance in connection with empire. This includes the main House, as its first description draws on tropes of Oriental exoticism with "a rich, spicy smell in the air of books and Oriental carpets and old wood and tobacco" (*Magicians* 20–21); its twin building on the Antarctic campus is located in Marie Byrd Land, which positions the campus within the imperial practice of exploring, claiming, and naming distant lands—a practice central to the colonialism of portal fantasies (Echterling 103).[14] More than any other building, though, it is The Cottage that is particularly emblematic of the institution's Anglophilia. A private retreat for students in the Physical discipline where Quentin spends much of his time as a student, the initial description of The Cottage presents what Bradford refers to as a "time capsule of imperialism" (201):

> In between the bookcases the walls were hung with the usual inexplicable artifacts that accumulate in private clubs: African masks, dreary landscape paintings, retired ceremonial daggers, glass cases full of maps and medals

3. Imperial Institutes

and the deteriorating corpses of exotic moths that had presumably been captured at great effort and expense [Magicians 100].

As Bradford outlines, the objects of colonial exploration and encounters embody both "regret and nostalgia" for a former era, implying a desire for renewed imperial dominance (Bradford 201–02). Though these colonial trappings and the room in which they are housed are past their prime—described as "battered," "dreary," "retired," and "deteriorating" (Magicians 100)—their presence both maintains and signifies the legacy of imperialism and serves to link this space on the Brakebills campus to empire writ large.

Other ways in which the physical space of Brakebills emphasizes the institution's imperial legacy include the ubiquitous presence of the school's coat of arms, which is "worked into carpets and curtains, carved into stone lintels, pieced into the corners of parquet floors" (Magicians 49), and the names ascribed to essentially every architectural feature or discrete space on the Brakebills campus. Many of these names denote the campus's legacies and lineages of power: the fountains, for instance, have "an official name, usually that of a deceased Dean, as well as a nickname generated by the collective unconsciousness of generations of Brakebillian undergraduates" (Magicians 45). As Chris Tiffin and Alan Lawson demonstrate, "Names and codes of naming are obvious, basic ways … to indicate who matters and who is subordinate" (3): the names of the fountains position Brakebills as dominant twice over, first through past administrators and then through the legacy of graduates who have subscribed to the institution's values and gone on to perpetuate them beyond its borders. Together, these features of the physical space of the campus and the repeated descriptions of them—which are emblematic of the portal fantasy mode and its descriptive tendencies (Mendlesohn *Rhetorics* xix)—ensure that no student can forget even for a moment that they are within the institution of Brakebills College for Magical Pedagogy and create for the reader an image of the school as an imperially dominant quasi–British institution.

Belonging at Brakebills

The positioning of Brakebills as a secondary world in a portal fantasy, accomplished through the foregrounding of the Fillory intratexts and the thematizing of the portal fantasy mode, welcomes consideration of the institution within a framework of empire and imperialism. Approaching an analysis of Brakebills within this framework, we can understand the school as an imperial system, as the center of a magical empire which colonizes those with magical aptitude and potential. Brakebills functions and is positioned as a colonial empire, and we can ask of it the same questions we can ask of any imperial nation: "Who is part of the nation? Who can claim citizenship? On what grounds do we make such claims? How are different subjects positioned?" (Dei 15).

In settler colonialism, the center is both a physical location and a reflection of the ideals and practices of the colonizer; within the magical community, Brakebills functions similarly as both a physical center of power and a simultaneous source and reflection of dominant norms and behaviors. To claim citizenship in the empire of Brakebills, prospective and current students must embody the colonizer's ideal, or at minimum demonstrate the potential to do so. How well each of the central characters embody this ideal or demonstrate this potential informs their relationship to Brakebills as the center of empire: those who most successfully emulate and conform occupy a position in or near the center, reaping the associated benefits of this privileged place. Those who fail to reflect key attributes find themselves closer to the margins—or entirely beyond the borders—and must contend with the inherent trauma of this distance.

The imperialist structures of Brakebills and its attendant ideology create categories of normality and deviance against which all students are measured, determining their citizenship status and their position in relation to the center; this status influences each individual's ability to access social, cultural, and economic capital through their schooling. Furthermore, these characters and their experiences within the institution demonstrate the ways in which the dominant colonizer is able to wield different types and amounts of power against individual colonized subjects based on the individual's historical and social position (Dei 8). As we shall see, students like Quentin who fit comfortably within the categories of normality, and are granted full citizenship status, are better able to access the capital available through Brakebills, while those labelled as entirely deviant, such as Julia, must work far harder to accrue capital through their educations from beyond the borders of the empire. The *Magicians* trilogy, by explicitly combining a school story narrative with a portal fantasy frame, foregrounds the imperialism of each and

3. Imperial Institutes

encourages interrogation of the ways in which students are positioned in relation to the imperial center and how this influences their educational experience.

As we consider the experiences of individual students within (and without) Brakebills, it is important to remember that education is an enactment of colonialism, as highlighted in the Gaile S. Cannella and Radhika Viruru epigraph. It is a particularly insidious and dangerous type of colonialism, as colonization through education subjugates "the minds, hearts, cultural perspective, and even desires of peoples" (Cannella and Viruru ["Euro-American"] 198). Schools indoctrinate students into the values of the dominant system and condition them to accept their position within it, thereby perpetuating the structures of power and oppression (Cannella and Viruru ["Euro-American"] 203); furthermore, as Mark Bray has outlined, imperial educational systems are structured to serve the ends of the colonizer, influencing who has access to an education and what their experience and success will be in the system (334).[15] The conceptual categories of "child" and "savage," or other terms for the native Other, are closely related; similarly connected to each is the conceptual category of "student." Certain educational practices and pedagogies are premised upon the understanding of students as empty vessels (*terra nullius*) requiring the guidance of teachers (superior humans), presenting the teacher's role as filling students with knowledge, done for the benefit and improvement of the student. These practices are what Paulo Freire would describe as "dominating praxis" and, more specifically, a "banking concept" of education, and they are inherently linked to imperialism both through the contexts of their enactment and through the similarities of their ideology, with these pedagogical beliefs mirroring the beliefs held by imperial colonizers.[16]

To earn citizenship in the empire of Brakebills, students must conform to the categories of normality established by the institution's ideology, embodying the ideal subject. Two key elements of this confirmation relate to students' beliefs and behaviors: academically, they must adopt an understanding of magic as a scientific practice; socially, they must accept the structures of the institution and abide by them without question or challenge. Examining how well particular characters are able to comply with these two requirements simultaneously reveals their position in relation to Brakebills as the center of the empire, as those who effectively embody these elements are located in or near the center, and those who deviate most significantly are furthest out at the edges.

More than any other character, Quentin proves to possess the qualities valued by the institution and displays a consistent willingness to conform to expectations, making him the ideal student as he achieves all the markers of normality. As noted above, educational systems are primarily designed to serve the colonizers and educate their own (Bray 334), and Quentin, exemplifying the "normal" student, is part of this privileged group: Quentin has the potential to entirely "outgrow" his status as a colonized individual and become a colonizer himself, earning full citizenship status and its attendant privileges. Quentin is best understood as simultaneously among the colonized students and belonging to and participating in the colonizing institution, exemplifying George J. Sefa Dei's assertion of the multiplicity of subject identities within colonialism (8). Consequently, Quentin serves primarily as an opportunity to understand the normative educational experience, examining the key imperialist ideology into which Brakebills indoctrinates its students and through which it evaluates them, and the desired trajectory for student development within the normative model of the institution; analyzing other characters and their experiences in contrast to Quentin explicates the consequences of deviance both minor and major.

One of Quentin's key accomplishments in his transition from colonized to colonizer is his embrace of the institution's conceptualization of magic as a scientific practice. Though Professor March, in his introductory lecture, claims that magic is "not a science"—nor is it art or religion, but rather a "craft" (Magicians 48)—the treatment of magic in the institution proves otherwise. Learning the practice of magic involves demonstration and then exact replication of extremely precise and technical hand gestures and incantations, executed primarily (alongside one's "lab partner") in a classroom with a highly scientific material environment: "[Practical Applications] was held in a room that resembled a college chemistry lab: indestructible gray stone tables; counters mottled with ancient unspeakable stains; deep, capacious sinks. ... It carried a whiff of ozone" (Magicians 59). While magic may not be *a science*, the practice of learning magic at Brakebills is distinctly *scientific*.[17] This conceptualization of magic as scientific is also evident in other aspects of the institution's pedagogical practice. This includes the Discipline

3. Imperial Institutes

system, which can be calculated on the basis of consistent factors but is easier to determine through pre-defined practical experiments (Magicians 91–94); it also includes the semester students spend at Brakebills South endlessly drilling minute variations of basic spells in order to "absorb and internalize" the myriad factors and permutations required for spellcasting (Magicians 149),[18] a practice that perfectly exemplifies the ways in which a scientific understanding of knowledge turns it into something that "can be extracted, as a fixed content, and employed in a mechanical, instrumental manner" (Thésée 27). Despite what Professor March claims, magic as taught at Brakebills and practiced by students and teachers alike is a distinctly scientific practice, informed by a belief in the application of constant factors and consistently replicable results.

As scholars such as Mary Louise Pratt and Gina Thésée have convincingly demonstrated, science and its conceptual trappings were central elements in imperial domination and dominion, and the positioning of magic as a scientific endeavor—in practice, if not in name—contributes to the colonial project enacted by Brakebills as an equivalent concept. Science as it developed alongside empire deliberately functioned to encourage the domination of nature by the European man (Thésée 28; Pratt 30–31); in nearly identical ways, the understanding of magic and its workings and purposes with which Brakebills students are indoctrinated encourages their domination of the world. Dean Fogg even goes so far as to suggest that the power and privilege inherent in magic is of nearly divine levels, giving magicians the power "to break the world" and make it over into the ideal as they perceive it (Magicians 217).[19]

Magic as an encouragement of domination is most evident in the pursuits Brakebills students pursue after graduation, as Quentin recounts that people "devoted years of their lives" to such pursuits: "It was considered chic to go undercover, to infiltrate governments and think tanks and NGOs, even the military, in order to get oneself into a position to influence real-world affairs magically from behind the scenes" (Magicians 210). While not all of this infiltration is inherently sinister, as there is recognition elsewhere that some graduates go into "public service—quietly promoting the success of humanitarian causes, or subtly propping up the balance of various failing ecosystems" (Magicians 181), the "chic" pursuit of using magic to manipulate the rest of the world is inherently imperialist. In the same way that science encouraged and supported colonial expansion, the teaching of magic at Brakebills presents it as a tool best employed in dominating the world and its non-magical population.[20]

To be "saved through education" means "to become an individual who intellectually conforms to notions of scientific progress and advancement" (Cannella and Viruru ["Euro-American"] 204), and we see Quentin adhere to this understanding of magic, its workings, and its goals, thereby satisfying the requirements to be considered "normal" within the institution's structures and securing for Quentin a place in the center of empire. For characters like Josh, however—who may subscribe to the understanding of magic as scientific but cannot realize this understanding in his practice—the failure to fully embody this key element of the institution's ideology sees him kept at a distance, hovering near the margins.

Josh is highly social, friendly, funny, and an astute social observer[21]; he embodies the key element of willing obedience discussed below, but he struggles with his sub-par magical abilities. Josh can never be sure that a spell will work: though he adopts the conceptualization of magic as a science, he is unable to achieve the consistent, replicable results in his practice that this conceptualization requires. This inconsistency with the results of his spellcasting is such a significant, persistent problem that it jeopardizes Josh's position within the institution, with only the Dean's intervention preventing Josh's dismissal from Brakebills (Magicians 130). Though his position within the social sphere of the institution is secure, Josh's sub-par magical abilities effectively marginalize him during his time at the school.

Forced by means beyond his control to a position permanently distant from the center, Josh responds by voluntarily moving further towards the margins: he moves beyond Brakebills' borders entirely, enacting the role of colonial explorer in his travels through the multiverse (Magician King 158–160), then settles on the border itself as an imperial administrator, facilitating commerce between those within and without the empire of Brakebills. Josh establishes himself as an intermediary between the network of hedge witches and Brakebills graduates, brokering trades of knowledge and artifacts between the two groups and exploiting the vulnerability of the hedge witches (Magician King 165–166). He considers himself to be a sort of "king" of the underground, and his attitude towards the hedge witches with whom he interacts is

3. Imperial Institutes

patronizing, belittling, and distinctly colonial (Magician King 165). Josh's experiences on the periphery during his education first compel him to enact the colonial explorer and then find a means to turn his peripheral status into a position valuable to the center, defining himself as a normative member of Brakebills through his juxtaposition against those definitively deviant and beyond the institution's borders.

Beyond the borders of Brakebills from start to finish, Julia develops an alternative conceptualization of magic as ceremony and ritual, which challenges the supremacy of the Brakebillian scientific conceptualization and undermines its presentation as the only or "natural" way to understand magic and its practice. As the privileging of science has resulted in a loss of cultural knowledge (Thésée 25), which Thésée understands as a deliberate "second phase" of colonization to support and consistently reinscribe imperial domination (33), so does the scientific practice of magic championed by Brakebills lead to the loss of other practices based in religion and mythology, which Julia and her peers studying collectively at the house in Murs recuperate through their resistance beyond the institution's borders.

First, though, Julia and the other Murs magicians must learn to reject the institution's insistence on magic as a scientific practice and anything else as based in inferior "folklore," having internalized the institution's values even from beyond the borders, as is common in colonial contexts (Thésée 34). We see Julia undertake this process, beginning with her initial skepticism and rejection of the Murs project as she struggles with the perception that "religion was just chaos, a complete junk pile" (Magician King 319). What begins as only pretend commitment to the concept, however, becomes true belief as they begin to experience first minor and then major magical successes via religion and mythology, discovering Our Lady Underground and working miraculous magics through prayer and ceremony related to this divine figure (Magician King 320–321, 324–331). While the final outcome of the ritual to call this divine figure is far from what was anticipated,[22] religion and mythology prove to be methods of accessing significant levels of magical power which have been forgotten by, and so are not available to, Brakebills and its students. Alone of all the characters, Julia ascends to divine status and gains access to powers far beyond the abilities of the Brakebills graduates through this alternative conceptualization.

Quentin can both believe that magic is a science and actualize this understanding in his practice, helping earn him a position in the imperial center; Josh, though he may believe it, cannot achieve it in practice, forever denying him a position in the center and driving him farther to the margins, where he can feel closest to the empire in contrast to those definitively beyond it. Julia, working beyond the borders of the empire, rejects the idea of magic as a science and rediscovers ritualistic practices which provide access to powers Brakebills has dismissed or forgotten: though they do not bring her into the imperial borders, they trouble the empire's very center, undermining the assertion that the Brakebillian conceptualization of magic is the only—or the superior—option.

Of equal importance to adopting the Brakebillian conceptualization of magic is social conformity to the institution's structures and norms, where we again see Quentin excel and can examine in contrast the consequences for those characters who do not so readily comply. An anti-colonial perspective, as Dei explains, is about identifying and challenging domination and the everyday practices in which it manifests (5); entering the institution with such a perspective, Penny secures a label of deviance from the outset. From his first interactions with Brakebills, we see Penny's tendency to challenge the institution's structures, as he discovers and exploits a flaw in the water-delivery system at the Entrance Exam, telling the others how much he enjoys testing and manipulating the system: "I love finding shit like that, where the system screws itself with its own rules" (Magicians 24). This critical mindset is not one desired by the institution—is, in fact, threatening to it—and so Penny cannot be welcomed into the imperial center. Penny's experiences throughout his education are shaped by the school's attempts to manage and mitigate the threat of his non-compliant deviance, first marginalizing him in an attempt to reduce possible harm and then, when this fails and the threat he presents increases, attempting to bring him closer to the center and encouraging him to adopt the institution's ideologies.

Penny is deliberately marginalized within the school throughout his first three years, maneuvered into a position of social isolation when he is identified as a candidate for potential advancement alongside Quentin and Alice and then alone denied this acceleration. Throughout this process, we once again see Penny's tendency to challenge the institution, as he is the only one of the trio who questions the inconsistencies, logistical flaws, and dubious motivation of the offer to advance

3. Imperial Institutes

(Magicians 60). We are given no indication that Penny is a less capable magician—in fact, he seems to be precisely on par with the other two—so we must locate another cause for his failure in the exam; seeing its effect in isolating Penny and thereby containing the threat presented by his critical non-compliance, it seems likely this has been a deliberate maneuver on the part of the institution.

Successfully rebuffed and sidelined by the institution's efforts to socially isolate him, Penny rebels against the center, including through a physical assault of Quentin, who he (rightfully) understands as representative of the ideal, normative Brakebills student, easily accessing all that Penny is denied. Following this altercation, we see Dean Fogg continue to actively marginalize Penny: Quentin receives no punishment and barely any chastisement, while Penny receives plenty of each (Magicians 88–89). While it may seem as if there are no positive outcomes for Penny in this incident, it does provide him with space to articulate his intentions regarding his relationship to the institution and their attempts to marginalize him:

> "I don't take things lying down, Quentin. ... I don't want trouble. But if you come after me, I swear to you that I will get right back in your face. That's just how it works. ... You try to walk all over me, Quentin. I'm going to come right back at you!" [Magicians 87]

Reading "Quentin" here as a stand-in for Brakebills itself, Penny proceeds to make good on this promise: he stays and he studies, but he rejects the conformity expected of him and exists on the periphery of the institution. Though the institution furthers his marginalization, assigning his Discipline as "independent" (Magicians 197–8),[23] Penny embraces this peripheral status and actively distances himself further. He becomes "a loner, a ghost," spending time alone and engaging with no one (Magicians 197): Penny's method of resistance becomes a deliberate perpetuation of the social isolation and marginalization that was initially forced upon him.

This isolation, however, does not successfully mitigate the threat posed to the institution by Penny's deviance, as Penny is pushed to a point at which his marginalization actually serves to increase this risk. "Colonialism," Tiffin and Lawson tell us, "alternately fetishized and feared its Others ... depending on its sense of the threat posed by the Other" (5), and Penny's active self-marginalization as he is rapidly developing unique and powerful magical knowledge presents a new threat: he has become "that Other which always threatens to expose the knowledge of itself as plural and complete and outside," beyond the discourses of Empire (Tiffin and Lawson 7). The potential that Penny will break away from the institution entirely and fundamentally challenge the system from beyond it becomes a greater threat than the risk he presents from within, and so we see Brakebills suddenly attempt to bring Penny back in towards the center. When he enters his Fourth Year, Penny is made one of the school's four prefects, surprising everyone (Magicians 197).

While this attempt to reintegrate Penny into the structures of Brakebills and neutralize the threat posed by his deviance is not completely successful, it does successfully prevent him from realizing his disruptive potential. Penny leaves Brakebills early, and his subsequent journey is one of slowly moving back towards the center, first accepting a marginal position among the group of Brakebills graduates—who represent the institutional center in the wider world, perpetuating and enacting its values and programs—and then finding a new center to which he can finally, fully, belong. Entering into "the warm, secret paper heart of the City" (Magicians 391), Penny joins the Library of the Neitherlands, where he participates in a different, though equally imperial, system dedicated to amassing and controlling knowledge. With his incorporation into an alternate imperial center, Penny no longer represents a threat to the institution of Brakebills and its representatives and actually becomes a powerful ally, acting on behalf of one powerful institution to aid another in the joint project of maintaining access to magic (Magician King 297–309).

The way Brakebills reacts to an internal threat is substantially different from its response to external threats, as we see with Julia. Julia's challenge of the institution, like Penny's, begins in the Entrance Exam: where Penny mostly complies, however, looking for flaws in the system only after he has finished writing, Julia freely admits that "The test was the least of her priorities" (Magician King 79). She is unable to focus on completing the exam because of her attention to the larger question of what, exactly, is happening:

> But she spent too much time looking around, trying to work it through, the implications of it. She didn't take it at face value the way Quentin did. The uppermost thought in her mind was, why are you all sitting here doing

3. Imperial Institutes

differential geometry and generally jumping through hoops when fundamental laws of thermodynamics and Newtonian physics are being broken left and right all around you? [Magician King 79]

Where Penny adopts some elements of the anti-colonial perspective, Julia's experience is anti-colonial from start to finish, focusing all of her energy on a critical consideration of the institution's structures and none on compliance with its seemingly arbitrary demands. As Dei explains:

> An anti-colonial perspective is about developing an awareness/consciousness of the varied conditions under which domination and oppression operate. Such a perspective seeks to subvert the dominant relations of knowledge production that sustain hierarchies and systems of power. It challenges the colonizer's sense of reason, authority and control [5].

As the embodiment of an anti-colonial perspective, the threat Julia poses to the institution is too great to countenance; where Brakebills felt able to manage Penny's minor non-conformity, Julia must be expelled entirely, and so her memory of the Exam is wiped and replaced with false memories of writing a class paper, with the essay itself available as evidence.

Brakebills, underestimating their opponent, is careless in creating the false essay, and the uncharacteristic error leads Julia down an investigative path that eventually uncovers her true memories of the Entrance Exam and the violation of her psyche.[24] Now aware of the institution and of her deliberate exclusion from it, Julia becomes a threat from beyond the Brakebills borders. Though Brakebills attempts to divert this threat early on, sending seven acceptance letters to elite universities to which Julia did not apply (Magician King 82), Julia rejects this alternative. Instead, she sacrifices her present, to both an obsessive search for access to magic beyond Brakebills (Magician King 121–125), including a plea to Quentin on one of his rare visits home (Magician King 145–7), and to more passive resistance as she remains committed to her challenge despite her lack of progress (Magician King 77–82, 120–121). While Julia's resistance is ultimately fruitful—as she discovers the Safe House system and is eventually invited to join the elite hedge witch community and participate in their project at the house in Murs—her education is defined by the limitations of studying outside the institution's monopolistic control and the significant, usually sexual, trauma and violence she experiences as a consequence of or even prerequisite to increasing her knowledge and ability.

What is it that makes Julia's pursuit of magic beyond the borders of Brakebills such a threat to the institution? First, Julia's success makes her impossible to ignore or dismiss, which runs counter to the institution's need to elide the existence of individuals like her. The concept of hedge witches is entirely absent in the narrative until Julia makes her re-appearance because Quentin, as the focalizing perspective, is positioned within an imperial institution that actively works to erase their existence. Brakebills considers Julia and the other hedge witches only when it must, and then only as less-than, subhuman—*never* as magicians. In this way, Brakebills is "conceptually depopulating" the magical world beyond the campus by denying the existence of those others with magical capabilities or, when it must acknowledge them, relegating them to categories of inferiority (Tiffin and Lawson 5). This strategy works to create and support the claim of *terra nullius* and make inhabited land available to colonizers; similarly, this erasure and denigration of the hedge witches and the Safe Houses maintains the world as entirely available for Brakebills graduates. When it is no longer possible to ignore Julia, it is no longer possible to pretend that the world is freely available for the colonization of Brakebills graduates, troubling the ideological underpinnings of the institution.

Second, to learn magic beyond the institution, Julia must understand magic better than the students at Brakebills: she must understand not just the practice of magic but also the curriculum of Brakebills, so that she may recognize the ways in which Brakebills regulates access to magic and identify the places where this control is imperfect and may be exploited to provide her with access. As part of this comprehensive understanding of magic, Julia also develops an alternative conceptualization of its practice as ritual and ceremony—which, as analyzed above, also threatens a foundational component of the institution's ideological practice. From her external vantage, Julia can see both where the borders of the institution are vulnerable and porous and where the very foundation of the imperial center is unsound, artificial, or arbitrary. Her existence forces an uncomfortable acknowledgment that the world beyond Brakebills is not empty and available, and her knowledge has the potential to undermine the institution's structures and dominance: recognizing these threats, it is no wonder that Brakebills works so hard to

3. Imperial Institutes

prevent individuals like Julia from realizing their potential beyond the borders, and the control, of the institutional empire.

The colonialism of educational institutions—their metaphorical position as imperial centers and their control over citizenship status for prospective and current students—is made uniquely available for consideration through the trilogy's foregrounding of its status as a portal fantasy, drawing attention to themes of imperialism in the school story and representations of education through its merger of these genres. Subsequently, so too is the impact of an individual student's position in relation to the institution as imperial center (at its heart, on the margins, or beyond the borders) presented for reader examination. Quentin, able to fully embody key elements of academic and social conformity in adopting the Brakebillian conceptualization of magic as science and displaying willing social conformity and obedience, occupies a secure position at the center of the empire, going so far as to realize his transition from colonized to colonizer when he joins the Brakebills faculty in the third novel. Other students, like Josh and Penny, are forced to the empire's margins as their abilities or attitudes prevent them from fully embodying the institution's ideal student, from whence they seek greater belonging by placing themselves in direct contrast with those outside the borders or by entering an alternative imperial center. And beyond the borders entirely stand hedge witches like Julia, a subjugated non-citizen who threatens the institution's very foundation through her resistance to the institution's desires for an empty and available world, her alternative conceptualization of magic, and her arguably greater power and abilities. The educational experiences of each of these students are intrinsically informed, for better or for worse, by the student's position in relation to Brakebills as the center of empire.

Socializing Critique

While Quentin makes the transition from colonized to colonizer with little awareness or critique, the series works to ensure that readers are not so complacent. Through both the thematizing of the portal fantasy mode—using the Fillory intratexts and Quentin's evolving relationship to them as a model for readers of how they might engage with the *Magicians* trilogy—and the multiple point-of-view narratives, which show a variety of ways that students are oppressed by the institution and their means of resistance, Grossman's trilogy encourages its readers to adopt a critical position and to question and critique Brakebills as an institution, particularly its imperialist ideology and assumptions.

The foregrounding of the portal fantasy mode through the Fillory intratexts include multiple moments of meditation on the series, in which readers are privy to Quentin's thoughts on the *Fillory and Further* books. Frequently, these moments of contemplation include a comparison of Quentin's experiences at Brakebills with those of the Chatwin children in Fillory and a consideration of the major themes or issues of these intratexts: readers see the ways in which Quentin uses the Fillory series as a framework for understanding his own experiences, and are implicitly asked to undertake a similar interrogation of the *Magicians* series, attending to what it has to say as a text, how it says it, and how the world would look if viewed through the framework Grossman's trilogy offers. In this way, the series is quite explicit with its thematizing of the portal fantasy genre and its invitation to readers to approach these books *as texts*.

Take, for instance, the opening of *The Magicians*. Before Quentin's alumni interview triggers the series of events which lead him to Brakebills, readers are presented with Quentin's meditation on what it is that books can accomplish, specifically a good portal fantasy narrative:

> But there was a more seductive, more dangerous truth to Fillory that Quentin couldn't let go of. It was almost like the Fillory books—especially the first one, *The World in the Walls*—were about reading itself. When the oldest Chatwin, melancholy Martin, opens the cabinet of the grandfather clock that stands in a dark, narrow back hallway in his aunt's house and slips through into Fillory ... it's like he's opening the covers of a book, but a book that did what books always promised to do and never actually quite did: get you out, really out, of where you were and into somewhere better [Magicians 7].

This passage, and others like it throughout the series, encourage readers to consider the allure and effect of reading, while also serving as a reminder that Quentin is a protagonist in just such a narrative, making his experiences as available for examination as the Chatwin children's adventures. Given the connections the series then goes on to foreground between portal fantasies and imperialism and the less-than-idealized representation of a secondary world with the "real" Fillory, readers are

3. Imperial Institutes

also prompted to question what is meant by "somewhere better" and the imperialist ideology of exploration and control which underlies the fantasy of travelling to a new world.

These metatextual musings and mentions of the Fillory intratexts are by no means a small component of the narrative: the Fillory novels feature prominently as Quentin's frame of reference throughout Book I of *The Magicians* detailing his studies at Brakebills. First querying whether this might actually be Fillory after all at the conclusion of his Entrance Exam (Magicians 33–34), Quentin then continues to compare Brakebills to Fillory throughout the remainder of the summer before his first term once he knows definitively that they are distinct (Magicians 42). When Quentin's formal education commences, he contrasts his experiences learning magic with those given in Fillory, noting it is nothing like he expected based on his reading (Magicians 55). Fillory is on his mind as he studies extra material to skip a year (Magicians 63) and when he and Alice step outside for a break (Magicians 67–68). Quentin uses them as a frame of reference again when he wakes in the infirmary, initially indirectly through his musings that he had passed through "another secret portal, this time into the world of the sick and injured" (Magicians 83) and then directly when he thinks about Jane Chatwin, with whom he has just unknowingly conversed (Magicians 83–85). Quentin thinks about Fillory when the Beast eats a classmate (Magicians 118) and—for the first time in "ages"—during his silent studies and final test at Brakebills South (Magicians 156, 160). Alice re-reads them in the Physical Cottage, after which she and Quentin discuss them in depth and even Janet admits her childhood love for the series (Magicians 177–9). Alice recognizes Quentin's persistent use of the Fillory narratives to inform his own expectations, worrying that this will result in nothing but disappointment for him following graduation (Magicians 206); this proves true, as Quentin begins despairing that he cannot imagine a future as satisfying as Fillory would be (Magicians 210, 213, 220). Through these moments, *The Magicians* both explicates and plays with expectations of genre, using the story-within-a-story of Fillory to keep readers consistently aware that they are reading a narrative themselves.

This effort to maintain a continual awareness of *The Magicians* as a text is paired with a model of critical reading practice: Quentin's periodic re-reading of the series throughout his studies provides an example of critical engagement with a portal fantasy text. Home for his first Christmas break, Quentin re-reads the Fillory series "for a taste of the magical world he'd just left," applying "a more critical eye" to the representation of magic as well as the narrative inconsistencies, unsatisfying gaps, and Martin's commentary on the portal fantasy structure (Magicians 73–75).[25] Quentin engages in another "Fillory binge" when he returns home for the summer following his Fourth Year: through this binge, readers are not only introduced to the boarding school frame of the second Fillory book, which brings Quentin's studies at Brakebills into yet another parallel with the Fillory narratives (Magicians 167–168), but also presented with another consideration of the portal fantasy structure and its insistence on a return at the end of the narrative, as well as the narrative difference of a portal one controls and those that appear independently (Magicians 168–169). While Quentin's critical engagement is relatively superficial, the fact that he interrogates the narratives at all is an invitation for readers to engage in the same process.

This invitation for interrogation is perhaps nowhere more explicit than with the unpublished manuscript of the sixth Fillory novel, titled: *The Magicians: Book Six of Fillory and Further*. Making the title of this most-interesting intratext the same as the title of the text itself explicitly draws the two narratives together, connecting the narrative of the text—the story of Quentin, *The Magicians*, with which we as readers are currently engaged—and the narratives within the text, the Fillory novels for which Quentin is the reader. Through these metatextual moments, which occur frequently throughout Quentin's time studying at Brakebills, and their explicit engagement with narrative expectations, readers are encouraged to approach the trilogy as a portal fantasy and to analyze it as such.

As readers engage critically and deliberately with Grossman's series, they are presented with multiple narratives of interaction between individuals and the institution of Brakebills and a variety of relationships, as examined above. The experiences of Quentin, Julia, and Plum are detailed first-hand through chapters in which they are the focalizing character, while the experiences of Alice, Penny, and Josh are all seen second-hand through their relationships and interactions with these focalizing characters, primarily Quentin. Primed by the thematization of the portal fantasy mode and the meta-textual foregrounding

3. Imperial Institutes

of Quentin's engagement with the Fillory texts, readers are encouraged to critically evaluate these disparate experiences and to recognize the harm and oppression perpetuated by Brakebills as an institution. While not every reader will recognize this harm as resulting from and contributing to an underlying imperialist ideology—present in both the institution of Brakebills and the portal fantasy narrative—readers are prepared through their deliberate positioning by the series itself to challenge and criticize the experiences of the characters within and beyond the boundaries of Brakebills, questioning even Quentin's seemingly simple experiences during his education there. In this way, readers are socialized into critique, rather than complacency.

Conclusion

Through the experiences of various characters as they undergo their education in magic, the imperialist elements of educational institutions are foregrounded. Through Quentin's normative experience at Brakebills, we see the institution's desire to transform colonized students in its own image and its conceptualization of magic as a scientific practice, including the ways in which this compels graduates to seek dominion over the mundane world. With the experiences of Alice and Plum, we see the significant impact that an individual's social position and history with the institution have in their ability to engage with the system and their experiences doing so. The marginalization Penny and Josh experience—the former as a result of the threat he presents to the institution, and the latter for his sub-par magical abilities—show us the ways in which being limited to only peripheral participation can create a desire for full membership and its inherent benefits rather than a rejection of the system and how individuals can seek to achieve this once their education has finished. Finally, with Julia, we see the ways in which exclusion from a system that maintains total control over access to power necessitates constant resistance if there is to be any learning. We witness the violence inherent in both Julia's exclusion and her resistance, but we also see that resistance can be successful and uncover knowledge lost to the institution and those within it.

In thematizing the portal fantasy structure through the intratexts *Fillory and Further*, Grossman's trilogy draws attention to it as a generic mode and foregrounds its inherent imperialism. Combining this with a school story narrative, and deliberately positioning the institution as a secondary world within the portal fantasy mode, transposes the consideration of imperialism to the institution and invites interrogation of the education represented within that lens. Through these metatextual meditations, readers are positioned to question and critique the imperialism inherent in education and the ways in which this ideology is manifest in the experiences of individuals within the institution, recognizing who is (dis)advantaged within the system and who is excluded entirely.

In Chapter 4, I demonstrate what happens when this process is reversed as Terry Pratchett's "Tiffany Aching" quintet plays with the generic expectations of the school story within a fantasy *Bildungsroman*, foregrounding structures and processes of education throughout the protagonist's maturation that may not otherwise receive critical attention. There, the metatextual meditations on the protagonist's anticipation of flying lessons position readers to recognize the ways in which Tiffany is socialized into the practice of witchcraft through her apprenticeships, before she changes her understanding of what it means to be a witch through her participation in the field.

Chapter 4

Nothing Exactly Like a Lesson

Legitimate Peripheral Participation in Terry Pratchett's "Tiffany Aching" Quintet

> "The thing about witchcraft," said Mistress Weatherwax, "is that it's not like school at all. *First* you get the test, and then afterward you spend years findin' out how you passed it. It's a bit like life in that respect."
> —Terry Pratchett, *The Wee Free Men*

> Whether such a process is incorporated into specialized institutions called schools or is carried on elsewhere and in less formal settings, the task of unraveling the patterns and mechanisms of intergenerational continuity is the first function of educational research.
> —Walter Feinberg, *Understanding Education: Toward a Reconstruction of Educational Inquiry*

In Chapter 3, I looked at the ways in which foregrounding the portal fantasy structure within a school story narrative in *The Magicians* trilogy draws attention to elements shared between these traditions, particularly the colonialism embedded in institutional education and the ways in which students' educational experiences are informed by their relationship to the school as imperial center. Turning our attention now to a subset of Terry Pratchett's expansive Discworld series, I examine the inverse: what happens when it is the school story narrative that is foregrounded and thematized in a typical young adult fantasy *Bildungsroman*? The "Tiffany Aching" quintet—*The Wee Free Men* (2003), *A Hat Full of Sky* (2004), *Wintersmith* (2006), *I Shall Wear Midnight* (2010), and *The Shepherd's Crown* (2015)—is a secondary world fantasy series detailing the maturation of a young protagonist; through pointed allusions to fantastic school story traditions in the first novel, readers are positioned to attend to the protagonist's education throughout her narrative arc from budding witch through apprentice to the new (non-)leader of all the witches.[1]

Here, too, we must consider the expanded versions of our key questions for analyzing the "deep structures" of education as consciously represented through a text, asking ourselves: what underlying meanings and ideologies are transmitted by the expectations and structures of genre along with the formal content of the narrative? How do authors and readers filter and distort knowledge, as teachers and administrators do? How do generic norms and expectations filter and distort knowledge alongside societal norms? Whose interests shape and inform narratives as well as educational institutions, processes, and outcomes? How do texts represent the distribution of social, cultural, and economic capital that occurs through the process of education?

Introduction

As with the *Harry Potter* series, there is a substantial and ever-growing body of scholarship on Pratchett's Discworld saga. Essay collections explore topics such as themes of identity and narrative (Noone and Leverett) and critical approaches to Pratchett's works from various disciplinary perspectives (Alton and Spruiell). Specific analyses of Pratchett's Discworld series include interrogations of: gender divisions and dynamics, particularly between witches and wizards (Çetiner-Öktem; Williams); Pratchett's employment of literary devices like satire, humor, allusion, and whimsy (Çetiner-Öktem; Haberkorn; Hunt "Terry"; Kochhar-Lindgren); the Discworld novels within the Urban Fantasy tradition (Young) and as situated between science and fiction (Sawyer). Other investigations work to put Pratchett's texts in conversation with other popular fantasy authors, including Pullman, Rowling, and Wynne Jones (Croft "Education"; Gruner "Teach"; Webb). The witches of the Discworld have been a particular focus, with scholars considering everything from their ethics and morality (Boulding; Croft "Nice"; McGillis), the ambiguous relationship between their witchcraft and their womanhood (Nuttall), and their particular practices and forms of magic (Martins) to Pratchett's subversive portrayal of the witch figure (Kittredge; Santaulària i Capdevila; Sayer; Sinclair; Webb) and

4. Nothing Exactly Like a Lesson

overviews of the Roundworld history that informs and underlies these representations (Sayer; Tykhomyrova).[2]

Looking specifically at the "Tiffany Aching" quintet, scholars have conversely explicated the series' critique of restrictive gender roles (Donaldson "Earning") and criticized Tiffany's internalization of "Pratchett's distrust of traditionally feminine traits" (Kittredge 676). Other investigations have analyzed Tiffany's connection to the worked landscape and the represented value of labor (Pandey) and the representations of religion (Gruner "Wrestling") and of selfhood (Moran) in the quintet. There has also been significant consideration of the series as a representation of education and as an education in its own right. Janet Brennan Croft compares Tiffany with Rowling's Hermione Granger, contrasting their educations in co-educational and gender-segregated spaces ("Education"), and Elisabeth Rose Gruner examines Tiffany's experiences alongside those of Harry Potter and Pullman's Lyra Belaqua as examples of "unschooling" or autonomous educations ("Teach"), while Maxi Steinbrück contrasts Tiffany's experiences with other Discworld characters to illuminate Pratchett's preference for experience-based learning. Other scholarship has included a consideration of various protagonists' educations in magic, including Tiffany's, as metaphorical representations of the work of adolescence (Haberkorn and Reinhardt) and explications of the ways in which the series demonstrates for young readers methods of resilience in the face of fear (Donaldson "Earning") and of addressing anxieties in the work of identity-formation (Donaldson "See").

In this chapter, we shall attend to the ways in which explicit references to fantastic school story traditions inform our reading of the quintet and bring forward distinct questions about Tiffany's vocational education as a witch and the ways in which intergenerational continuity in the witches' community of practice is achieved. This attention to Tiffany's education, in turn, helps us to see the series' challenge of aetonormativity and adult supremacy. By means of foregrounding the school story in *The Wee Free Men*, the "Tiffany Aching" quintet helps readers to recognize that Tiffany's apprenticeship and work as a witch are educational experiences; Jean Lave and Etienne Wenger's scholarship on learning through legitimate peripheral participation in a community of practice gives us valuable language to investigate the ways in which Tiffany learns from, among, and with the broader community of witches on the Discworld, constituting in its own fashion a structured education into the vocation of witchcraft. With this awareness of Tiffany's learning through practice, we recognize the ways in which Tiffany replicates some elements of the witches' vocational habitus while contesting and ultimately changing others—and, as a result, can see the ways in which the quintet challenges the aetonormativity usually present in both school stories and children's and young adult fantasy literature.

The Hidden Curriculum of School Stories

Foregrounding the School Story

Examining the ways in which the quintet foregrounds and explicitly plays with the conventions of fairy tales, Caroline Webb asserts that "Pratchett's fiction emphasises its own literary framework, inviting a comparatively sophisticated response from a reader implied to be consciously intelligent and analytical" (24). The "Tiffany Aching" quintet also plays with the tropes of the fantastic school story, deliberately introducing the idea of a school for witches and playing with readers' expectations by means of Tiffany's own imaginings and hopes. In this way, *The Wee Free Men* establishes the frame through which readers will approach and understand the remainder of Tiffany's series and primes readers to interrogate Tiffany's subsequent apprenticeships and her work as a witch as an education, even as it is simultaneously a fantastic adventure and a job that looks a lot like doing chores. *The Wee Free Men* foregrounds and thematizes the school story, thereby positioning readers to recognize the learning that happens during Tiffany's apprenticeships and her work as a witch, which in turn allows for an interrogation of her participation in the community of witches and the ways in which this community imparts a distinct vocational habitus, thereby ensuring intergenerational continuity.

Those familiar with the Discworld series at large might know of a number of opportunities for learning across this fantasy world, including the Unseen University; Quirm College for Young Ladies; the Assassin's Guild; roving bands of itinerant teachers; private schools; in-home tutoring with governesses; reading the Almanack; and apprenticeships, sometimes to Death himself.[3] While two of these options are introduced

4. Nothing Exactly Like a Lesson

to readers early in *The Wee Free Men*—a band of itinerant teachers passes through the Chalk, offerings facts in exchange for food and hand-me-downs, and Miss Tick the witch-finder is an alumna of Quirm College—we learn relatively little about these two educational institutions in this text alone. Beyond the explicit knowledge that Miss Tick earned a Gold Swimming Certificate there (Wee 42), most of what can be learned about Quirm College in *The Wee Free Men* is implied in Miss Tick's understanding of what it means to be a teacher, which includes lists, assessments, and neat handwriting (Wee 50). A more detailed picture is provided of the itinerant teachers, who move between far-flung communities with their carts and donkeys to sell "invisible things," giving short lessons on many subjects and answering such pressing questions as "What's on the other side of the mountain?" and "How come rain falls out of the sky?" (Wee 17–19).[4] While it is generally agreed among these rural communities that the teachers play a useful role in "[teaching] children enough to shut them up" (Wee 19), their ragged appearance and foraged diet indicates that education is not a lucrative career choice. With more humor than detail, these two brief examples nevertheless introduce the idea of formal schooling on the Discworld. Even for those coming to this secondary-world setting for the first time, there is an awareness that schools *exist*, that education can be deliberately structured and delivered, and that at least some people get it. When Miss Tick teases a mention of the school for witches, therefore, it seems entirely plausible that such an institution exists, most likely in some brick-and-mortar form—in fact, given what most readers know about fantasy stories detailing a protagonist's education, it feels far more than merely plausible.

Readers familiar with the genre know what to expect as the story develops from this first mention of the witches' school: namely, a journey to this school, where Tiffany will make friends, break rules, rise to the challenge, and don her black hat to ride upon her broomstick in flying lessons. The answers Miss Tick provides about the "special school" invite readers to fill in the considerable gaps with their own "white knowledge" of fantastic schools and to speculate alongside Tiffany[5]:

"There really is a school for witches?" said Tiffany.
"In a manner of speaking, yes," said Miss Tick.
"Where?"
"Very close."

Schools of Magic

> [...]
> "Can I go there by magic? Does, like, a unicorn turn up to carry me there or something?"
> "Why should it? A unicorn is nothing more than a big horse that comes to a point, anyway. Nothing to get so excited about," said Miss Tick [Wee 43].

In this exchange, we see Tiffany move from generalized speculation to specific questions about the first step in the familiar process, the journey to the magical school.

While Miss Tick dismisses Tiffany's first guess, when Tiffany presses with another question about where she can find the school, Miss Tick gives an answer that, again, encourages both Tiffany and the reader to continue imagining a typical fantasy school accessed by magic means.[6]

> "To find the school for witches, go to a high place near here, climb to the top, open your eyes...." Miss Tick hesitated.
> "Yes?"
> "...and then open your eyes again" [Wee 44, ellipses in original].

Everything about these instructions and their delivery—the dramatic hesitations, Tiffany's prompting, the vague specifics—creates space for and indirectly affirms readers' expectations; when Tiffany tries to follow these instructions that night, both she and readers anticipate that it just *might* reveal something:

> She closed her eyes and opened them again. And blinked, and opened them *again*.
> There was no magic door, no hidden building revealed, no strange signs.
> For a moment, though, the air buzzed and smelled of snow [Wee 47, emphasis in original].

Though nothing happens this time, there is everything there to suggest that next time might be different and that this act of twice opening one's eyes is one of power and potential. Readers turn to the next chapter expecting to read about Tiffany accomplishing some qualifying task, receiving some indication that her next attempt will be successful, or perhaps accidentally meeting the conditions and performing these ritualistic steps in some unexpected way and opening the portal when she least expects.

In addition to this thematizing of the means of accessing the witches' school, Tiffany's subsequent speculations continue to draw upon familiar fantastic school story tropes:

4. Nothing Exactly Like a Lesson

> But maybe there were magical doors. That's what she'd make, if she had a magical school. There should be secret doorways everywhere, even hundreds of miles away. Look at a special rock by, say, moonlight, and there would be yet another door.
> But the school, now, the school. There would be lessons in broomstick riding and how to sharpen your hat to a point, and magical meals, and lots of new friends [Wee 54, emphasis in original].

Note how little attention Tiffany gives to imagining the classes at this school, beyond the standard tropes of lessons in broomstick flying and another she imagines in hat-sharpening, which focuses more on the typical uniform of a witch than actual skills or knowledge. Tiffany's focus—and, therefore, the readers' focus—is on the extra-curricular aspects of a *school story* over and above the particulars of a *school*. Again, we see Tiffany's attention to magical and secrets means of transportation and access, to which we now add food and friendship, two more cornerstones of the school story narrative. Just as *The Magicians* works deliberately to prepare protagonist and readers alike for a portal fantasy narrative, *The Wee Free Men* prepares both for a school story, albeit with the common fantastic twists.

The school, however, fails to materialize. As Tiffany becomes further involved in the Fairy Queen's incursion into her homeland and both the danger and the stakes grow higher, Tiffany's failure to discover the door into the school becomes a point of insecurity and doubt, along with her consequent lack of spell knowledge and the absence of a pointy hat (Wee 97). Still, the imminent appearance of the school is constantly teased, ensuring that it does not fade from awareness: there are continual hints that the grand moment of entrance and discovery still lies before Tiffany, just around the next corner, such as the old kelda's insistence that believing in only one world is "a good thought for sheep and *mortals who dinna open their eyes*" (Wee 141, emphasis added).[7] In addition to echoing Miss Tick's instructions about opening one's eyes, the kelda affirms the presence of magic doors throughout the world:

> Some ye can see an' some ye canna, but there are doors, Tiffan. They might be a hill or a tree or a stone or a turn in the road, or they might e'en be a thought in yer heid, but they are there, all around ya. You'll have to learn to see 'em, because you walk among them and dinna know it [Wee 141].

Delivered in a thick brogue from a definitively fantastic source, coming as it does from the leader of the local Nac Mac Feegle "pictsie" clan, this assertion by the kelda reads as both an explicit confirmation of the existence of magic portals and an indirect confirmation of the existence of the school for witches and the method by which Tiffany must access it.

The moment of pay-off comes not long after, when Tiffany successfully applies the instructions to open her eyes and discovers, at last, a magical door. With a helpful reminder to "Use yer eyes. Use yer heid" from a nearby Feegle (Wee 174), Tiffany is able to find a magical doorway among the trilithons on the Chalk—though first she once again laments her failure to find the witches' school and her resulting lack of preparation: "I haven't got any training for this. I haven't even been to the witch school! I can't even find *that*!" (Wee 175, emphasis in original). Thinking critically about how to make her next passage under the stone arch different from her previous attempts, Tiffany closes her eyes, steps slowly through, and then opens her eyes—and, at last, finds herself in another place, magically transported via a hidden portal (Wee 180). Having opened her eyes once metaphorically to the information that close observation of her surroundings can impart, Tiffany opens her eyes a second time literally, successfully accessing a magical door.

The door that Tiffany opens, however, leads to fairyland; it is the Queen's country that Tiffany enters, not the campus of a witches' school. Though readers understand the importance of Tiffany's mission to rescue her brother from the Queen of the fairies and know that it was Tiffany's intention to travel to this land, there is still a moment of disappointment that we have not come to the school unintentionally after all. Expecting, perhaps, the long-awaited moment of successful entry, where Tiffany will learn the spells and skills she needs to successfully face the Queen of the Fairies (prompted by the reminder of the witches' school immediately prior) readers are once again left imagining a school that does not appear. Though Tiffany again employs her newfound ability to think a doorway into existence as part of her adventures in rescuing her brother and the baron's son (Wee 256–7), and successfully defends the Chalk from a fairy incursion, neither the necessary doorway nor the school for witches ever materializes.

As it turns out, this is actually the point. There never was a school for witches, as is revealed to Tiffany when Miss Tick returns with Nanny Ogg and Granny Weatherwax, the most senior and well-respected of the Discworld witches. Once Granny Weatherwax, the (non-)leader of

4. Nothing Exactly Like a Lesson

the witches, has received a satisfactory recount of the events, Tiffany inquires whether *this* is the moment where she learns about the witches' school, a question which leaves Granny Weatherwax quite perplexed: the elder witch's confusion, combined with Miss Tick's guilty "Um," are the final pieces Tiffany needs to confirm her slowly-developed understanding of this supposed school (Wee 313). Tiffany recognizes now that Miss Tick was being metaphorical:

> "It's like stories," said Tiffany. "It's all right. I worked it out. *This* is the school, isn't it? The magic place? The world. Here. And you don't realize it until you look. [...] We just don't look. You can't give lessons on witchcraft. Not properly. It's all about how you are … you, I suppose" [Wee 313–14, emphasis and second ellipsis in original].

Granny Weatherwax confirms this understanding of the nature of witchcraft and learning the practice; then, Tiffany *does* learn about the witches' school, at least in the sense that the work and the way it is learned are finally explained to her. New and aspiring witches learn magic and how to "look to the edges" and care for a local community as part of an apprenticeship to another witch (Wee 314–5). This, the apprenticeship of a newcomer to an experienced practitioner, is the real educational institution of the witches, which Granny Weatherwax lays out quickly and simply: "'There're elderly witches up in the mountains who'll pass on what they know in exchange for a bit of help around the cottage. [...] you'll get three meals a day, your own bed, use of a broomstick … that's the way we do it'" (Wee 315–6, second ellipsis in original). With her parting assertion that learning witchcraft is far more like life than school (see the epigraph at the start of this chapter), Granny Weatherwax gives Tiffany an invisible pointed hat and instructions to come seek out an apprenticeship when she feels old enough to leave home.

And just like that, the great trick of the quintet is accomplished: both Tiffany and readers now understand unequivocally that Tiffany's critical thinking, her reading, her taking responsibility and doing what must be done, and her apprenticeship yet to come are all an apprenticeship in witchcraft, an education in a complex practice. Life and the world itself become the educational institution and working alongside an experienced witch is positioned as the structure in which learning—which would be happening anyways and all the time—is supported and deliberately achieved in the community of practice. It is possible, of course, to make this evident without foregrounding the trappings of the school story and thematizing the stereotypical fantastic school, and it may even be possible to do so as effectively without these elements; yet, by explicitly filtering this coming-of-age fantasy narrative through the school story lens and inviting readers to speculate and to anticipate alongside Tiffany, Pratchett's first novel in the quintet ensures that readers will understand Tiffany's entire journey as an ongoing education in witchcraft by means of her participation in an institution that is informal, geographically-dispersed, and frequently chaotic, but which is nevertheless effective in teaching new witches all they need to know to care for the edges in a community of their own.

Peripheral Participation

At the start of the next book, Tiffany begins an apprenticeship under the witch Miss Level, quickly discovering that learning witchcraft is primarily completing mundane chores: "Endless chores. You could look in vain for much broomstick tuition, spelling lessons or pointy-hat management. They were, mostly, the kind of chores that are just ... chores" (Hat 77, ellipsis in original). While Tiffany is occasionally taught something explicit by another witch, or certain moments or events are presented as a deliberate lesson, the majority of Tiffany's education in witchcraft continues to look like life, rather than school. Operating largely independently, Tiffany employs critical thinking and reasoning with keen observation and the information thereby gleaned to do the best she can with whatever task is set before her. The ways in which Tiffany learns in the remainder of the quintet, in comparison with her initial education in *The Wee Free Men*, is not substantially different except for one key factor: Tiffany now recognizes herself as a witch regardless of her level of experience, and in presenting herself this way, she is treated as one by others in turn.

Tiffany's feats over the remainder of the quintet include being possessed by and expelling a Hiver spirit in *A Hat Full of Sky*, killing the Wintersmith in order to end the harsh winter and bring the spring in *Wintersmith,* facing the anti-witch sentiments aroused by the Cunning Man and defeating him to save all of witchcraft in *I Shall Wear Midnight,* and then rallying the witches to defend the Discworld from

4. Nothing Exactly Like a Lesson

an all-out fairyland assault following the death of Granny Weatherwax in *The Shepherd's Crown*. While it would be easy to focus solely on Tiffany's adventures as a witch in each of the remaining books, the framing of Tiffany's experiences established in the first text ensures that the mundane chores and the less-adventurous activities in which she engages are not dismissed as either unimportant or incidental. These everyday moments are also part of Tiffany's education, as a consequence of which she is equipped to undertake these monumental tasks.

Reading the remainder of the quintet as the story of Tiffany's education in witchcraft—as, essentially, a non-school school story—what is it that we find? What is the hidden curriculum of apprenticeships and applied learning in the witches' community, and what is Tiffany learning beyond skills and spells? In attending to Tiffany's education, we are able to interrogate the underlying meanings and the categories of normality and deviance through which knowledge is filtered, employing the key questions for interrogating the "deep structures" of education from the Introduction. To undertake a successful investigation of the hidden curriculum of the witches, however, we must first understand the structure of Tiffany's education and the ways in which learning happens in these apprenticeship contexts. Recognizing Tiffany's experiences as a vocational education, we can then consider additional questions posed by Helen Colley and colleagues to "rende[r] visible aspects of the hidden curriculum in these learning sites" (492): "What is it that makes learners feel they are suited to particular jobs? What are their experiences of the community of practice they seek to enter? How does their sense of identity change as they become a member of that community?" (475). In considering these questions, we can see the way in which Tiffany's prior experiences and dispositions in the first book identify her—to herself and to others—as a desirable candidate for the occupation of witchcraft, the understanding she gains about what it means to be a witch by means of her participation in the work and the ways in which these explicit and implicit lessons are imparted, and how Tiffany comes to change both herself and the field of practice as a consequence of her work as a witch throughout the quintet.

With apprenticeships, "there is very little observable teaching; the more basic phenomenon is learning" (Lave and Wenger 112). This perfectly describes Tiffany's experience, as she finds that "There was no school and nothing that was exactly like a lesson" (Wintersmith 20) but that she is nevertheless gaining knowledge, skill, and confidence as a witch owing to her interactions with other practitioners and her own performance of the work of witchcraft. Tiffany's education is representative of what Lave and Wenger describe as legitimate peripheral participation in a community of practice. Community here does not imply "co-presence, a well-defined, identifiable group, or socially visible boundaries"—rather, it speaks to "participation in an activity system about which participants share understandings concerning what they are doing and what that means in their lives and for their communities" (Lave and Wenger 115). The witches' community of practice fits this description precisely; rather than attending a school or completing defined lessons and assessments, it is Tiffany's ongoing participation in the general work of witchcraft, and therefore in the witches' community of practice, that constitute the learning opportunities for her training as a witch.

Assisting an elderly witch with the tasks around her cottage and the local community she serves—functionally, an apprenticeship to an established member—is the means by which Tiffany secures legitimate access to the community of practice. This access, in turn, provides Tiffany with opportunities to participate, not merely to observe; through this participation, Tiffany is "both absorbing and being absorbed in" the culture of practice in the community (Lave and Wenger 113). In assisting the established witches, Tiffany engages in the work of the community of practice from the periphery, but nevertheless authentically. Assessing Tiffany's experiences, we can see key elements of an education via legitimate peripheral participation, including a curriculum based on practice, an absence of formal tests, and the importance of a network of fellow newcomers.

What Tiffany learns is informed by what it is the community of witches does: they look to the edges, care for those who need it, and uphold justice in the communities in which they reside. This work, then, as with all learning by way of legitimate peripheral participation, creates "the potential 'curriculum' in the broadest sense" and determines what beliefs, skills, information, and values are available for newcomers to learn as part of their participation (Lave and Wenger 112). Tiffany understands what there is to be learned, how this learning will be applied, and why it is important to learn it because her participation in

4. Nothing Exactly Like a Lesson

the work of witchcraft provides a holistic view of the occupation and the application of practitioner's knowledge and expertise (Lave and Wenger 112).

Though Tiffany understands herself to be under constant scrutiny and evaluation—frequently repeating to herself that "Everything is a test!" (Wintersmith 157)—this is a consequence of the individual pride of practitioners and the constant status negotiations between colleagues which characterize the community of practice, and not a situation at all unique to newcomers. Little besides Tiffany's own pride and her status within the witches' hierarchy is on the line in these tests— except, of course, where the stakes are also life and death, for herself and for the Discworld. Nothing in the behavior of the community of practice, however, differentiates the small tests from the big ones, with Tiffany held to the same standards of self-reliance, responsibility, and skill whether she is evaluating the truth of Miss Level's claim that farting shortens your lifespan (Wintersmith 157) or confronting the Cunning Man to save witchcraft itself (Midnight 360). None of these tests is capable of, nor understood as, determining whether or not Tiffany *is* a witch, merely how respected she is as one; Tiffany has already taken the only test capable of making this determination by deciding to become a witch in the first place. This, too, is typical of apprenticeships, following from the legitimacy of the apprentice as a participant in the community who is not being assessed for eligibility or entrance once their peripheral participation begins (Lave and Wenger 121).

Where Tiffany does a great deal of her learning—in particular, the work of reflecting on and talking about her experiences so that she might translate them into explicit knowledge and skills gained—is also characteristic of an education via legitimate peripheral participation. Similarly to the tailors Lave and Wenger studied, a fundamental aspect of apprenticing to an experienced witch is securing access to a network of other apprentices, among whom a great deal of the learning happens (112). When established members of the community are too distant or too respected "to engage with in awkward attempts at a new activity," as is most certainly the case with Tiffany's relationship to Granny Weatherwax, for instance,[8] it is among fellow apprentices that such attempts can be productively made (Lave and Wenger 112). As Lave and Wenger note, "It seems typical of apprenticeships that apprentices learn mostly in relation with other apprentices," and that knowledge creation

Schools of Magic

and circulation among these networks is effective and efficient (112). These apprenticeship networks can be understood as spaces of "benign community neglect," where room is deliberately created by means of the absence of experienced practitioners to allow newcomers to organize and engage in learning opportunities with one another (Lave and Wenger 112).

The coven of young witches in which Tiffany participates is just such a network,[9] and is of great value to both Tiffany and the other apprentices. In this coven of newcomers, the members comment on and celebrate one another's successes, share their otherworldly and mundane experiences, complain and brag in turn about their mentors, speculate about possibilities for advancement into their own cottages— and, when the need arises, they mobilize to support one another. For instance, Tiffany receives confirmation from this network that witches can, in fact, predict their own deaths and, subsequently, invaluable assistance hosting Miss Treason's pre-emptive funeral (Wintersmith 118, 124, 139–40).

It is not Tiffany herself, however, but fellow apprentice Annagramma who receives the greatest benefit from, and education through, her participation in this network of apprentices. When Annagramma is given the late Miss Treason's cottage, Tiffany recognizes that her peer's training under the unorthodox witch Mrs. Earwig has left her wholly unprepared, and soon enough, Annagramma shows up at Nanny Ogg's cottage in a tizzy seeking Tiffany's help. Tiffany agrees to help Annagramma with her immediate tasks and subtly introduces her to the art of Boffo (Wintersmith 245–6),[10] guides Annagramma in her first time sitting up with the dead and delivering a baby (Wintersmith 248–53), counsels her on the squabbles and habits of the locals and how to learn about them so she can care for them (Wintersmith 270–2), and enlists the rest of the apprentices' network to help fill in the other gaps in Annagramma's knowledge (Wintersmith 273–5, 300–1). Though none of the young witches are eager to help their peer, the other apprentices nevertheless agree to help Annagramma not only because people might get hurt due to her incompetence, but also because the failure of one young witch would reflect poorly on the whole group of newcomers (Wintersmith 275–80). The coven of apprentices fills in the space left by the experienced witches' benign neglect, which Tiffany comes to realize is exactly what Granny Weatherwax had anticipated (Wintersmith

4. Nothing Exactly Like a Lesson

396), deliberately leveraging the network of newcomers to ensure Annagramma becomes a functional member of the community and, in the process, to indirectly undermine Mrs. Earwig's alternative practice of witchcraft.

Understanding the ways in which Tiffany's education conforms to these basic structures of learning through legitimate peripheral practice is a necessary foundation for analyzing the hidden curriculum. This mode and method of learning through participation is closely linked to vocational education and training, defined as "the development and application of knowledge and skills for middle level occupations" (Moodie 260),[11] but perhaps most simply understood as a method for and a goal-oriented process of learning a particular occupation or trade (Schaap, Baartman, and de Bruijn 100). The process of vocational education and training has, at its core, an emphasis on inculcating within individuals certain beliefs, practices, and attitudes that are associated with the profession, shaping students into the "right kind of person" for the occupation (Colley 19). As has been repeatedly demonstrated, the process of vocational training attempts to draw upon, mediate, and reconceptualize the previous experiences and dispositions of newcomers and encourage them to adopt particular outlooks, beliefs, and attitudes common—and often thought necessary—in the occupational field (Bates; Colley; Skeggs).

By recognizing Tiffany's experiences learning through work as a particular form of vocational training, we can then attend to this process of shaping Tiffany undergoes throughout her education, explicating and interrogating the beliefs about the work of witchcraft and the place of witches within the community of practice. In this way, we can analyze the hidden curriculum of Tiffany's education by addressing the foundational questions and the additional ones brought to us by Colley and colleagues: why does Tiffany feel she would make a good witch, what is it she already knows of witchcraft, and how does her identity change as she develops her sense of self as a practitioner? In answering these questions, we can understand the ways in which the shaping of a newcomer's vocational habitus is a central element of the hidden curriculum, and how this habitus replicates the existing structures and values of the community of practice and ensures intergenerational continuity for the witches—except, of course, where elements are contested and changed by individuals such as Tiffany.

Schools of Magic

Working Among the Witches

"Education is neither the mirror of society (it mirrors only some parts and aims to change others) nor the origin of change (as alleged by some who describe progressive educational reforms as 'social engineering')," Stephen Kemmis and Christine Edwards-Groves explain. Rather, education "always has elements of reproduction, maintaining understandings, skills and values from the past, and elements of transformation, stimulating change towards new kinds of understandings, skills and values" (101). The education that Tiffany and her peers receive through their legitimate peripheral participation, like all educational processes, functions to reproduce and preserve societal structures and norms, maintaining the witches' collective social identity across generations by imparting skills, behaviors, defined relationships, and shared understandings (Kemmis and Edwards-Groves 86–7); in internalizing the vocational habitus and replicating the personal sacrifice implicitly required for dedicated witches, Tiffany participates in the maintenance of these beliefs and structures in the community of practice. Simultaneously, however, Tiffany contests and changes other elements of witchcraft, namely the gendered division of magic on the Discworld. Tiffany does not passively receive the hidden curriculum imparted alongside the practical skills of witchcraft: even as she adopts the vocational habitus which values both self-sacrifice and agentic action, she questions both the elements that she replicates and those that she challenges.

The key norm replicated in Tiffany's identity and practice is the vocational habitus of the witches, which itself is the bulk of the hidden curriculum imparted to apprentice witches and serves a key role in facilitating intergenerational continuity in the community of practice. As Lave and Wenger note, a newcomer's first and most foundational learning upon gaining legitimate access to a community of practice is knowledge of the shape of the field itself, compiling a "general sketch" of the occupation in which they now participate. In compiling this semiconscious sketch, newcomers attend to details including:

> who is involved; what they do; what everyday life is like; how masters walk, talk, work and generally conduct their lives; how people who are not part of the community of practice interact with it; what other learners are doing; and what learners need to learn to become full practitioners. It includes an increasing understanding of how, when, and about what old-timers

4. Nothing Exactly Like a Lesson

collaborate, collude and collide, and what they enjoy, dislike, respect and admire [Lave and Wenger 113–4].

By means of her legitimate peripheral participation, Tiffany develops a keen and nuanced understanding of witchcraft, how witches relate to one another, and what it means to *be* a witch—she is socialized into the practice of witchcraft (Gruner "Teach" 225), developing the mindset of a witch and an understanding of their social structures over and above particular skills.

This "witch's mindset" and the understanding of how the community of practice operates is the vocational habitus of witchcraft. Drawing on the work of Pierre Bourdieu, Colley and colleagues define the term "vocational habitus" as follows:

> Vocational habitus proposes that the learner aspires to a certain combination of dispositions demanded by the vocational culture. It operates in disciplinary ways to dictate how one should properly feel, look and act, as well as the values, attitudes and beliefs that one should espouse [488].

Identifying this "process of orientation to a particular identity" as an essential component of vocational education, Colley and colleagues outline a complex process of acculturation which occurs as part of a newcomer's legitimate peripheral participation in an occupational field (488). Learning to be a witch involves immersion in and a gradual adoption of the witches' vocational habitus, a process of becoming the "right kind of person" that is an integral component of vocational education and training (Colley 19). This process is broad and wide-reaching, influencing an individual's wardrobe and appearance, their emotional labor and management,[12] their goals and future aspirations, their orientation to and adoption of societal structures and cultural norms, and their fundamental sense of self (Colley; Skeggs). With Colley and colleagues' questions in mind—what makes Tiffany feel she is suited to the work of witchcraft? How does her sense of identity change as she becomes a full practitioner in the witches' community?—we can explicate what makes someone the "right kind of person" to be a witch, and then attend to the ways in which Tiffany replicates or contests elements of the witches' vocational habitus.

Other scholars have indirectly examined the vocational habitus of the witches or other communities of practice on the Discworld, including Lucas Boulding's assertion that the actions of the witches in assisting others are informed by "professional values, external to the individual" (para. 1) and Karen Sayer's interrogation of this same premise with her analysis of the ways in which Granny Weatherwax is fundamentally shaped by the needs, expectations, and desires of her community (140). Looking to another example of apprenticeship learning in Prachett's *Mort*, Steinbrück's comments regarding Mort's apprenticeship with Death are equally applicable to Tiffany's education; the representation of this apprenticeship learning, as Steinbrück explains,

> implicitly discusses the socializing effects of professional work and education. The confrontation with the requirements and conditions of the workplace leads to the development of personality structures, despite the fact that these social processes *are not* pedagogically planned or executed in a controlled fashion [96–7, emphasis in original].

These personality-shaping outcomes are "accompanying effects of other learning and working processes" (Steinbrück 97), what we can recognize as a hidden curriculum. As Steinbrück elucidates, "The main part of Tiffany's apprenticeship is [...] not based on knowledge, but is moreover a kind of *social education* that aims to show Tiffany that being a witch is all about doing for those who can not" (100, emphasis in original). Attending to the ways in which the witches' community of practice understands their work and themselves in relation to their labor, and the attitudes Tiffany comes to recognize and embody, we can see a highly gendered understanding of the value of care work and whose responsibility it is to provide this care: the perhaps not-so-hidden curriculum of witchcraft on the Discworld encapsulated in the community's vocational habitus, which Tiffany largely—though critically—replicates.

There is, as it turns out, a great deal of care work involved in witchcraft, more than there is actual magic. Contrary to what Mrs. Earwig tells her apprentices about "cosmic balances and stars and circles and colours and wands and ... and *toys*," the true "soul and centre" of witchcraft is caring for people (Hat 235–6, emphasis and ellipsis in original). This fundamental understanding of witchcraft is sometimes presented as the more abstract "speaking up for them as has no voices" and "seeing to the edges," but these more philosophical tenets are embodied in the community's practice of "going around the houses." This passage from *Wintersmith* is among the more concise descriptions of the work of witchcraft, introduced by Nanny Ogg:

4. Nothing Exactly Like a Lesson

"Now, our next little favour is—"

—giving an old lady a bath, as much as was possible with a couple of tin basins and some washcloths. And that was witchcraft. Then they looked in on a woman who'd just had a baby, and that was witchcraft, and a man with a very nasty leg injury that Nanny Ogg said was doing very well, and that was witchcraft too, and then in an out-of-the-way group of huddled little cottages, they climbed the cramped wooden stairs to a tiny little bedroom where an old man shot at them with a crossbow [Wintersmith 228–9].

As Katherine Kittredge elaborates, Pratchett's witch figures are "environmentally sensitive caretakers for the disadvantaged," performing health care and social service roles encompassing "herbalist, elder care provider, midwife, nurse, hospice worker, dispute resolution counsellor, veterinarian, therapist, and all-around first-responder" (675).[13] The majority of Tiffany's labor, and the labor of her peers, is in seeing to the care needs of individuals in these relatively rural and isolated communities; one little favor after another, the witches of the Discworld provide for those who are in need, seek justice for those who have been wronged, and keep a protective eye on those otherwise forgotten.[14]

Here on the Roundworld as on the Discworld, such care work and the vocational education and training that prepare new practitioners are part of a highly gendered field. Women are understood as the ideal candidates for caring occupations, since both the labor and the desire to perform it are uncritically understood as "inherent capacities of women, undifferentiated by class or race" (Colley 16). Women are both more likely to enter caring occupations and to have previous relevant experience caring for members of their family (Colley 23; Skeggs 136–8). Femininity—normally a trait hard to celebrate, given its typical lack of cultural value and association with powerlessness—is presented and championed within the context of care work as an essential trait of the successful care worker (Skeggs 133), and Beverley Skeggs has found that electing to enter a vocational education program for care work is often motivated by a desire "to gain some autonomy within class and gender structures using the cultural resources available" to women who may not perceive or have access to other employment opportunities, or at least not ones which align with their culturally-mediated identity as a woman (138). Women are figured as the ideal care workers because they are assumed to possess, by default, the desirable traits of care workers. This, in turn, positions women as qualified by default to train as care workers, and their choice to do so then reinforces the perception of women as ideal care workers.

As with the students who enter vocational training programs for care work on the Roundworld, Tiffany has prior experiences and examples within her family that contribute to her initial understanding of the work of witchcraft and her own likely suitability for the role. Her Granny Aching, who—though not formally a witch herself—served the same function for the community of shepherds on the Chalk, provides for Tiffany a model of the profession even before she meets her first "real" witch in Miss Tick. With the example of Granny Aching, Tiffany internalizes the idea that an elder matriarch is the best possible authority figure for a community, as her grandmother provided guidance, assistance, and judgement more effectively and compassionately than the local Baron (as detailed in Tiffany's memories of her Granny throughout *The Wee Free Men*). In addition to this example of the value of a witch's role, Tiffany has practical experience in care work from tending to her younger brother Wentworth and working alongside her family on their sheep farm, both of which mimic the domestic experiences which lead young women into care work training programs (Colley; Skeggs).

Beyond this initial understanding and her relevant experience, Tiffany also already displays many of the attributes which make someone the "right type of person" to become a witch. The initial description Miss Tick gives of a witch is a one-to-one description of who readers discover Tiffany to be throughout the first novel:

> "Witches don't use magic unless they really have to. [...] A witch pays attention to everything that's going on. A witch uses her head. A witch is sure of herself. A witch always has a piece of string [...] A witch delights in small details. A witch sees through things and around things. A witch sees farther than most. A witch sees things from the other side. A witch knows where she is, who she is, and *when* she is" [Wee 28–9, emphasis in original].

With relevant prior experiences and a well-suited predisposition, Tiffany registers to Miss Tick as a witch from the outset (TWee 2).

However, while the predisposition mediated by societal gender norms and expectations is a vital component of the vocational habitus of care work, these predispositions are not alone sufficient: there is still identity-work to be done in refining the vocational habitus through

4. Nothing Exactly Like a Lesson

educational training programs (Colley et al. 488). As Skeggs elaborates, in these programs, "The primary 'raw material' on which these girls learned to labour was *themselves*" (26, emphasis in original). By the time their training is finished, graduates have internalized the vocational habitus of care work that tells them to value their "natural" nurturing instincts as women but to mediate this compassion with a level of professional remove, and have come to understand themselves as care workers, making their new occupation an integral component of their identity both within and beyond the workplace (Colley; Skeggs).

Tiffany's adventures and her work alongside established witches expand her experiences, equip her with new tools, and mold the raw material of her identity into the vocational habitus of the ideal witch. Throughout the quintet, Tiffany comes to internalize the witches' shared understanding of the value of the care work they perform in their communities, and she makes "witch" and its associated traits the central component of her identity as she performs this identity-work upon herself. By the time Tiffany has taken on the Chalk as her own steading and is working independently to serve the communities there, she has internalized not just the conceptualization of care work as a witch's work, but also the value of doing this labor. After Tiffany has just done the difficult work of caring for a young teenage girl who has had a miscarriage following a beating from her father, Tiffany's own father questions why she not only *does* the work, but *likes* it. As Tiffany explains:

> "Well, Dad, you know how Granny Aching always used to say, 'Feed them as is hungry, clothe them as is naked, and speak up for them as has no voices'? Well, I reckon there is room in there for 'Grasp for them as can't bend, reach for them as can't stretch, wipe for them as can't twist,' don't you? And because sometimes you get a good day, that makes up for all the bad days and, just for a moment, you hear the world turning," said Tiffany. "I can't put it any other way" [Midnight 36].

This is the vocational habitus of the witches, internalized so completely by Tiffany that she feels unable to fully articulate her understanding to someone outside the profession.

In fact, Tiffany has so thoroughly internalized the idea that her role, her very identity as a witch, is to do for others where they cannot or do not do for themselves that one of the pivotal lessons she learns in the fourth book is when *not* to do for others, even when and where she perceives a clear need for care and assistance, precipitated by her counterproductive visit to Mrs. Petty. This is a fundamental tension within witchcraft, as its proper practice requires both that witches recognize and respect the rights of individuals *and* that they do for those who cannot, taking on the responsibility of and for others (Croft "Nice" 162)—the balance is in learning where this assumption of agency is and is not warranted or welcome.

As a full practitioner following her various apprenticeships, Tiffany works to impart her understanding of witchcraft as an essential service to others. Returning full-time to the Chalk to become their first resident witch, Tiffany takes deliberate measures to teach the communities there that they *do* need the care she provides. When the magically-induced anti-witch sentiment spreading through the community leads to Tiffany's (ineffectual) imprisonment in *I Shall Wear Midnight*, she goes willingly, seeing it as an opportunity to highlight precisely what the community will lack in her absence as all of her necessary labor goes undone. As she says to the Sergeant when he locks her in the cell: "'Of course, when I'm locked in here I can't be out there. I can't make medicines. I can't clip toenails. I can't help'" (Midnight 283). In enumerating all those who will go without care and aid because she has been locked up, Tiffany expresses her fundamental belief that her work is vital, that there are literal lives at stake if she cannot perform her role, and that there is no one else who can or will do them in her absence (Midnight 295–6)—a belief which she very much desires the rest of the community to adopt, as well, and which we see them begin to take on.

"Witch" becomes Tiffany's identity, subsuming and replacing earlier identities like "daughter of shepherds" and "cheese maker." At the beginning of *The Shepherd's Crown*, we see the ways in which Tiffany has made "witch" her identity expressed in her comment about herself and her beau Preston, explaining that "we like our work, both of us, in fact you might say we *are* our work" (Shepherd's 21, emphasis in original). This conflation of occupation and identity is a facilitating factor in the self-sacrifice and self-denial that are central components of the vocational habitus of witchcraft: as Stephen Billett and Margaret Somerville assert, the ways in which a vocational habitus makes work part of an individual's identity are "the basis of care worker's engagement in, and commitment to, a low-status, poorly paid job with stressful and often physically arduous working conditions" (314). Though she questions the necessity of it, we see Tiffany replicate the restrictive elements of the

4. Nothing Exactly Like a Lesson

vocational habitus alongside her belief in the value of care work, making sacrifices in her personal life that are implied requirements for true greatness as a witch.

Throughout *The Shepherd's Crown*, events demonstrate and characters specifically warn that Tiffany's identity *as* her work may be limiting, preventing her from accessing other valuable experiences and developing parts of her identity not directly related to witchcraft. Jeannie, the new kelda of the Nac Mac Feegle, urges Tiffany to consider what is important and where she might make space in her life for things, and people, that are not her work (Shepherd's 19–20), while her parents raise the question of whether her profession will leave her space to have and enjoy her family (Shepherd's 100–4). Tiffany, demonstrating critical awareness of the self-denial implicit in witchcraft, talks with Mrs. Proust about her desire to work as a witch and her seemingly incompatible desire to build a life with Preston (Shepherd's 186–91). Standing alongside, and perhaps precipitating, these conversations is Tiffany's witness to the grief of Mustrum Ridcully, Archchancellor of the Unseen University, as he mourns the relationship he and Granny Weatherwax never had time to develop (Shepherd's 67–8, 76–9); Ridcully's grief stands simultaneously as a cautionary tale for Tiffany and as evidence that the most powerful and dedicated of witches are *only* witches, sacrificing aspects of their lives that are not directly related to their work in and for their communities. The witches who combine their identity as a witch with something else—like Mrs. Earwig, who is also a wife, or Nanny Ogg, who is a wife and a mother many times over—are not the ones portrayed by the text as the most committed to their craft or the most powerful. An identity as a witch, particularly a *great* witch, is presented as all-consuming, leaving little room to identify as anything else: as a friend, a partner, a parent.

Despite these cautions and Tiffany's own doubts about whether she wants her work to be her entire identity and her entire life, at the end of the quintet, Tiffany's decision to build a shepherding hut and live up on the downs where she can serve her community and be at its center seems to imply that, for those who truly embody the vocational habitus of a witch, love, companionship, and a life among family *are* incompatible with a dedication to the craft and the care of the community. Though Tiffany's assertion that she will live alone "For now" and her thoughts of the future in relation to Preston's latest letter leave open the possibility for a less solitary existence in days to come (Shepherd's 325), the series ends—and Pratchett dies—without providing readers with a representation of Tiffany successfully balancing her identity and role as (non-)leader of the witches with other, family-centered identities. Tiffany's situation at the end of the quintet is characteristic of the separation and distance of the witch's role: as Alice Nuttall observes, though witches serve and are integral to their communities, they are also always removed from them (32). The conclusion of Tiffany's story seems to almost entirely reject the possibility that she can be *more* than a witch while still being the guiding example of witchcraft in the community of practice, actualizing the tenets of self-sacrifice and self-denial she has internalized through her adoption of the vocational habitus. Tiffany's isolated shepherding-hut-for-one maintains intergenerational continuity in the community of practice and the ways in which it understands and embodies dedication to the craft, as Tiffany prepares to live and work alone as both Granny Weatherwax and Granny Aching did before her—whether additional novels would have seen Tiffany formalize a relationship with Preston or someone else, we can only speculate.

At one and the same time, however, with the induction of Geoffrey into the community of practice, Tiffany contests and eventually changes the dictate that witchcraft is exclusively the domain of women; replicating some elements does not preclude modifying others. First and foremost, witchcraft on the Discworld has traditionally been presented and understood as women's work (Gruner "Wrestling" 289; Nuttall). The magic of men and women is portrayed as fundamentally different: as Steinbrück elucidates, "wizards study higher magic, a purely intellectual practice, while witches concentrate on practical requirements by using their magic to foster social cohesion and assume traditional 'female' duties such as midwifery and domestic aid" (106–7).[15] Granny Weatherwax herself asserts this distinction as an immutable truth in *Equal Rites*, the third Discworld novel: "Female wizards aren't right either! It's the wrong kind of magic for women, is wizard magic, it's all books and stars and jommetry. [sic] She'd never grasp it. Whoever heard of a female wizard?" (Pratchett 21). Witchcraft, the labor of care work in the domestic sphere, is the exclusive domain of women on the Discworld; wizardry, the labor of intellect and academia in the public sphere, is the exclusive domain of men, and witches who get too close to wizardly

4. Nothing Exactly Like a Lesson

practices—like Mrs. Earwig and Annagramma—are demonstrated to be less capable practitioners.

In addition to perpetuating limiting gender roles along a flawed understanding of gender as binary, the gendered division of magic contributes to the restrictive and traditional gendering of care work in what Kittredge acknowledges as an otherwise positive recognition of the importance of this labor,[16] perpetuating "underlying assumptions that a woman's ultimate identity will be based on her status as wife or mother, and that deviating from a traditionally feminine role will make them outliers from society" (676). It is this gender division which Tiffany contests and changes in the community of practice, partly during her own education but primarily through her instruction of newcomers to the practice when in the role of (non-)leader.

Transformation in an occupation is often precipitated by an event which creates questions for an individual about their work practices, their identity as a practitioner, or both, which in turn results in a disidentification with the work or their identity and changes how the individual responds to the demands and social pressures of their occupation (Billett and Somerville 319–20). From this moment, the actions of the individual in response to this change in themselves and their work "constitute the vanguard of cultural transformation" in the community of practice: when one practitioner makes or advocates for a change, it can then grow to change the entire occupation (Billett and Somerville 318). Tiffany, faced with just such a precipitating moment by the arrival of Geoffrey in *The Shepherd's Crown*, makes just such a change.[17] In moments like these, we see the "fundamental" tension and conflict between continuity and displacement within any community of practice play out (Lave and Wenger 123–4). Shaped by and shaping the field in turn (Hodkinson and Hodkinson 177), the work of the witches on the Discworld evolves over time as new practitioners enter the field—but Tiffany's assumption of the role of (non-)leader precipitates a more dramatic and wide-reaching change than those wrought by individuals in their everyday practice.

Citing the precedent of Eskarina Smith, the witch who became a wizard in *Equal Rites*,[18] Geoffrey argues that Tiffany should give him a chance because he is "the right type of person" to be a witch: he has a thirst for knowledge, a deep understanding of people, skill with animals, and an interest in and respect for the everyday concerns and chores of everyday people (Shepherd's 153). Like Tiffany herself, Geoffrey has prior experiences and a predisposition which indicate his suitability to be a witch. Geoffrey—who decides to be a witch, and then, when he is told men cannot be witches, decides he wants to know *why* (Shepherd's 29)—requires Tiffany to make a choice: to continue in the traditional way and direct the young Geoffrey to the Unseen University, or to take up Geoffrey's question for herself and consider *why* men cannot be witches, contesting the structures and norms imparted to her.

As Tiffany ponders why Geoffrey should not be able to make the same choice to be a witch that she herself had made, she realizes that her opinion here *matters*, and that "If she was going to be a sort of head witch, she should be able to decide this. She didn't have to ask any other witches. It could be her decision. Her responsibility. Perhaps a first step towards doing things differently?" (Shepherd's 153). As Kemmis and Edwards-Groves note, teachers have a "professional responsibility" to consider consciously the elements they reproduce and those which they contest in their education practice (102); stepping into the role of teacher as she takes on her own apprentices, Tiffany must be deliberate in her actions if she wishes to avoid uncritically perpetuating potentially problematic structures. Embracing her role as (non-)leader and her inherent responsibility to guide the future of the practice, Tiffany decides to make a change and challenge a central tradition of witchcraft.

Guided by the two criteria Kemmis and Edwards-Groves explicate as implied by the double purpose of education—"what will be in the interests of individuals (and not just particular groups taken alone) and what is in the interests of a good society and the good for humankind" (102)—Tiffany makes her decisions regarding Geoffrey on the basis of what is good for him as an individual and what is good for the communities that the witches serve. Geoffrey's narrative arc throughout *The Shepherd's Crown* affirms Tiffany's choice and Geoffrey's desires: in bringing Geoffrey into the community of practice, Tiffany enables him to discover and address a problem of which the other witches were unaware, that of the old men who are in the way in their own homes and left at loose ends (Shepherd's 164–7, 261–5, 272–4). Geoffrey encourages them in their hobbies, helps them find community with one another, and improves their lives in ways that are less medically-based than traditional witchcraft but no less important for their overall wellbeing.

With her acceptance of Geoffrey, Tiffany contests the gendered structures of magic which have been presented to her throughout her education and precipitates change in the witches' community of practice.[19] Though Ana Rita Martins notes that both Geoffrey's and Eskarina's storylines are underdeveloped, in part due to Pratchett's death, she nevertheless asserts that their experiences "indicate that the lines separating witches and wizards are slowly disappearing from the Disc" (124). While it is only a small step, this seems a first step with a promising future, though one we will not see play out in future texts by Pratchett. At the conclusion of Tiffany's story, even as we see her replicate limiting aspects of the witches' vocational habitus with her isolation and self-denial of any identity beyond "witch," we can celebrate the ways in which Tiffany has successfully contested and changed the community of practice to begin to undo the restrictive gendering of both magic and care work on the Discworld. Attending to the hidden curriculum within the vocational habitus imparted to Tiffany through her apprenticeship learning, we can recognize the elements of reproduction and of transformation which are present in the representation of Tiffany's education, and which are made available for critical analysis and interrogation by readers by means of the series' foregrounding of the school story in the first novel.

Socializing Critique

In addition to expanding readers' understanding of where and how education happens, the deliberate play with the expectations of fantastic school stories allows the quintet to challenge the assumed inferiority of youth: as less capable, less responsible, and less powerful. The recognition of Tiffany's capability and responsibility as a professional, even though she is still a child and then a teenager,[20] challenges the aetonormativity usually present in both school stories and children's and young adult fantasy literature. The fact that it is Tiffany who precipitates fundamental change in the community of practice and the conceptualization of magic on the Discworld, successfully contesting the gender-exclusivity of witchcraft, is the final piece of the quintet's consistent challenge of aetonormativity.

Drawing on the concept of heteronormativity used in queer theory to understand the ways in which heterosexuality is understood to be the default, Maria Nikolajeva uses the term "aetonormativity" to address the comparable ways in which adult, in opposition to child, is a societal default (*Power* 8). This "adult normativity" is a pervasive influence, not only in children's and young adult literature, but in the ways in which children and youth are understood by and treated within sociocultural structures (Nikolajeva *Power* 8). As Marah Gubar notes, an aetonormative society understands adult as the standard, compared with which children are the aberration (300). This not only presents children and youth as an undifferentiated collective all possessing "essential characteristics that differentiate them decisively from adults" (Gubar 294), but also positions them as the Other, a distinction which carries with it all the attendant risks of idealization or demonization when groups are othered based on their perceived alterity from a commonly-accepted norm (Gubar 297).

Applying this theory to the study of children's agency, Lorenzo Bordonaro argues that adult-normativity influences the ways in which the actions of children and youth are analyzed, with conceptualizations of children's agency informed by adults' perceptions of what is moral; expanding upon this, Gubar argues that "If we adults do not conceive of young people as possible exercisers of the same sort of agency that we possess, then we are less likely to treat them in ways that help them to develop the competencies associated with that sort of agency" (297). This assertion of the impact that the conceptualization of children and youth has on the practice of understanding their agency is merely one example of the "looping effect" which makes these models and discourses so important to address: discourse informs action,[21] and it therefore "genuinely matters" how society thinks about and talks about young people, particularly among those credited as experts (Gubar 302).

To leave aetonormativity unacknowledged and unchallenged, even in literature, is to elide the impact on children and youth. Children's literature, however, has the power "to question the adults as the norm" through challenging aetonormative structures and assumptions (Nikolajeva *Power* 11), demonstrating that all norms are arbitrary and all conditions are equally normal (Nikolajeva *Power* 9). The substantial subversive potential of children's and young adult literature is achieved primarily by means of the empowerment of child protagonists, particularly in fantasy texts.[22] Here, they are given the ability and the agency to challenge adult authority and shape the world according to their own

4. Nothing Exactly Like a Lesson

understandings and desires, exposing in the process the artificiality of the adult norms against which they are able to successfully rebel (Nikolajeva *Power* 41–2).

Despite this potential, Nikolajeva laments that the majority of children's and young adult texts do not make full use of their opportunity to challenge adult normativity and domination, engaging instead with the carnivalesque's "circular movement" that produces a temporary state of empowerment before the ultimate return to the originating norms and structures (*Power* 203–4)—though, at least, this temporary suspension foregrounds the fact that adult norms are far from absolute (*Power* 204). With the "Tiffany Aching" quintet, however, we see a break with the common carnival structure: Tiffany is not temporarily empowered by the events of the narrative but is instead *always and already* empowered through her own predispositions and desires to be a witch, and this empowerment results in a steady growth of her skills and knowledge, her agency, and her authority in the world. At the end of her narrative arc, rather than being forced to give up her temporary power and return to a place lower in the hierarchy, Tiffany steps into the position at the top of the structure, displacing older and more senior practitioners, and begins to make changes to the structure itself.

As Eileen Donaldson notes, the witches are a rarity on the Discworld for their belief that children and youth are capable as a general rule ("Earning" 154), a perspective which stands in contrast with that of the majority of the adults represented in the series and which is magnified in regard to their own apprentices. The series' challenge of aetonormativity is present throughout Tiffany's education: while the quintet largely re-creates a fairly traditional apprenticeship model, the complexity and significance of the tasks Tiffany performs from the very beginning of her participation in the community run counter to the common assumption that the inexperienced—which includes, by default, the young—must start with simple and low-stakes tasks. According to Lave and Wenger, the initial participation of newcomers "requires less demands on time, effort and responsibility" compared to the practice of full members (121); "A newcomers' [sic] tasks are short and simple," Lave and Wenger assert, "the costs of errors are small, the apprentice has little responsibility for the task as a whole" (121). With Tiffany's apprenticeship, however, this is fundamentally untrue: her tasks are long and complex, the cost of error is often death for herself or others, and she is expected to take ownership of the problem, her solution, and any consequences from beginning to end. Tiffany's trajectory as an apprentice is one of demanding to more demanding, from risk to more risk, and never one of ease and safety to challenge and danger. Beginning immediately with complicated tasks that have potentially staggering repercussions at the age of nine, Tiffany's responsibility and capability only grow.

Following her defeat of the Hiver at eleven years old, Tiffany understands that her growth in skill and ability has been and will continue to be exponential: already she has outstripped the other, more experienced, apprentices, and her path will see her "beat" Granny Weatherwax sooner than later (Hat 326–7). Even before Tiffany has concluded her first apprenticeship placement, the community of practice as a collective understands that Tiffany's age has no bearing on her skill. She is good, and in short order, she may well be the best. In recognition of Tiffany's abilities, Granny Weatherwax puts forward Tiffany's name in *Wintersmith* to inherit a vacant cottage even though Tiffany is only thirteen and, traditionally, cottages are given to the oldest and most experienced apprentice (Wintersmith 140)—a fundamentally ageist practice that, upon the basis of aetonormative understandings of youth and age, assumes older witches are by default the most capable. Though Granny Weatherwax knows Tiffany will not get the cottage, her sponsorship is a statement to the community of practice that Tiffany is a skilled practitioner who has the acknowledgment and respect of their (non-)leader.

Nor is it just Granny Weatherwax who sees Tiffany's exceptional skill. When Tiffany meets Eskarina Smith, Eskarina recognizes the effort and commitment Tiffany has put into honing her craft. Forcefully asserting that Tiffany "[was] not born with a talent for witchcraft" (Midnight 358), Eskarina expounds upon the importance of this fact:

> "I said you weren't *born* with a talent for witchcraft: It didn't come easily; you worked hard at it because you wanted it. You forced the world to give it to you, no matter the price, and the price is, and will always be, high. Have you heard the saying 'The reward you get for digging holes is a bigger shovel'? [...] People say you don't find witchcraft; witchcraft finds you. But you've found it, even if at the time you didn't know what it was you were finding, and you grabbed it by its scrawny neck and made it work for you" [Midnight 359, emphasis in original].

What Eskarina's speech makes clear is that Tiffany is not an exceptionally capable witch by some matter of fate, accident, birthright, or luck,

4. Nothing Exactly Like a Lesson

as is so often the case for empowered young protagonists in fantasy literature. Her skill is a direct result of her desire, her dedication, and her willingness to do the work. The implication is that anyone could have done the same and achieved the same results, reiterating for readers that Tiffany is not a chosen one, a prodigy, an exception, or anyone special at all, really. She has done the work of digging the hole, and now she has earned the reward of the larger shovel—and there is no age requirement for wielding a spade.

In *I Shall Wear Midnight*, the novel in which Tiffany is positioned between apprentice and (non-)leader as she serves her steading on the Chalk, Tiffany's age is raised as a potential barrier, as a point of concern among the community of practice. This is notable timing, for not only does it come for Tiffany towards the end of her first life-or-death challenge as a full practitioner in her own right, but also it comes for readers right before the final book in which Tiffany will advance to a leadership position. Her final challenge here has significant repercussions, where failure will mean not only her own death, but the continued persecution and death of other witches until someone can succeed where she will have failed. Of all the possible times to accept help from the other witches, this would be the time to do so, for in doing it alone Tiffany is taking on the responsibility for protecting the lives of all witches and their patients, as well as her own. The decision to accept help, though, is positioned as akin to admitting that, as a consequence of her youth, Tiffany is a less capable witch than her colleagues:

> In twenty years' time, perhaps, if she asked for help, people would think, Well, even an experienced witch can run up against something really unusual. And they would help as a matter of course. But now, if she asked for help, well ... people would help. Witches always helped other witches. But everyone would think, Was she really any good? Can't she last the distance? Is she strong enough for the long haul? No one would say anything, but everyone would think it [Midnight 379, ellipsis in original].

As Tiffany asserts, it is "a matter of age" (Midnight 379)—and, in saying such, it becomes true, in the eyes of her colleagues and in the minds of readers. From here, however, rather than accept that her age is a potential limitation, Tiffany makes her youth a conscious decision: she will not be rushed into maturity or pressured into behaving as if she is any older than she is, and she will not allow anyone to imply that her age is a barrier or an indication of inability or inexperience. Cleverly defeating the Cunning Man, Tiffany dispels any doubt that her age will prevent her from succeeding in even the most high-stakes situations.

The conclusion of *I Shall Wear Midnight* affirms Tiffany's skill despite her youth and is the culmination of the development and demonstration of her ability throughout the previous three novels. With this declaration, readers and witches alike understand that Tiffany has become, if not the equal of Granny Weatherwax, second only to the (non-)leader. When Granny Weatherwax dies at the opening of *The Shepherd's Crown*, then, and leaves "all" to Tiffany (60), it is only a surprise that the community of witches does not create more of a fuss about this break with tradition by not allowing the most senior witches to compete amongst their select group to decide who will assume the role of (non-)leader.[23] Nanny Ogg, approximately equal with Granny Weatherwax in both age and respect among the community, does not consider for a moment that she should be the successor (Shepherd's 74); Mrs. Proust, highly regarded among the witches of the city Ankh-Morpork, feels utter conviction that "it will surely be young Tiffany Aching who gets that steading," as they all know her capabilities (Shepherd's 65), and the young witches who worked as apprentices alongside Tiffany are similarly a united front of support and encouragement (Shepherd's 83).

When Tiffany herself protests that she is "far too young" and implies that Nanny Ogg—who is "older, more experienced" and "knows a lot more"—would be a better fit for the role, Nanny dismisses this vehemently: "'You're not too young,' she said. 'Years ain't what's important here. Granny Weatherwax said to me as you is the one who's to deal with the future. An' bein' young means you've got a lot of future'" (Shepherd's 75–6). Tiffany's own Second Thoughts corroborate this understanding: "Why not do things differently? Why should we do things how they have always been done before?" (Shepherd's 76). Rather than an impediment, a reason why Tiffany *cannot* become the new head of the witches, Tiffany's youth is presented as a central reason why she is the best choice.

With Tiffany's promotion to (non-)leader, the community of witches embraces a change in how they select their head witch: based on skill and ability alone, disregarding age and seniority. In doing so, the community takes the first step in dismantling their ageist and aetonormative structures of advancement. We know that this is not a one-off alteration in their practice: at the conclusion of *The Shepherd's Crown*, when

4. Nothing Exactly Like a Lesson

Tiffany decides to dedicate herself solely to the Chalk steading, it is Geoffrey who is given care of Granny Weatherwax's steading in recognition of his skill and connection with the people there (320), despite the availability of older and more experienced apprentices who might previously have felt entitled to occupy the vacancy.

In the role of (non-)leader, as analyzed above, Tiffany precipitates important change, seemingly succeeding where Granny Weatherwax's earlier attempts with Eskarina Smith failed in *Equal Rites*.[24] At sixteen years of age, Tiffany leads the community of practice into a less restrictive, more inclusive, and demonstrably improved direction: Geoffrey's inclusion in the community has already created positive change for the people in his steading, and we can only speculate about the further good to come from even more diversity of perspective and experience in the witches' community of practice. As Mrs. Proust (and Nanny Ogg) reiterate often to Tiffany throughout *The Shepherd's Crown*, the future of the practice is hers to dictate: "'it is your way, Tiffany, your time. And Esme Weatherwax was no fool. She could see the future coming'" (Shepherd's 185). While it is unlikely that Granny Weatherwax foresaw this particular change of challenging the gendered division of magic, Mrs. Proust's comments imply that part of the reason Tiffany was chosen as her successor was because Granny Weatherwax trusted her to make the right choice, whatever that happened to be, giving tacit approval to everything Tiffany does as (non-)leader. In the end, with even Mrs. Earwig agreeing that Geoffrey makes a fine sort of witch and should be allowed to look after Granny Weatherwax's steading (Shepherd's 319–20), we receive every indication that Tiffany's choices have been the right ones, and that her openness to change—a consequence, at least in part, of her youth—has made these successes possible.

Attending to what is happening with education in the quintet not only foregrounds but also adds new dimensions to the challenge of aetonormativity presented throughout the series. Through their engagement with the Discworld novels, which themselves reflect upon how stories shape our worlds, selves, and actions, readers are better able to understand our own sources of value, the forces that influence our identities, and the structures in which we are situated (Boulding para. 2). This opportunity to critically consider societal structures and ideologies is further supported by the subversion of the traditional witch figure and the subsequent invitation this presents for readers to challenge other stereotypes and prejudices (Donaldson "Earning" 150). With Tiffany's accension to the (non-)leader of the witches, the series critiques and challenges aetonormativity, socializing readers into critical interrogations of structures such as age-based promotions and adult authority.

Conclusion

Before Tiffany meets Miss Tick the witchfinder and learns about the (admittedly metaphorical) school for witches, before she performs her first bit of magic protecting the Chalk from the Fairy Queen, before she goes around the houses with an established witch, before she even wears a pointy hat, Tiffany *is* a witch. As Tiffany explains to Mrs. Proust, she was about eight years of age when she recognized the injustice of how her community treated Mrs. Snapperly—who was *not* a witch—and thereby became a witch herself (Midnight 173, 210). What Mrs. Snapperly needed was care, and on the Discworld, care work is witchcraft, understood as powerful and important labor by those who perform it and by the communities who benefit from their labor. The five novels comprising Tiffany's narrative arc detail her growth from newcomer to full practitioner to (non-)leader of the community of practice, throughout which Tiffany internalizes the vocational habitus of the witches and makes "witch" the soul and center of her identity, culminating with Tiffany's expansion of the community to encompass more diverse perspectives and experiences and to allow others to assume the identity of witch for themselves.

In thematizing the school story and playing with readers' expectations of a witches' school alongside Tiffany's, *The Wee Free Men* draws attention to the quintet as a representation of education foregrounding issues inherent in vocational education and apprenticeship structures. Emphasizing these elements in an otherwise typical young adult fantasy *Bildungsroman* and positioning her work in witchcraft as legitimate peripheral participation in a community of practice, the series transposes the consideration of the hidden curriculum of vocational education to the fantasy narrative and invites critical analysis of Tiffany's education. Readers are invited to recognize and to question the vocational habitus of the witches—which understands care work as witchcraft, witchcraft as essential, and women as witches—and to consider

4. Nothing Exactly Like a Lesson

the ways in which Tiffany replicates some elements and contests others, ensuring widespread intergenerational continuity even as she changes the shape of the practice. As with *The Magicians*, the metatextual meditations on a school for witches position readers to interrogate and critique the gendered norms inherent in vocational education for care work and, furthermore, to engage with the series' critique of aetonormativity and the gendered division of labor which informs the vocational habitus of the witches.

Conclusion

Using the three-part framework, which attends to fantastic school stories simultaneously as school stories, fantasy narratives, and representations of education, enables us—as scholars, critics, and fans alike—to recognize the ways in which these texts engage in complex and sophisticated ways with the processes and products of education and the societal issues and structures that inform these schooling practices. As outlined in the Introduction, we achieve a holistic means of analyzing fantastic school stories by simultaneously attending to themes and characteristics from the three genres and traditions on which fantastic school story texts draw: the attention to broader themes of socialization and attitudes towards schools and schooling from criticism on the school story genre; the method of thematic criticism, foregrounding fantasy's commentary and critique on real world issues, from the field of fantasy literature, and an awareness of hidden curricula and their impacts and implications from scholarship on schools and education, as well as a set of key questions for interrogating these deeper structures.

Focusing our analysis at the level of the text, as in Chapters 1 and 2, explicates issues related to education which the fantastic elements draw forth from the usually mundane processes of institutional teaching and learning. Demonstrating the use and value of the holistic framework presented in Chapter 1, I examined the testing practices at Hogwarts through this lens, concluding that the prioritization of rote memorization and repetition of decontextualized facts and routines inform the teaching practices of Hogwarts staff and that, furthermore, the use of OWL and NEWT scores to determine career eligibility function as gate-keeping measures to ensure that political and economic capital is distributed primarily to Pureblood individuals, maintaining the status quo hierarchy of wizarding Britain even as the characters supposedly fight against the oppression of Muggleborns and even Halfbloods

Conclusion

in the fight against Voldemort and his Death Eaters. While the fantastic elements of the *Harry Potter* series do effectively bring forward the issues inherent in these standardized testing practices, drawing attention to an otherwise mundane educational practice, the series ultimately fails to capitalize on the subversive potential of its carnivalesque structure; as with many school stories, Rowling's series is far more likely to socialize readers into a complacent acceptance of these testing practices as an unproblematic norm than it is to generate critical awareness of such issues and foster a challenge of this educational practice where it appears beyond the text.

Repeating the process in Chapter 2, I once again employed the three-part framework in analyzing a fantastic school story, this time Patrick Rothfuss's in-progress *Kingkiller Chronicle* trilogy. Here, I explicated the series' challenge of postsecondary education as a means of social mobility, developed through the focus on the protagonist's financial hardships throughout his education and the ways in which his lack of economic capital constrains and prevents his access to an education through the University institution and therefore to the increased social, cultural, and economic capital promised as a result of a postsecondary education. Readers' attention is drawn to the requirement for capital as a prerequisite for education through the defamiliarization of the familiar structures—including monetary denominations and postsecondary institutions—within the fantasy landscape. With readers attending to the issues of Kvothe's economic status in relation to his education, the series presents an explicit critique of the function of capital in education through Kvothe's commentary on his hardship and through the theme of performativity that runs throughout the series, as Kvothe frequently and explicitly engages in cross-class performances that highlight for readers the gate-keeping function of capital in the fictional University. The awareness thereby generated may then spread to the role and use of capital in other, mundane educational structures.

When we shift our examination to consider also the level of genre, as in Chapters 3 and 4, we see the ways in which deliberate generic play can further enhance the critical awareness engendered by the fantastic school story's unique elements and consequent opportunities for engagement. Analyzing Lev Grossman's *Magicians* trilogy in Chapter 3, with a focus on *The Magicians*, I demonstrated the effect of foregrounding the Fillory intratexts in this fantastic school story, which thematize

Conclusion

the portal fantasy narrative structure and subsequently invite readers to consider the representation of education at Brakebills College for Magical Pedagogy through the lens of a portal fantasy. This lens then transposes the attention to imperialism and colonization that scholarship has recently brought to the portal fantasy structure, drawing out the imperialism inherent in the intensely and self-consciously Anglophilic education structures of Brakebills. Examining the school story narrative of the trilogy with issues of imperialism at front of mind, we can recognize Brakebills as an imperial institution, the center of the magical empire, and can see the ways in which the education process is a process of colonization and domination. Characters like Quentin, who resemble the colonizer's ideal subject and who can themselves become colonizers after their socialization into the empire's center, have vastly different—and less traumatic—experiences within the educational institution than characters who fail to meet this ideal due to their social position or history, or who are marginalized within the institution for their failure to perform or as result of the threat they pose. We can also recognize the harm done to characters like Julia, who experiences significant violence as a result of her forceful exclusion from the borders of the Brakebills empire, as well as the alternative systems of knowledge that exist beyond the imperial center and which are elided within it.

Examining the opposite in the final chapter, I demonstrate the ways in which Terry Pratchett's *The Wee Free Men* thematizes the school story genre—specifically, the fantastic school story subgenre, with its "school for witches"—and subsequently encourages readers to attend to the text and the remainder of the "Tiffany Aching" quintet as a process of education for the young protagonist. Consequently, what might be read only as a fantasy *Bildungsroman* is available for consideration as a school story and a representation of education, and we can recognize the community of witches on the Discworld as a dispersed institution which creates and oversees the process and structures of education for new practitioners. The field of witchcraft itself, focused on care work, is highly gendered, and both the overt and the hidden curriculum of learning witchcraft is informed by the understanding of care work as women's work; furthermore, it is positioned within the witches' community as necessary work which requires great personal sacrifice. As Tiffany contests the vocational habitus of the witches through her choices as an apprentice and then as a full practitioner, her representation in the text

Conclusion

also challenges the aetonormativity so often present in children's and young adult literature, which assumes that older always knows better. This challenge to aetonormative assumptions means that, when Tiffany works to enact change in the gendered field of witchcraft, readers are positioned to understand this not as the impulsive actions of an ignorant child, who will learn over time the error of their actions and the reasons for the established norms, but as a thoughtful and deliberate action of the most powerful of witches on the Discworld, who is acting to correct a major source of inequity in her society.

The framework presented and used here for analyzing fantastic school stories takes us beyond mere analysis of the ways in which the combined features of school stories, fantasy literature, and representations of education operate within the text to demonstrate the ways in which the unique characteristics of the subgenre present an opportunity for fostering critical awareness in readers; in doing so, this framework participates in the project of an emancipatory Childhood Studies approach to literary analysis,[1] as well as in the project of consciousness-raising regarding hidden curricula and the relationship between power and education.

The emancipatory approach to analyzing children's and young adult literature for which Mary Galbraith calls, drawing on the emancipatory model of Jürgen Habermas, outlines three goals:

> understanding the situation of babies and children from a first-person point of view, exploring the contingent forces that block children's full emergence as expressive subjects, and discovering how these forces can be overcome [188].

While youth continue in their schooling, we can understand them as remaining within the elastic boundaries of childhood as a social construct, since the process of schooling is central to the conceptualization of childhood (Gruner "Teach"; Hunt *Introduction*), and can adapt these goals to consider the experiences of students at large alongside babies and children in Galbraith's goals for an emancipatory approach. The "primary project" of this approach is, after all, to "change adults, especially as parents, *teachers*, and therapists" (Galbraith 188, emphasis added). By examining the ways in which power and control are created and presented in fantastic school stories as a subgenre of children's and young adult literature, the framework developed here contributes

Conclusion

to the goals of understanding the situation of children and youth within educational institutions and the forces oppressing and limiting them throughout their schooling.[2]

By also participating in the project of consciousness-raising regarding hidden curricula in the process of school and the ways in which educational institutions function to distribute and deny power, this framework also participates in the third goal of the emancipatory approach to children's and young adult literature, that of discovering how to overcome these forces. Jane Martin asserts that consciousness-raising—"showing" the underlying ideologies and structures to the destined recipients through explication, analysis, and open discussion (136)—is the most realistic, immediate, and positive response to the presence of these systems of power and control in education.[3] The program of consciousness-raising Martin envisions has four goals:

> realizing that a given setting has a hidden curriculum, knowing what that hidden curriculum is, knowing which practices of the setting are responsible for the various learning states [outcomes or lessons] of its hidden curriculum, and understanding the significance of these learning states for one's own life and for the larger society [137]

Through explicating the presence of hidden curricula and analyzing the informing ideologies, the creation and transmission of norms and structures, and the impact of these elements in fantastic school stories as representations of education, the holistic, three-part framework for analysis furthers the work of consciousness-raising while simultaneously contributing to the third goal of emancipatory literary analysis to address and overcome the forces limiting students.

The analysis undertaken here of works in the fantastic school story subgenre by Grossman, Pratchett, Rothfuss, Rowling, and Yolen help us recognize the hidden curricula of each of these fantastic institutions, giving us practice in explicating the "deep structures" of education and the structures of power and oppression which underly these institutions. Furthermore, the ways in which the unique features of the subgenre foreground the elements of the hidden curricula and make them readily available for examination better enable us to recognize these underlying structures and ideologies as forces limiting the full expression and well-being of students, with significant repercussions for both the individuals and the societies in which they are located.

Conclusion

Testing practices, particularly the use of standardized testing as employment credentials, reinforces the dominance of the privileged group in *Harry Potter*'s wizarding Britain, preventing Muggleborn and even Halfblood students from discovering, let alone reaching, their potential at Hogwarts or in their post-graduate careers. Without access to stable financial resources, Kvothe is limited in his ability to access the University of the Four Corners world within *The Kingkiller Chronicle*, constrained in his development as a Sympathist and negatively affected in terms of his physical and mental health and well-being during his studies by his lack of economic capital. Brakebills College for Magical Pedagogy in the *Magicians* trilogy admits only those who resemble its ideal student, enacting violence on those it excludes and doling out access to power to its students based on how well they conform to the unspoken requirements for conduct and how well they internalize the values of the institution. To become a witch on the Discworld, one must be a woman, at least until Tiffany discards this rule—but to be a *good* witch, one must be nothing else, sacrificing other interests and pursuits, as well as personal relationships.

Future analyses of fantastic school stories using the holistic three-part framework presented here promise to reveal new hidden curricula, new relationships between power and education practices, new forces constraining students—particularly those written by Black authors, and others who are marginalized for their race, disability, sexuality, or gender. Fantastic school stories by racialized authors offer opportunities to analyze the systemic racism in our educational institutions and the ways in which alternative practices can empower those deliberately disadvantaged within the traditional system; texts written by those beyond a British and North American context expand our understanding of what constitutes an education, how learning best happens, and what the goals of schooling should be in the first place.

In Nnedi Okorafor's *Akata Witch*, we see the ways in which Sunny's education in the mundane system is informed by the British colonization of Nigeria, which stands in stark contrast to her education in juju among the Leopard People. It is Sunny's magical education, her instructors, and her peers who help her to build connections with her Nigerian roots and her family heritage, and which help her embrace her identity as albino, as an American-born Nigerian, and as a Free Agent; her mundane schooling, in contrast, is a site of bullying, torment, and physical

Conclusion

abuse (for Orlu as well as Sunny). Learning juju and joining the community of Leopard People empowers Sunny in a way that her mundane schooling cannot possibly achieve, inviting critique of the traditional schooling system by showing us the ways in which an alternative structure and subject provides Sunny access to agency and a sense of identity that is out of reach in the traditional classroom.

Tracy Deonn's *Legendborn* critiques the white supremacy inherent in the American postsecondary school system, addressing the Anglocentrism (and even Anglophilia) of these institutions by explicitly linking institutional elements like legacy admissions and campus administration to the myths of King Arthur. The fantastic nature of a war against Shadowborn demons fought by the reanimated spirits of the Knights of the Round Table creates a backdrop against which it is impossible for readers to miss the racism embedded within this secret society and the university which this chapter calls home, and which is enacted by the Legendborn and their network. As Bree learns about her abilities with Rootcraft and the experiences of her ancestors—both those directly related to her, and those in her larger Black community—we see two opposing ways of engaging with history: where Rootcraft honors those who came before and borrows power temporarily for efforts like healing and understanding, the Legendborn bind themselves to their forebears permanently, a choice which has direct physical consequences for all those whose lives are cut short and also indirect sociocultural limitations imposed by the hierarchies and structures that have grown up around these lineages. When Bree accepts the Call of Arthur and takes up a position of leadership within the Round Table, she alters the position through her inclusion of her Rootcraft heritage and her own personal beliefs and desires, inviting readers to enter historically white institutions in ways that honor their identities and shape the institutions to fit themselves, and not the other way around.

By engaging in this work as we analyze fantastic school stories from a variety of origins, particularly those which expand the borders of and bring new voices into the subgenre, we all can participate in the project of conscious-raising by drawing attention to the hidden curriculum wherever we find one, and also in the project of emancipatory analysis of children's and young adult literature through looking closely at magical schools as a means of revealing the mundane—though by no means inconsequential—forces at work that limit and oppress students.

Chapter Notes

Preface

1. For a discussion of these "habits of whiteness," see Helen Young's *Race and Popular Fantasy Literature*.
2. See Gaile S. Cannella and Rahika Viruru's "(Euro-American Constructions of) Education of Children (and Adults) Around the World: A Postcolonial Critique" for an analysis of the dominance of the European-American educational agenda across the globe and the indirect colonization which results.

Introduction

1. For a discussion of the persistent didactic tendency of children's literature, see, for instance, Perry Nodelman's *The Hidden Adult*.
2. This socializing element is, of course, not limited to either school or texts about school, but is rather at play in all children's and young adult literature (see, for instance, Coats) and in all popular fiction (see Richards).
3. Richards identifies this elevation and glorification of school institutions as the central purpose of school stories at the birth of the genre, explicating the ways in which these literary depictions of public school and the socialization undergone by the protagonist present "a glamorous substitute for the often grim reality of [the readers'] own schools, a wish-fulfillment of a particularly potent and beguiling kind" and function as second-hand socialization for readers who would never experience it first-hand (13–14). Kirkpatrick also acknowledges the role of school stories in socializing their readers, asserting that the genre has served as an essential method "to promulgate the ideals and dogmas of the adult world" throughout its history (3).
4. Maria Nikolajeva also recognizes this tendency for rebellious stories—particularly in the school story genre—to conclude with conformity, marking the protagonist's entry into adulthood with their acceptance of whatever norm or system against which they have been rebelling and ultimately positioning them as supporters of that which they once challenged, complicating and even undermining any anti-socialization messages otherwise presented (*Power* 7).
5. See, for instance, Elizabeth A. Galway's recognition that schooling in *Tom Brown* and other traditional school stories is primarily focused on preparing students for their future social roles in the upper classes of British society (67–69).
6. Whether or not there is also an assumption that gender is linked exclusively to biological sex is unclear, as this issue is never raised in the text—but, as readers, we can certainly raise the question of what would happen in the case of a non-binary or transgender student. Could a non-binary student walk either direction, or neither? Which direction would a transgender student be forced to walk? Would an exception need to be made for them, and would this be done?

Notes—Chapter 1

Would they even be admitted to study at the institution?

7. The wizard names of Thornmallow's peers suggest far more positive characters: Tansy is named after a bright yellow flower "because she has such a sunny disposition," and Willoweed "manages to plant himself anywhere" (Yolen 93). Were these names to be similarly treated as self-fulfilling prophecies, others would be biased towards understanding Tansy's behavior as cheerful and warm, and Willoweed should find himself treated immediately as a member of the community. Whether or not these wizard names are accurate reflections of who these individuals are when they arrive at Wizard's Hall, they certainly serve to dictate how they will be received and will influence the ways in which each student develops and comes to understand themselves.

Chapter 1

1. Authentic learning refers to instructional approaches which are grounded in real-world applications or contexts that are relevant to the specific learners, explicitly working to draw connections between the skills and knowledge learned in the classroom and the "real world" with the understanding that this will increase student interest and engagement and better prepare them for later schooling and life outside the educational institution.

2. As Hermione is able to access OWL practice papers in her fourth year (Goblet 296), it is entirely plausible that similar materials are available to Hogwarts instructors to help them determine what topics and skills are likely to be covered. The fact that Hermione removes her exam booklet from the written portion of her Charms exam (Order 628), and that Snape did the same in his Defense Against the Dark Arts exam in his youth (Order 566–8), suggests that there is likely a wealth of previous years' written tests from which instructors may draw, as well. Using these practice and previous tests to inform their curriculum for the year, and perhaps even as instructional tasks or tools in the classroom, would be in keeping with research findings that demonstrate teachers' reliance on test items, such as externally provided sample questions or commercially produced practice tests, to determine the focus of their instruction to prepare their students (Firestone et al., viii; Schorr and Firestone, 160).

3. Unfortunately, the majority of subjects offered at Hogwarts are not readily available for this analysis. There is not enough detail given on Astronomy or Herbology lessons in Harry's fifth year to draw any conclusions about the test preparation practices of Professors Sinistra and Sprout, though we do know that Sprout mentions the OWLs in the first class (Order 237). History of Magic similarly lacks detailed representation, though we are told that the course has not been changed at all, nor is there any mention made by Professor Binns of the approaching OWLs (Order 206, 317). Defense Against the Dark Arts, meanwhile, has not had a consistent teacher from one year to the next, and Harry does not take Ancient Runes, Muggle Studies, or Arithmancy and we are provided with only the sparsest details of these courses through Hermione.

4. As Jennifer Sattaur notes, the issue of blood status in Rowling's series draws metaphorically upon both issues of racism and classism; Sattaur asserts that the "fantasy re-telling makes both issues ambiguous, and forces her readers to actively consider it" (4). Elizabeth Galway, however, challenges this conclusion, suggesting that this ambiguity does not prevent the series itself from perpetuating elitist ideologies and that this implied metaphorical connection is not enough alone to force readers into an active consideration of their own or the series' assumptions regarding race and class (77). For further considerations of the

Notes—Chapter 2

ways in which Rowling presents racial issues through the metaphor of blood purity—and the problems with this conflation and the depiction of the issue—as well as the representation of race in the series, in general, see, for instance, Anatol; Ostry. For examinations of the non-human creatures who are presented as an additional metaphor for race; see, for instance, Rana.

5. Nikolajeva notes the frequency of these carnival structures in children's and young adult literature and the value of attending to them, particularly when considering youth empowerment and agency in and through literature: "Carnival theory is highly relevant for children's literature. Children in our society are oppressed and powerless, having no economic resources of their own, no voice in political or social decisions and subject to laws and rules that the adults expect them to obey without interrogation. Yet, paradoxically enough, children and youth are allowed, in fiction written for their enlightenment and enjoyment *by adults,* to become strong, brave, rich, powerful, independent—on certain conditions and for a limited time" ("Harry" 227, emphasis in original). Importantly, these structures have a "subversive effect, showing that the rules imposed on the child by the adults are in fact arbitrary" ("Harry" 227).

6. Jack Zipes also asserts that the *Harry Potter* series fails to challenge conventional morality and foster critical reading, which other "good" children's and young adult literature achieves ("Radical").

Chapter 2

1. While some might contest the categorization of these novels as fantasy school stories, since they fit with equal ease under the umbrella of high or epic fantasy, I argue that the prominent role of the educational institution and the significant portion of the plot dedicated to the protagonist's education places them within the "fuzzy set" of fantasy school stories, to borrow Brian Attebery's term for defining the broader genre first introduced in *Strategies of Fantasy*. In fact, readers expecting high fantasy may well find themselves disappointed to discover how much these books are actually a school story: as Giebert recounts, numerous reviewers have lamented how Kvothe gets "'stuck' at a university ... and seems to forget about his quest for periods of time altogether" (106).

2. Pierre Bourdieu's foundational work on capital informs later definitions and analyses of capital, including Cecilia Rios-Aguilar and Judy Marquez Kiyama's work. See "Cultural Reproduction and Social Reproduction" in *Knowledge, Education and Cultural Change* (ed. Richard Brown, 1973); *Outline of a Theory of Practice* (1977); "Forms of Capital" in *Handbook of Theory and Research for the Sociology of Education* (ed. John G. Richardson, 1986), as well as *Reproduction in Education, Society, and Culture* with Jean-Claude Passeron (1977).

3. It is almost impossible not to sense the asymmetry in interactions between Kvothe and his peers, with the greater capital and privileged backgrounds of his peers on display in the text in a reflection of the realities at postsecondary institutions: it can be seen in their clothes and belongings, their means of transport, their discretionary funds and spending on food, goods, and services, their access to academic supports and supplies, their prior education, and on-campus meal plans and housing (Aries and Seider 425, 427–8; Ostrove and Long 365). All of these function as markers of difference and heighten awareness of differing levels of capital for students like Kvothe (Aries and Seider 425–6, 439), and Kvothe himself feels these differences and remarks upon them in his later recounting of his time at the University.

4. The term "first-generation student" does not have a consistent definition and is used to identify an ever-shifting group

Notes—Chapter 2

of individuals. Always based on the educational attainment of an individual's parents, definitions variously specify both parents have a high school diploma or less, have some postsecondary experience but no terminal degree, or more generally do not have a bachelor's degree (Nguyen and Nguyen 147). Rebecca Taylor et al. echo the concern expressed by Thai-Huy Nguyen and Bach Mai Dolly Nguyen, noting the issues with treating first-generation students "as a homogeneous, deficient group" and the ways in which this (re)produces understandings of these students as "less prepared, less supported by families, and less engaged in their studies" (350), essentializing first-generation students by assigning them particular detrimental traits (352). By not considering the intersectional identities of those students who qualify as first-generation, studies cannot attend to the influence that other facets of students' identities have on students' experiences and the ways in which these may mitigate or exacerbate the challenges of being a first-generation student—we cannot and should not assume that being a first-generation student "has an effect that is unique from gender, race, social class, and other salient categories," and we must also acknowledge that parental education attainment is influenced by these same structures and social forces (Nguyen and Nguyen 148). Recognizing the intersectionality within the first-generation student cohort and the difficulty of isolating the impact of being first-generation from other categories of identity, we can attend to the specifics of students' backgrounds and identities, their institutional context, and their educational experiences and outcomes as individuals (Nguyen and Nguyen 148–9). While it is important to recognize that this category of "first-generation students," like any other, is composed of individuals whose social locations, lived experiences, and outcomes will differ greatly, there are common characteristics that first-generation students often share: they are likely to be women; from low-income households; mature students; and—in the United States—Hispanic, Black, or Native American (Nguyen and Nguyen 148).

5. Kris Gutiérrez and Barbara Rogoff caution against making assumptions about how students will learn and engage with institutions based on their background, as such generalized assumptions do not reflect the reality of individuals and the ways in which experiences and engagement change across contexts (19–20). Any conceptualization which homogenizes a group based on a single shared trait is inherently flawed, failing to account for individual experience and variation, and so we must attend to the particulars of Kvothe's experiences in relation to his unique background and identity, analyzing the ways in which these influence one another without assuming a direct causal relationship between his background and his educational experiences and attainment.

6. Research has shown that underrepresented students experience and encounter a variety of barriers and hardships as they pursue postsecondary education, including: discrimination, academic disadvantages, negative feelings such as apprehension and alienation, a difficult transition to school, psychological distress, challenges persisting to graduation, constraints resulting from needing to work, lower grades, less extracurricular involvement, fewer friendships, greater separation from campus and academic life, and more limited career prospects and earning potential than their peers (Aries and Seider 420–1; Granfield 331–2; Lehmann "In a class" 103 and "Working-class" 527; Ostrove and Long 365–8; Pascarella et al.; Stuber 34–35; Walpole 46).

7. Habitus is "a durable, but not entirely inflexible, system of learned attitudes, perceptions, and behaviours towards one's probabilities and possibilities in life" (Rios-Aguilar and Kiyama 14), or "the system of durable,

Notes—Chapter 2

transposable dispositions that form the basis of perception and appreciation of one's social experience" (Stuber 3). Habitus shapes and is shaped by an individual's practice within the field, informing their standing—and their understanding of this standing—within its networks and structures; habitus is not deterministic and can be altered, but it is definitively shaped by an individual's past and present, creating and offering some possibilities while obscuring others based on the interplay between an individual's agency and the structures of the field (Rios-Aguilar and Kiyama 14–15). Just as capital can be understood only in relation to a field, so it must also be considered in relation to an individual's habitus in particular, which informs their acquisition and use of capital and their engagement with a field such as a post-secondary institution (Rios-Aguilar and Kiyama 15).

8. The primary currency used in the texts is that of the fictional nation of Ceald. As explained in the Kingkiller Fandom Wiki: "The official denominations are the iron drab, the copper jot, the silver talent, and the gold mark. The conversion system is decimal; ten drabs make a jot, ten jots make a talent, and ten talents make a mark" ("Currency").

9. It is interesting to note that Kvothe's decision to advocate for himself arises from his mismatched habitus, as he elects to take advantage of an opportunity other students do not perceive, as they are predisposed to conceptualize the final question—"Is there anything else you would like to say?"—as rhetorical and ritualistic as opposed to a genuine invitation for dialogue (Name 256–7). The fact that Kvothe knows almost nothing about the masters, the admissions process, and the larger systems of the University and the Arcanum means he does not understand the precise nature of the risk he takes when he chooses to advocate for himself in this moment.

10. As Rios-Aguilar et al. note, having social and cultural capital is not sufficient without activation (173), and access to capital does not automatically lead to such activation and mobilization (170). Noting the contexts in which capital is successfully activated, the actions taken by individuals to achieve this, and the institutional response to this activation—as well as moments in which attempts at activation are unsuccessful—we see moments in which cultural and social reproduction occurs (Rios-Aguilar et al. 174).

11. Artificing, overseen by Master Kilvin, is the process of inventing and replicating products powered or enhanced by sympathy, accomplished through the use of materials both mundane and magical and driven by the art of sygaldry: a set of runes with inherent magic powers that can be inscribed onto objects as part of their construction to achieve particular results, many of which would be impossible otherwise. Artificing products include lamps that cast light without fire, contraptions that stop arrows in flight, and specialized tokens that protect individuals from harmful magics targeting them.

12. Advancement from E'lir to Re'lar requires sponsorship by one of the masters, and each master sets their own requirements. Almost immediately after advancing into the Arcanum to the rank of E'lir, Simmon advises Kvothe "'to figure out who you're going to suck up to'" and then "'stick to him like shit on his shoe'" (Name 326), indelicately urging Kvothe to begin cultivating a relationship and acquiring the necessary capital to secure sponsorship. Kvothe remarks wryly upon the non-choice of targeting Kilvin as the most expedient option—"'And that is when I decided to pursue the noble art of artificing. Not that I had a lot of other options'" (Name 345)—acknowledging the constraints resulting from his need to advance quickly, itself a consequence of his limited capital and, therefore, limited time within the institution.

13. It is worth noting here that, even where the time available for socialization

Notes—Chapter 2

is not prohibitively constrained by the need to work, socialization with peers is a challenge for students in positions like Kvothe's (Aries and Seider 428). Their inability to participate in social events like trips to restaurants can hinder their ability to be part of the school community and prevent full membership (Aries and Seider 429), and some may avoid social contact that would reveal their class status (Granfield 338). Further challenges arise from living off-campus and a lack of available economic capital, which generate their need to work and an inability to participate in certain social events or outings, as well as from a perceived difference in background and discrimination from peers and from these students' tendency to focus on outside relationships where these barriers are not present (Stuber 51–56). The latter is certainly true of Kvothe, as he makes more substantive and costly efforts to maintain his relationship with Denna, which exists beyond the boundaries of the institution, than he does to socialize with his peers. While this does limit Kvothe's opportunities to gain social and cultural capital within the field through the network of his peers, it is important to acknowledge the benefits Kvothe derives from this relationship with Denna and not conceptualize them as primarily or only "maladaptive and inhibiting" (Stuber 59). Kvothe's relationship with Denna is also demonstrative of the challenges under-represented students face maintaining these prior or external relationships, as they navigate tensions of code-switching (Aries and Seider 435), as well as the general changes and conflicts in relationships with parents and old friends (Lehmann "Habitus" 9), which can result in lost access to old networks and their forms of social capital and funds of knowledge (Lehmann "Habitus" 12; Walpole 50).

14. The availability of time to dedicate to these non-earning pursuits functions as what Armstrong calls "social sorting" and informs which students gain membership in which networks and communities, distributing further capital to those students who already have considerable stocks (Armstrong quoted in Stuber 61–2). Kvothe, who must work to support himself while at school and so necessarily prioritize time spent earning an income, must relegate his academic work to secondary priority and can make no time for leisure, socialization, or self-care. This makes him appear to be a less dedicated and less engaged student, as we see with Kilvin's conclusion that Kvothe is not dedicated to his studies of artificery despite the many hours Kvothe spends working there, since efforts to acquire economic capital to afford continued enrollment are incompatible with social participation in the institution's networks.

15. Kvothe's experiences studying in Ademre also call into question the implied need for the University to charge tuition and require students to have access to existing economic capital if they are to access and persist in their studies. Education for the Adem in the path of the Letantha, in the school at Haert, is free; only after they have attained the social and cultural capital of their studies, enabling them to "take the Red" and earn economic capital as elite mercenaries throughout the Four Corners, are graduates expected to contribute financially to the school as a proportion of their income. This system removes economic barriers to accessing education in these specialized martial arts—though we must acknowledge the existence of social and cultural barriers to access, with which Kvothe must attend.

16. With this insult, we also see Kvothe has learned to navigate the social and punitive structures of the University through his increased understanding of the hidden curriculum in operation. He carefully drives up his tuition without generating too significant a disciplinary consequence: for insulting Hemme, he is charged with Improper Address of a Master, the punishment for which is a

Notes—Chapter 2

letter of apology and a single silver talent. With all the money he will earn back from his high tuition cost, Kvothe considers this talent "[m]oney well spent" (Wise 1040); and, as we have seen with his apology letter to Ambrose, Kvothe is able to manipulate and even weaponize these public apologies to his own ends.

17. Kucich draws on the work of Margaret Archer, Andrew Sayer, Peter Bailey, Patrick Joyce, Anthony Giddens, and Bourdieu to present this understanding of cross-class performance.

18. As Cristine M. Varholy asserts, sumptuary laws and legal proceedings in seventeenth-century London against those found to be cross-class dressing speak to the viability of this strategy for cross-class performance, as successful presentation through dress "produced a crisis of interpretation by blurring the boundaries between that which is "real" and that which is performed" and called into question the immutability of the class hierarchy and markers of class status (11). Both sumptuary laws and play plots involving cross-class dressing implied that an individual's identity could be changed through the consumption of clothing and the performance of a particular class status, thereby achieving transgressive social mobility (Varholy).

19. Additional examples of the reputation and persecution of the Edema Ruh include the group of criminals posing as Edema Ruh Kvothe meets while travelling, who actively embody the poor reputation of the Edema Ruh as rapists, thieves, and charlatans and see their assumed identity as license to behave illegally and immorally (Wise 944–63). The Edema Ruh are hated by members of the Modegan nobility (Wise 503–4)—most notably Lady Meluan Lackless, who repeats the slur Hemme used (Wise 1023)—and Kvothe's refusal to speak ill of them and the revelation of his own identity as Edema Ruh sees him ejected from the court of Maer Alveron, where he had previously been in favor (Wise 1022–6).

20. Readers can also understand Kvothe's desire to "pass" specifically by concealing his identity as Edema Ruh as a method of self-preservation to avoid persecution.

21. Bast himself consciously performs as a man, rather than a Fae being, paralleling and drawing greater attention to Kvothe's own performance in this present-day timeline of the trilogy. Bast's performance, similar to Kvothe's, is best understood as passing within the narrative and—if we understand Fae creatures to be superior to humans in terms of their innate power—slumming from the perspective of the reader and the occasional knowing character, like Kvothe. Choosing to reveal the artificiality of his performance, as he does during his late-night visit to the Chronicler, serves as an effective intimidation tactic (Name 718–9), as the abrupt change from seemingly playful young man to powerful Fae with eyes of solid, changeable blue is an uncomfortable reminder of Bast's raw power, of his ability to manipulate the perceptions of others to suit his desires, and of how little others actually know of his true self.

22. The fact that Kvothe refers to the admissions exam as a "performance" or "performing" also draws attention to the fact that Kvothe is playing the role of a student as expected by the institution (Name 352–3; Wise 37), as does the location of the exams on "the stage of an empty theater" (Name 248; Wise 91, 1040).

23. Readers are also reminded of Kvothe's class performance in moments where he forgets to drop the act, as it were, such as when he leaves the social circle of the University chasing after rumors of the Chandrian and, still performing a middle-class identity in his speech, alienates a group of lower-class gentlemen in a tavern from whom he had hoped to glean information (Name 528–9).

24. These strategies of concealment and the attendant assimilation generate

Notes—Chapter 3

both positive and negative results: while students note a subsequent attainment of "new forms of self-confidence and self-respect that came along with diminished feelings of difference, inadequacy and exclusion" (Aries and Seider 432), the conscious attempt to mimic wealthier peers makes it difficult for students of similar backgrounds to find one another as support (Aries and Seider 340–1).

25. It is important to recognize, as Foster does, that recognizing and discussing class as performative does not invalidate or dismiss the "real class differences, real consequences, real hardships, and real privileges that come with class" (*Class-Passing* 7).

Chapter 3

1. Mendlesohn most often uses the term "portal-quest fantasy," in accordance with her argument that the majority of portal fantasy narratives are also quest narratives and that the "rhetorical position" of the author is the same in each (*Rhetoric* 1). I prefer the term "portal fantasy," however, as I agree with Paul Kincaid's assessment that these are in fact separate concerns, with portal fantasy being a particular mode while the quest is a narrative strategy which can be employed with equal success in any mode (264).

2. Secondary worlds are defined in *The Encyclopedia of Fantasy* "as an autonomous world or venue which is not bound to mundane reality ... which is impossible according to common sense and which is self-coherent as a venue for Story (i.e., the rules by which reality is defined can be learned by living them, and are not arbitrary like those of a Wonderland can be)" (Clute "Secondary World" 847). Both Fillory and Brakebills meet these criteria, being distinct from mundane reality, having many impossible elements, and operating on consistent rules.

3. See, for example, the interviews Grossman has done for *Flavorwire, The Millions, Entertainment Weekly,* and *Vox.*

4. See: Hand; A. Himes; J.B. Himes; Kramer; Nester; Vinci "Mourning" and "Post."

5. One notable difference in Grossman's adaptation is the nationality of the fictional author: where Lewis was British, Plover is American. Specifically, Plover is a rich American who moved to England and conspicuously enacted the identity of an English gentleman during his life: "he embraced Anglophilia, began pronouncing his name the English way ("Pluvver"), and set himself up as a country squire in a vast home crammed with staff" (TM 74). As we learn in the final novel through Rupert Chatwin's memoir, Plover was not particularly comfortable in this role, unable to perfect the intricacies and in-group markers of a British identity and lacking the confidence to confront the "truly" British, even children. On his first meeting with the Chatwin children, Plover offers them tea—a stereotypically British act, but one which the natively–British children recognize as mistimed and misinformed—and the children take up this imperfect invitation as an opportunity for both eating and exploiting the deficiencies of their neighbor (Land 214). While Plover "wasn't even really English," as the narrative voice insists, "[o]nly an American Anglophile could have created a world as definitively English, more English than England, as Fillory" (TM 74). This difference, rather than distancing Grossman's American reimagining of the portal fantasy from its British roots, serves to reinforce the legacy and explicitly insist that Fillory, and the *Magicians* series which contains it, is definitively part of this British tradition.

6. In this chapter, I follow Donnarae MacCann's use of the terms "imperialism" and "colonialism." As MacCann explains: "Colonialism and imperialism are commonly used synonymously, although imperialism is the term often applied to the whole colonial structure—

Notes—Chapter 3

an empire's array of countries, relationships, political controls, etc. Colonialism involves the domination of one group over another, or over culturally unrelated groups" (Note 6, 205). Imperialism, as used in this chapter, refers to the larger structures and ideologies in which the narratives and schooling practices participate, while colonialism will be used in reference to specific, smaller-scale actions, usually in reference to the students and teachers of Brakebills.

7. Both MacCann and Bradford insist that imperialist ideologies continue to exist within twenty-first century children's literature.

8. Hunt and Sands note the connection between imperialism and the school story and the public school system which informed the genre (44), and Jeffrey Richards explicates the relationship of both the imperial adventure narrative and the school story to sustaining and justifying the British empire, remarking on their coinciding declines (5–6).

9. As Marcia Langton, Maureen Tehan, and Lisa Palmer assert, imperial treaties between indigenous populations and imperial agents from countries such as Britain, France, Spain, and Portugal were sites of exploitation and double standards. Treaties were an apparatus of the *ad hoc* imperial law codes developed "to justify conquest, trade, safe passage and other exigencies of imperialism" (Langton et al. 4), and while these agreements officially brought the indigenous populations within or at least adjacent to the law of the imperial centre, separate law codes were developed so different regulations and standards applied to settler and indigenous populations (Langton et al. 6), and imperial agents modified rules and agreements frequently to better suit the needs and desires of settler populations (Langton et al. 5). While treaties were employed and weaponized in different ways across the globe, making it impossible "to reduce the international relations between the Europeans and Indigenous peoples as a whole to a single pattern" (Langton et al. 13), there are nevertheless similarities in how treaties were made in the interests of the colonizing power and then broken to the detriment of the subjugated party, with Indigenous peoples "disadvantaged, even in apparently consensual arrangements" (Langton et al. 25).

10. Gaile S. Cannella and Radhika Viruru in *Childhood and Postcolonization* assert the connection between imperial ideology and the construction of childhood (3–5), as does Wallace.

11. See, for example, DuPlessis, who notes that education is an essential part of the colonizer's "strategy of suppression/oppression" (121).

12. Note that this timing coincides with the publication of *The Chronicles of Narnia*, as does the outdated kitchen in the Cottage (TM 102).

13. Taking up Hamish Bax's performative Anglophilia through the lens of Homi Bhabha's "colonial mimicry" offers a dual reading of this deliberate presentation, explicating the ways in which Bax presents himself as the "reformed, recognizable Other" (122), who closely approximates the ideal of the colonizer, while simultaneously disrupting colonial authority by mocking, through his exaggerated mimicry, the power of Britain as an imitable model (125). "Mimicry conceals no presence of identity behind its mask," Bhabha explains—Bax's plus fours do not attempt to obscure his identity as a Black man; rather, in partially producing the colonizer's ideal, his performative Anglophilia resists colonial appropriation by destabilizing the notions of origin and identity (126–7).

14. Marie Byrd Land was named for the wife of American naval officer and explorer Admiral Richard E. Byrd in 1929.

15. Postsecondary institutions, of which Brakebills is one, are particularly important to consider within an imperial educational system: as Bray explains, they are the "apex" of the system and are where future leaders receive their training (340).

175

Notes—Chapter 3

16. For a discussion of these beliefs in general, see, for instance, Tiffin and Lawson. For an examination of the ways in which the educational practices at Brakebills exemplify a "dominating praxis," as well as how the alternate un-schooling educational experiences of Julia exemplify a "liberating praxis," see my previous work on the series.

17. Consequently, this practice devalues the learning process and elides the socially-constructed aspect of knowledge in the same ways as a science-centred pedagogy (Thésée 35). As Arlo Kempf demonstrates in his study of history curricula and instruction, "[t]here is strategic importance in the *who, why, where* and *how* of knowledge production" (129, emphasis in original), and Brakebills students are denied participation in knowledge-production and knowledge produced in certain fields, primarily the *theory* of magic. See my previous work on the series for an examination of the ways in which this control of knowledge-production and the denial of theoretical understanding functions in the institution, serving to discourage critical engagement among students by fostering a sense of fatality and hopelessness.

18. It is interesting to note that, while science was of value in the imperial system because it was understood as "de-contextualized, neutral, asocial, a-historical and universal" (Thésée 26), this system of Circumstance and Exceptions explicitly contextualizes the working of magic, requiring the caster to account for the context of the casting in numerous ways, including the time of day, the season, the geographic location, and the gender of the magician (TM 150–151). As a result, magic in this world has power not because it is de-contextualized, but rather because magicians are inherently able to account for its context.

19. Fogg speculates that magic and the powers attendant in its mastery were never intended for humans and might be better off forsworn (TM 217), but this does not prevent him from presiding over an institution designed to provide a secret elite with these powers and abilities. The possibility that magic was never intended for human use and is rather "divine" is borne out in interesting ways throughout the rest of the series, through the narrative thread of Julia and the Murs magicians pursuing divine ascension as a means to access greater levels of magical ability in *The Magician King*, and through Julia's realized ascension to demi-goddess and Quentin's temporary possession of godly powers in *The Magician's Land*.

20. When Quentin actualizes his transition to colonizer by joining the Brakebills staff, his research similarly actualizes this understanding of the purpose of magic: he uses his power to literally create a land which is entirely his to shape and control. The time and resources provided through his faculty position enable Quentin to decipher the Neitherlands page, providing the necessary knowledge to create a magical secondary world of his own, which he enters as colonizer at the close of the trilogy (Land 396–401).

21. In addition to being all of these things, Josh is also, as we are consistently reminded, fat. An examination of the ways in which Josh's fatness is represented in the text would be a fruitful analysis, particularly as it is represented through his uniform and the implications this has for his belonging within the institution and the institution's policing of bodies (TM 107).

22. The unanticipated outcomes go beyond the immediate consequence of summoning Reynard, who murders most of the Murs magicians and rapes Julia as a means of imparting divine power to her: their call to the gods draws the attention of all the divine beings, whose awakening threatens to remove magic from human use entirely. This threat is the focus of the present-day timeline of *The Magician King*; metaphorically,

it is a fight to maintain the power of empire and the ability to subjugate the world.

23. The official reason behind this decision is that Penny's Discipline is "so arcane and outlandish it couldn't be classified according to any of the conventional schemes" (TM 198), but we know from Quentin's example of being assigned to the Physical group despite not having a defined Discipline that the rules can be and are bent for other students (TM 95). Designating Penny as "independent" is a deliberate choice the institution has made, one which cements his social isolation and marginalization within the institution's structures.

24. This is an enactment of a particular form of colonial violence as Brakebills attempts to "amputate" Julia from her past, thereby constraining her present and future (Kempf 132). As Tony M. Vinci notes, the repeated allusions to and direct mentions of rape throughout this portion of the narrative rightfully frame the institution's actions as an assault ("Mourning" 374, 376), and Julia's attempts to process the trauma of this mental violation create a bifurcation of her personality and identity (King 76–78) and trigger a depressive episode (King 77–82).

25. During this re-read, Quentin speculates that the answer to Martin's disappearance may have been contained in *The Magicians* manuscript he had so briefly possessed (TM 75): Quentin is unknowingly correct, as *The Magicians*—this text, which also contains Quentin's story—does contain the rest of Martin's history, and readers are once again reminded that this text is a portal fantasy and welcomed to interrogate it as such. Quentin himself, we are told via the paramedic (who is secretly Jane Chatwin), is not ready yet to know this part of the story, though she promises that he will find it and know it eventually, if he seeks it. This, Quentin notes, is "the kind of thing people always said about Fillory" (TM 84).

Chapter 4

1. As is frequently noted throughout not just the "Tiffany Aching" quintet but any of the Discworld novels in which the witches feature, there is no leader of the witches, as no witch would ever allow any of their colleagues to be placed above them in any sort of hierarchy, explicit or implied. Nevertheless, Granny Weatherwax is acknowledged as the leader they do not have, the most senior and accomplished witch against whom all others are judged and to which the others turn in times of crisis or uncertainty—the quintessential witch who defines the practice of witchcraft with her own actions and attitudes. When Granny Weatherwax dies in *The Shepherd's Crown*, Tiffany becomes the new non-leader of the witches.

2. In the context of the Discworld saga, Roundworld refers to this world (the planet Earth) and our reality and experiences here.

3. Gideon Haberkorn and Verena Reinhardt note that the more an educational opportunity on the Discworld is institutionalized, the less likely it is to be represented as either practical or useful (42).

4. As Steinbrück explicates, the wandering teachers turn education into "a commodity to be bought, marketed, sold and passed on," a free market good where the type, quality, amount, and price are all variable and only those with material wealth can secure it, resulting in "social inequality, exclusion and education poverty" (99).

5. "White knowledge" is Pratchett's term for the general knowledge and awareness of common cultural references, narratives, tropes, stereotypes, character archetypes, plots, devices, etc.—"the sort of stuff that fills up your brain without you really knowing where it came from" (Pratchett quoted in "Words from the Master").

6. Croft comments upon these allusions, connecting them specifically to Hogwarts in the *Harry Potter* series

Notes—Chapter 4

("Education" 133), as does Gruner with her observation that Tiffany's imaginings sound "almost as if she's been reading J.K. Rowling" ("Teach" 224).

7. Pratchett writes the brogue of the Feegles phonetically; all of the original spellings are maintained when the Feegles are quoted throughout this chapter.

8. While Tiffany never apprentices directly to Granny Weatherwax, there is a general consensus among scholars that Granny Weatherwax nevertheless oversees Tiffany's education at a remove and serves unofficially as Tiffany's mentor (Haberkorn and Reinhardt; Steinbrück).

9. The relationships in this group are not founded upon personal affinity: the purpose of the coven, as fellow newcomer Petulia explains, is to "keep in touch" and "make contacts" (Hat 122), which Tiffany later reiterates as an opportunity to "see friends, even if they were friends simply because they were, really, the only people you could talk to freely because they had the same problems and would understand what you were moaning about" (Wintersmith 117). This network is created and maintained on the basis of their shared status as up-and-coming witches in the community of practice, who need knowing listeners for their complaints and safe spaces to express their frustrations and disappointments as they develop as practitioners.

10. Boffo is another way Pratchett plays with genre expectations and cultural stereotypes throughout the quintet: it is the name of a novelty and joke shop selling props like skulls, bubbling cauldrons, and warts. Miss Treason, who makes liberal use of Boffo's products, calls it "the art of expectations," elaborating on the importance of showing people what they expect to see and maintaining one's reputation (Wintersmith 81). None of these products are essential to, or even used in, the practice of witchcraft, but as Annagramma learns and Tiffany intuitively understands, they are a viable means of earning respect: fundamentally, "Miss Treason had power because people thought she did" (Wintersmith 83), and any witch can generate this respect by deliberately creating an appearance of power using stereotypes as building materials.

11. As Gavin Moodie makes clear, such a concise definition of vocational education leaves out a great deal. Vocational education is variably understood through a focus on its epistemological aspects, developing a "distinctive way of knowing" for practitioners in a given field, its teleological aspects, emphasizing on the purpose it serves in producing capable technicians in the field, its hierarchical aspects, distinguishing vocational from general education by way of comparisons of educational or cognitive level, and its pragmatic aspects, recognizing its liminal position between secondary and postsecondary education and its uniqueness from other, better defined education sectors. Rightfully concluding that none of these aspects alone adequately define and capture vocational education at any given time, and that attempting to definitively codify it in theory risks losing its flexibility and adaptability in practice, Moodie thereby presents a *possible* definition encompassing a variety of key characters.

12. Alice Nuttall analyzes the emotional labor involved in witchcraft on the Discworld, commenting on its connection with traditional gender roles for women and the domestic sphere and the ways in which its portrayal both celebrates womanhood and domesticity and demonstrates the ways in which women's opportunities are limited under patriarchy.

13. Other apt descriptions of witchcraft include Steinbrück's "medical outpatient village pastoral care" (100) and Gruner's "traditional parish priest—though with a uniquely Pratchettian twist" ("Wrestling" 278).

14. As part of providing this care, witches must also be willing to make the hard choices, accepting the conse-

Notes—Chapter 4

quences and allowing others to be "innocent of responsibility" for difficult decisions, bearing these burdens often for an entire community (Croft "Nice" 159). As Croft explicates, the morality of the witches is focused on doing Right, which Croft explicates as "making decisions that are just but not necessarily merciful, morally correct but not necessarily pleasant" ("Nice" 155).

15. Croft notes that the structures of education are similarly divided, with the training of wizards at the Unseen University and of witches by apprenticeship perpetuating a home school/classroom dichotomy that replicates the domestic/public dichotomy often associated with the binary genders ("Education" 131, note 3). L. Kaitlin Williams also analyzes this "educational ideology" of magic on the Discworld, noting the association of the Unseen University with the British public school system, academic elitism, male privilege, and traditional power hierarchies, in contrast with the witches' subversion of societal norms throughout the self-education of their apprentices.

16. Lian Sinclair also addresses the positive representation of domestic labor and "women's work," arguing that the major theme of the Witches novels is balancing personal desire with the expectation of gender roles, intervening with a subversive reimagining of the witch figure and a celebration of domestic labor to demonstrate the ways in which gendered narratives and expectations constrict individuals.

17. Tiffany is not the only witch to face a precipitating moment and change the nature of witchcraft as a result: fellow newcomer Petulia contests and changes the community of practice's taboo of discussing Death and the final door at the end of *A Hat Full of Sky*. Petulia insists that "'It is a time to talk about it, just here, just us!'" because this is an exceptionally important and dangerous part of witchcraft, and it must be discussed if they are to be prepared to render this service when called upon to do so (Hat 304). Following Petulia's initial challenge, the truth of Tiffany's experiences spreads quickly, including explicit mention of the desert and the dust beyond the door (Hat 305–8); Petulia's actions break the taboo, changing the field.

18. Züleyha Çetiner-Öktem has explored Eskarina's representation, including her engagement with "women's work" as a means to enter the "men's space" of the Unseen University and the "personal hybrid space" she thereby creates so she may pursue her education in wizardry informally, asserting that Eskarina's position between the dichotomous positions of witch and wizard begins to diffuse this border and offers "the possibility of a genderless, or even multi-gendered, occupation" (102). While Eskarina's study of wizardry is an important first step in changing the gendered division of magic, it is disappointing that Eskarina's initial challenge precipitated no noticeable change in the practice of either witches or wizards in the following thirty-seven novels, until Tiffany and Geoffrey's new first step on the other side of the magical division in the forty-first and final novel.

19. This change in the gender-exclusive nature of witchcraft is made possible, in part, by the concurrent societal changes within the community of practice: internally, there is the change represented by the passing of Granny Weatherwax and Tiffany's assumption of the role of (non-)leader; externally, the Discworld itself is changing with the development of the railroads. As Kemmis and Edwards-Groves explain, "When there is a new realignment or confluence of ideas, economic processes and developments, and the emergence of new or reshaped social and political orders, then there is a good chance that major transformations—in education as in other aspects of society—will develop and gain widespread acceptance" (98). Combining the larger destabilization of structures and norms on the Discworld resulting from the railroads with the more

immediate upheaval of the community of practice's hierarchy with Granny Weatherwax's death and Tiffany's assumption of the role of non-leader, conditions are favorable for enacting lasting changes in the practice of witchcraft.

20. Tiffany is nine years old during the events of *The Wee Free Men* (with flashbacks to her at age eight) and sixteen years old by the events of *The Shepherd's Crown*.

21. We find additional evidence in the long-standing dismissal of children's and young adult literature as a subject of serious study in the academy, arising from a flawed assumption that literature produced for children and youth cannot be substantive enough to support critical analysis or interrogation through various theoretical frameworks, which Beverly Lyon Clark has comprehensively catalogued and refuted in texts such as *Kiddie Lit*.

22. Understanding the power hierarchy which informs aetonormativity as "non-negotiable" given the social conditions surrounding childhood, Nikolajeva asserts that "The only way to circumvent adult normativity completely is through non-mimetic modes" (*Power* 203).

23. Only Mrs. Earwig—who, by this point, has been thoroughly established as the odd-woman-out in the practice, who has the least true understanding of the work and none of the respect usually attendant with seniority—sees an opportunity to advance herself and her girls (Shepherd's 64–5), challenging Tiffany for the position and losing to her in a quiet game of politics and work ethic throughout the remainder of the book.

24. Though scholars like Sinclair have argued for a recognition of Eskarina's narrative arc in *Equal Rites* as a successful challenge of gender essentialism, in which both Eskarina and Granny Weatherwax "effectively contest the institution that is the Unseen University both by beating the men at their own game and by retaining their femininity" (14), the fact remains that this singular triumph does little to change the witches' (or wizards') community of practice despite the many Discworld volumes following *Equal Rites*.

Conclusion

1. Childhood Studies takes, as its foundation, the fact that childhood is "socio-historically and culturally constructed" (Kassem, Murphy, and Taylor 1). The field emerged from a widespread dissatisfaction with the treatment of childhood as a subject of study in various fields, which ignored the context and constructedness of childhood as well as privileging a focus on the "indoctrination" of children and youth into society, excluding them as social actors (Prout 1), resulting in failure to provide a "holistic conceptualization of children as individuals and as a class" (Lenzer 182). The intention of Childhood Studies is to "contribute to the well-being of children by promoting a knowledge-based and improved understanding among the educated public and in society at large of children's capacities, capabilities, needs, and desires, as well as of their civil, political, economic, and cultural human rights" (Lenzer 185) by addressing the limitations in earlier studies and considering children, youth, and childhood in all of its contexts.

2. It is worth noting that children's and young adult literature as representations of the lived experiences of youth is a contentious issue. Some critics see children's and young adult literature as a site of worthwhile, though not universal, representation, a place to begin developing an understanding of childhood: Gertrude Lenzer, for instance, asserts that "much of our most intimate knowledge of children and childhood has traditionally come from writers, poets, and artists and not from scholars, educators, and policy makers" (185–186), while Galbraith claims that literature "has been the real pioneer in presenting the experience

of individual child SELVES [*sic*]" and can help to "'lift out' and characterize the phenomenon we seek to study" in non-literary childhoods (194). On the other side of the debate, Peter Hunt warns that these texts are "highly unreliable guides to what childhood was or is" and are "more likely to portray *attitudes* to childhood" than actual experience ("Children's" 51, emphasis in original). Analyzing these attitudes, however, is a valuable undertaking, and is an essential part of understanding the forces limiting children and youth—for, as Hunt himself acknowledges, while these texts may not reflect reality, they do come to influence it ("Children's" 52), and children's and young adult literature function as "a barometer of the pressures on childhood" ("Children's" 69), positioning these texts to aid in the goal of understanding the factors limiting the full expression of children and youth as subjects and agents.

3. Others, including Lisa Delpit and Terry Wrigley, have also addressed the importance of consciousness-raising: for Wrigley, it is a key step towards being able to enact change (136), and for Delpit, it is both a step towards change and an immediate need for students who come to education systems from outside the dominant culture and must develop an awareness of its hidden rules and structures before they can succeed within them.

Bibliography

Primary Sources

Deonn, Tracy. *Legendborn*. Margaret K. McElderry Books, 2020.

Grossman, Lev. *The Magician King*. Viking, 2011.

——. *The Magicians*. Viking, 2009.

——. *The Magician's Land*. Viking, 2014.

Okorafor, Nnedi. *Akata Witch*. Viking, 2011.

Pratchett, Terry. *Equal Rites*. Corgi Books, 1987.

——. *A Hat Full of Sky*. Doubleday, 2004.

——. *I Shall Wear Midnight*. Doubleday, 2010.

——. *The Shepherd's Crown*. Doubleday, 2015.

——. *The Wee Free Men*. Doubleday, 2003.

——. *Wintersmith*. Doubleday, 2006.

Rothfuss, Patrick. *The Name of the Wind*. DAW Books, 2007.

——. *The Wise Man's Fear*. DAW Books, 2011.

Rowling, J.K. *Harry Potter and the Chamber of Secrets*. Bloomsbury, 1998.

——. *Harry Potter and the Deathly Hallows*. Bloomsbury, 2007.

——. *Harry Potter and the Goblet of Fire*. Bloomsbury, 2000.

——. *Harry Potter and the Half-Blood Prince*. Bloomsbury, 2005.

——. *Harry Potter and the Order of the Phoenix*. Bloomsbury, 2003.

——. *Harry Potter and the Philosopher's Stone*. Bloomsbury, 1997.

——. *Harry Potter and the Prisoner of Azkaban*. Bloomsbury, 1999.

Rowling, J.K., Jack Thorne, and John Tiffany. *Harry Potter and the Cursed Child*. Scholastic, 2017.

Yolen, Jane. *Wizard's Hall*. 1991. Magic Carpet Books, 1999.

Secondary Sources

Ahsan, Sumera, and William C. Smith. "Facilitating Student Learning: A Comparison of Classroom and Accountability Assessment." Smith, pp. 131–51.

Al Ghoraibi, Amani Mansi. "The Narrative Techniques Used by Patrick Rothfuss in *The Name of the Wind*." *Narratology*, vol. 29, 2018, pp. 77–92. *Egyptian Journals*, https://journals.ekb.eg/article_89147.html. Accessed 26 Jul. 2020.

Alexander, Jonathan, and Rebecca Black. "The Darker Side of the Sorting Hat: Presentations of Educational Testing in Dystopian Young Adult Fiction." *Children's Literature*, vol. 43, 2015, pp. 208–34. *Project Muse*, doi:10.1353/chl.215.0019. Accessed 12 Aug. 2020.

Alfitra, Yonanda. *Makna Referensial Implisit Dan Makna Situasional Implisit Novel the Magicians Karya Lev Grossman Dan Analisis Terjemahannya*, 2013. Padjadjaran University, Undergraduate thesis. *Unpad Repository*, https://repository.unpad.ac.id/frontdoor/index/index/year/2020/docId/25647. Accessed 16 Feb. 2021.

Alton, Anne Hiebert. "Playing the Genre Game: Generic Fusions of the Harry

Bibliography

Potter Series." Heilman *Critical*, pp. 199–223.

Alton, Ann Hiebert, and William C. Spruiell, editors. *Discworld and the Disciplines: Critical Approaches to the Terry Pratchett Works*. McFarland, 2014.

Anatol, Giselle Liza. "The Fallen Empire: Exploring Ethnic Otherness in the World of Harry Potter." Anatol, pp. 163–78.

Anatol, Giselle Liza, editor. *Reading Harry Potter: Critical Essays*. Praeger, 2003.

Apple, Michael, and Nancy King. "What Do Schools Teach?" Giroux and Purpel, pp. 82–99.

Aries, Elizabeth, and Maynard Seider. "The Interactive Relationship Between Class Identity and the College Experience: The Case of Lower Income Students." *Qualitative Sociology*, vol. 28, no. 4, 2005, pp. 419–43. *Springer*, doi: 10.1007/s11133–005–8366–1. Accessed 12 Feb. 2020.

Attebery, Brian. *The Fantasy Tradition in American Literature: From Irving to Le Guin*. Indiana UP, 1980.

———. *Strategies of Fantasy*. Indiana UP, 1992.

Bathmaker, Ann-Marie, and James Avis. "Becoming a Lecturer in Further Education in England: The Construction of Professional Identity and the Role of Communities of Practice." *Journal of Education for Teaching*, vol. 31, no. 1, 2005, pp. 47–62. *Taylor & Francis Online*, doi: 10.1080/02607470500043771. Accessed 5 Mar. 2021.

Battis, Jes. "Trans Magic: The Radical Performance of the Young Wizards in YA Literature." *Over the Rainbow: Queer Children's and Young Adult Literature*, edited by Michelle Ann Abate and Kenneth B. Kidd, U Michigan P, 2011, pp. 314–28.

Beaton, Tisha. "Taking Time: Harry Potter as a Context for Interdisciplinary Studies." *The English Journal*, vol. 95, no. 3, 2006, pp. 100–03. *JSTOR*, www.jstor.org/stable/30047053. Accessed 18 Sep. 2015.

Bell, Christopher E, editor. *Legilimens!: Perspectives in Harry Potter Studies*. Cambridge Scholars, 2013.

Bhabha, Homi. *The Location of Culture*. 1994. Routledge, 2004.

Billett, Stephen, and Margaret Somerville. "Transformation at Work: Identity and Learning." *Studies in Continuing Education*, vol. 26, no. 2, 2004, pp. 309–26. *Taylor & Francis Online*, doi: 10.1080/158037042000225272. Accessed 5 Mar. 2021.

Birch, Megan L. "Schooling Harry Potter: Teachers and Learning, Power and Knowledge." Heilman *Critical*, pp. 103–20.

Bishop, Katherine E. "The Pedagogical Fantastic: Active Learning Through and in Fantasy Literature." *Comparative Culture*, vol. 22, no. 2, 2018, pp. 46–51. Accessed 26 Jul. 2020.

Black, Mary S., and Marilyn J. Eisenwine. "Education of the Young Harry Potter: Socialization and Schooling for Wizards." *Educational Forum*, vol. 66, no. 1, 2002, pp. 32–7. *Scholars Portal*, doi:10.1080/00131720108984797. Accessed 20 Jan. 2016.

Bordonaro, Lorenzo I. "Agency Does Not Mean Freedom. Cape Verdean Street Children and the Politics of Children's Agency." *Children's Geographies*, vol. 10, no. 4, 2012, pp. 413–26. *Taylor & Francis Online*, doi: 10.1080/14733285.2012.726068. Accessed 28 Oct. 2015.

Boulding, Lucas. "'I Can't Be Having with That': The Ethical Implications of Professional Witchcraft in Pratchett's Fiction." *Terry Pratchett*, special issue of *Gender Forum*, vol. 52, 2015, n.p. *Gender Forum*, http://genderforum.org/special-issue-terry-pratchett-issue-52-2015/. Accessed 17 Feb. 2021.

Bourdieu, Pierre. "Cultural Reproduction and Social Reproduction." *Knowledge, Education and Cultural Change: Papers in the Sociology of Education*,

Bibliography

edited by Richard Brown. 1973. Routledge, 2018, pp. 71–112.

———. "Forms of Capital." *Handbook of Theory and Research for the Sociology of Education*, edited by John G. Richardson, Greenwood Press, 1986, pp. 241–58.

———. *Outline of a Theory of Practice*. Translated by Richard Nice, Cambridge UP, 1977.

Bourdieu, Pierre, and Jean-Claude Passeron. *Reproduction in Education, Society, and Culture*. Translated by Richard Nice, Sage Publications, 1977.

Bradford, Clare. "The End of Empire? Colonial and Postcolonial Journeys in Children's Books." *Children's Literature*, vol. 29, 2001, pp. 196–218. Project Muse, doi.org/10.1353/chl.0.0796. Accessed 26 Jun. 2019.

Bray, Mark. "Education and the Vestiges of Colonialism: Self-Determination, Neocolonialism and Dependency in the South Pacific." *Comparative Education*, vol. 29, no. 3, 1993, pp. 333–48. JSTOR, www.jstor.org/stable/3099333. Accessed 2 Jul. 2019.

Bryson, Colin. "Clarifying the Concept of Student Engagement." *Understanding and Developing Student Engagement*, edited by Bryson, Routledge, 2014, pp. 1–22.

Camilli, Gregory, and Lora F. Monfils. "Test Scores and Equity." Firestone et al., pp. 143–57.

Cannella, Gaile S., and Radhika Viruru. *Childhood and Postcolonization: Power, Education, and Contemporary Practice*. Routledge Falmer, 2004.

———. "(Euro-American Constructions Of) Education of Children (and Adults) Around the World: A Postcolonial Critique." *Kidworld: Childhood Studies, Global Perspectives, and Education*, edited by Cannella and Joe L. Kincheloe, Peter Lang, 2002, pp. 197–213.

Cecire, Maria Sachiko. "English Exploration and Textual Travel in *The Voyage of The Dawn Treader*." *Space and Place in Children's Literature, 1789 to the Present*, edited by Cecire, Hannah Field, and Malini Roy, Routledge, 2019, pp. 111–28.

Çetiner-Öktem, Züleyha. "Creating a Space of One's Own: Dialogues of Gender in Terry Pratchett's Discworld." *Languages, Cultures, and Gender*, edited by Çetiner-Öktem, Begüm Tuğlu, and Erkin Kiryaman, Ege UP, 2017, pp. 100–12.

Chappell, Drew. "Sneaking Out After Dark: Resistance, Agency, and the Postmodern Child in JK Rowling's Harry Potter Series." *Children's Literature in Education*, vol. 39, 2008, pp. 281–93. Springer, doi:10.1007/s10583-007-9060-6. Accessed 26 Oct. 2015.

Choudry, Sophina, and Julian Williams. "Figured Worlds in the Field of Power." *Mind, Culture, and Activity*, vol. 24, no. 3, 2017, pp. 247–57. Taylor & Francis Online, doi: 10.1080/10749039. 2016.1183132. Accessed 12 Feb. 2020.

Clark, Beverly Lyon. *Kiddie Lit: The Cultural Construction of Children's Literature in America*. Johns Hopkins UP, 2003.

———. *Regendering the School Story: Sassy Sissies and Tattling Tomboys*. Routledge, 2001.

Clute, John. "Club Story." *The Encyclopedia of Fantasy*, edited by Clute and John Grant, St. Martin's P, 1997, p. 207.

———. "Portals." *The Encyclopedia of Fantasy*, edited by Clute and John Grant, St. Martin's P, 1997, p. 776.

———. "Secondary World." *The Encyclopedia of Fantasy*, edited by Clute and John Grant, St. Martin's P, 1997, p. 847.

Coats, Karen. *Looking Glasses and Neverlands: Lacan, Desire, and Subjectivity in Children's Literature*. U Iowa P, 2004.

Cockrell, Amanda. "Harry Potter and the Secret Password: Finding Our Way in the Magical Genre." Whited *Ivory*, pp. 15–26.

Colley, Helen. "Learning to Labour with Feeling: Class, Gender and Emotion in Childcare Education and Training." *Contemporary Issues in Early Childhood*, vol. 7, no. 1, 2006, pp. 15–29. Sage,

Bibliography

doi: 10.2304/ciec.2006.7.1.15. Accessed 5 Mar. 2021.

Colley, Helen, et al. "Learning as Becoming in Vocational Education and Training: Class, Gender, and the Role of Vocational Habitus." *Journal of Vocational Education and Training*, vol. 55, no. 4, 2003, pp. 471–97. *Scholars Portal*, doi: 10.1080/13636820300200240. Accessed 12 Feb. 2020.

Conn, Jennifer. "What Can Clinical Teachers Learn from *Harry Potter and the Philosopher's Stone*?." *Medical Education*, vol. 36, no. 12, 2002, pp. 1176–181. *Scholars Portal*, doi:10.1046/j.1365–2923.2002.01376.x. Accessed 20 Jan. 2016.

Conn, Jennifer, and Susan Elliot. "Harry Potter and Assessment." *The Clinical Teacher*, vol. 2, no. 1, 2005, pp. 31–6. *Scholars Portal*, doi:10.1111/j.1743–498X.2005.00052.x. Accessed 20 Jan. 2016.

Copp, Derek T. "Teaching to the Test: A Mixed Methods Study of Instructional Change from Large-scale Testing in Canadian Schools." *Assessment in Education: Principles, Policy and Practice*, vol. 25, no. 5, 2018, pp. 468–87. *Scholars Portal*, doi: 10.1080/0969594X.2016.1244042. Accessed 27 Sep. 2019.

Croft, Janet Brennan. "The Education of a Witch: Tiffany Aching, Hermione Granger, and Gendered Magic in Discworld and Potterworld." *Mythlore*, vol. 27, no. 3/4, 2009, pp. 129–42. *JSTOR*, https://www.jstor.org/stable/26815565. Accessed 17 Feb. 2021.

———. "Nice, Good, or Right: Faces of the Wise Woman in Terry Pratchett's "Witches" Novels." *Mythlore*, vol. 26, no. 3, 2008, pp. 151–64. *JSTOR*, https://www.jstor.org/stable/26814590. Accessed 17 Feb. 2021.

"Currency of Ceald." *The Kingkiller Wiki*, https://kingkiller.fandom.com/wiki/Currency_of_Ceald#cite_note-:0-0. Accessed 27 Mar. 2020.

Dei, George J. Sefa. "Introduction: Mapping the Terrain—Towards a New Politics of Resistance." Dei and Kempf, pp. 1–23.

Dei, George J. Sefa, and Arlo Kempf, editors. *Anti-Colonialism and Education: The Politics of Resistance*, Sense Publishers, 2006.

Delpit, Lisa D. "The Silenced Dialogue: Power and Pedagogy in Educating Other People's Children." *Other People's Children: Cultural Conflict in the Classroom*. New Press, 1995, pp. 21–47.

de Vita, Novella Brooks. "Wiz Kids: An Exploration of Pedagogy in the World of *Harry Potter*, from Remus Lupin's Differentiated Reconstructionism to Dolores Umbridge's Discipline-Focused Essentialism." *Teaching and Learning on Screen: Mediated Pedagogies*, edited by Mark Readman, Palgrave Macmillan, 2016, pp. 63–82.

Dickinson, Renée. "Harry Potter Pedagogy: What We Learn About Teaching and Learning from J.K. Rowling." *The Clearing House*, vol. 79, no. 6, 2006, pp. 240–44. *JSTOR*, www.jstor.org/stable/30182136. Accessed 18 Sep. 2015.

Donaldson, Eileen. "Earning the Right to Wear Midnight." *The Gothic Fairy Tale in Young Adult Literature: Essays on Stories from Grimm to Gaiman*, edited by Joseph Abbruscato and Tanya Jones, McFarland, 2014, pp. 145–64.

———. "'See Me': How the Uncanny Double Supports Maturing Girlhood in Terry Pratchett's *Tiffany Aching* Series." *Mousaion: South African Journal of Information Studies*, vol. 35, no. 2, 2017, pp. 1–16. *Unisa Press Journals*, 10.25159/0027–2639/1359. Accessed 17 Feb. 2021.

Doughty, Terri. "Locating Harry Potter in the 'Boys Book' Market." *Whited Ivory*, pp. 243–57.

DuPlessis, Nicole M. "ecoLewis: Conservationism and Anticolonialism in *The Chronicles of Narnia*." *Wild Things: Children's Culture and Ecocriticsm*, edited by Sidney I. Dobrin and Kenneth B. Kidd, Wayne State UP, 2004, pp. 115–27.

Eccleshare, Julia. *A Guide to the Harry Potter Novels*. Continuum, 2002.

Bibliography

Echterling, Clare. "Postcolonial Ecocriticism, Classic Children's Literature, and the Imperial-Environmental Imagination in 'The Chronicles of Narnia.'" *The Journal of the Midwest Modern Language Association*, Vol. 49, No. 1, 2016, Pp. 93–117. *JSTOR*, Www.jstor.org/stable/44134678. Accessed 17 Jun. 2019.

Elster, Charles. "The Seeker of Secrets: Images of Learning, Knowing, and Schooling." Heilman *Harry*, pp. 203–20.

Esteban-Guitart, Moisès, and Luis C. Moll. "Funds of Identity: A New Concept Based on the Funds of Knowledge Approach." *Culture & Psychology*, vol. 20, no. 1, 2014, pp. 31–48. *Sage*, doi: 10.1177/1354067X13515934. Accessed 12 Feb. 2020.

Feinberg, Walter. *Understanding Education: Toward a Reconstruction of Educational Inquiry*. Cambridge UP, 1983.

Firestone, William A., et al. Preface. Firestone et al., pp. vii–xi.

Firestone, William A., et al., editors. *The Ambiguity of Teaching to the Test: Standards, Assessment, and Educational Reform*. L. Erlbaum Associates, 2004.

Firestone, William A., and Roberta Y. Schorr. Introduction. Firestone et al., pp. 1–17.

Fisher, Linda. "Pedagogy and the Curriculum 2000 Reforms at Post–16: The 'Learn It, Forget It' Culture?" *The Curriculum Journal*, vol. 18, no. 1, 2007, pp. 103–14. *Scholars Portal*, doi: 10.1080/09585170701292257. Accessed 17 Oct. 2019.

Forsberg, Jennifer H. "'A Jack-of-All-Trades': Jack Kerouac's Fashionable Practice of Working-Class Drag." *The Journal of Popular Culture*, vol. 50, no. 6, 2017, pp. 1213–229. *Scholars Portal*, doi:10.1111/jpcu.12618. Accessed 22 Sep. 2020.

Foster, Gwendolyn Audrey. *Class-Passing: Social Mobility in Film and Popular Culture*. Southern Illinois UP, 2005.

———. *Performing Whiteness: Postmodern Re/Constructions in the Cinema*. SUNY P, 2003.

Froese-Germain, Bernie. "Educational Accountability: ... as If Education Mattered." Moll, pp. 276–93.

Fusellas Busquets, Isaac. *Análisis De La Traducción De La Novela "The Name of the Wind."* 2015. Universitat Autònoma de Barcelona, Bachelor thesis. *dipòsit Digital De Documents De La UAB*, https://ddd.uab.cat/record/146991. Accessed 26 Jul. 2020.

Galbraith, Mary. "Hear My Cry: A Manifesto for an Emancipatory Childhood Studies Approach to Children's Literature." *The Lion and the Unicorn*, vol. 25, no. 2, 2001, pp. 187–205. *Project Muse*, doi: 10.1353/uni.2001.0019. Accessed 28 May 2018.

Galway, Elizabeth A. "Reminders of Rugby in the Halls of Hogwarts: The Insidious Influence of the School Story Genre on the Works of J.K. Rowling." *Children's Literature Association Quarterly*, vol. 37, no. 1, 2012, pp. 66–85. *Project Muse*, doi:10.1353/chq.2012.0011.

Giebert, Stefanie. "Boxes Within Boxes and a Useless Map: Spatial (and Temporal) Phenomena in the *Kingkiller Chronicle*." *Weltenwürfe Des Fantastischen: Erzählen—Schreiben—Spielen*, special issue of *Komparatistik Online*, 2013, pp. 106–14. *Komparatistik Online*, https://www.komparatistik-online.de/index.php/komparatistik_online/article/view/103. Accessed 26 Jul. 2020.

Giroux, Henry, and Anthony Penna. "Social Education in the Classroom: The Dynamics of the Hidden Curriculum." Giroux and Purpel, pp. 100–21.

Giroux, Henry, and David Purpel, editors. *The Hidden Curriculum and Moral Education: Deception or Discovery?* McCutchan, 1983.

Granfield, Robert. "Making It by Faking It: Working-Class Students in an Elite Academic Environment." *Journal of Contemporary Ethnography*, vol. 20,

Bibliography

no. 3, 1991, pp. 331–51. *Scholars Portal*, doi:10.1177/089124191020003005. Accessed 12 Feb. 2020.

Grenfell, Michael. "Being Critical: The Practical Logic of Bourdieu's Metanoia." *Critical Studies in Education*, vol. 51, no. 1, 2010, pp. 85–99. *Scholars Portal*, doi:10.1080/17508480903450240. Accessed 12 Feb. 2021.

Grossman, Lev. "A Brief Guide to the Hidden Allusions in *The Magicians*." *Tor.com*, 11 Aug. 2011, https://www.tor.com/2011/08/11/a-brief-guide-to-the-hidden-allusions-in-the-magicians/. Accessed 8 Feb. 2021.

———. "Exclusive: Time Magazine's Lev Grossman on His New Book, *The Magicians*." By Caroline Stanley, *Flavorwire*, 17 Aug. 2009, http://flavorwire.com/34037/exclusive-time-magazines-lev-grossman-on-his-new-book-the-magicians. Accessed 4 July 2019.

———. "Homage Vs. Rip-off: An Interview with Lev Grossman and a Guide to Literary Allusions in *The Magician King*." By Cassandra Neace, *The Millions*, 10 Aug. 2011, https://themillions.com/2011/08/homage-vs-rip-off-an-interview-with-lev-grossman-and-a-guide-to-literary-allusions-in-the-magician-king.html. Accessed 4 July 2019.

———. "Lev Grossman on 'The Magician's Land': 'It Felt Like a World Ending.'" By Jacob Shamsian, *Entertainment Weekly*, 5 Aug. 2014, https://ew.com/article/2014/08/05/lev-grossman-on-the-magicians-land-it-felt-like-a-world-ending/. Accessed 4 July 2019.

———. "*The Magicians*' Lev Grossman on Seeing His Remix of Narnia and Harry Potter Get Remixed." By Constance Grady, *Vox*, 18 Jan. 2018, https://www.vox.com/culture/2018/1/18/16883082/magicians-lev-grossman-syfy-narnia-harry-potter-remix. Accessed 4 July 2019.

———. Response to question from Will Whiskey. *GoodReads*, https://www.goodreads.com/questions/127247-it-s-obvious-fillory-is-heavily-influenced. Accessed 8 Feb. 2021.

Gruner, Elisabeth Rose. "Teach the Children: Education and Knowledge in Recent Children's Fantasy." *Children's Literature*, vol. 37, 2009, pp. 216–35. *Project Muse*, doi:10.1353/chl.0.0815. Accessed 24 Oct. 2015.

———. "Wrestling with Religion: Pullman, Pratchett, and the Uses of Story." *Children's Literature Association Quarterly*, vol. 36, no. 3, 2011, pp. 276–95. *Project Muse*, doi:10.1353/chl.0.0815. Accessed 17 Feb. 2021.

Gubar, Marah. "The Hermeneutics of Recuperation: What a Kinship-Model Approach to Children's Agency Could Do for Children's Literature and Childhood Studies." *Jeunesse: Young People. Texts, Cultures*, vol. 8, no. 1, 2016, pp. 291–310. *Project MUSE*, doi: 10.1353/jeu.2016.0015. Accessed 3 July 2018.

Gutiérrez, Kris D., and Barbara Rogoff. "Cultural Ways of Learning: Individual Traits or Repertoires of Practice." *Educational Researcher*, vol. 32, no. 5, 2003, pp. 19–25. *Scholars Portal*, doi:10.3102/0013189X032005019. Accessed 12 Feb. 2020.

Gutiérrez, Peter. "School as the Real Star: Harry Potter and the Half-Blood Millennials." *Screen Education*, vol. 55, 2009, pp. 26–31. *EBShepherd'sOhost*, search.ebscohost.com/login.aspx?direct=true&db=cms&AN=44328131&site=ehost-live&scope=site. Accessed 20 Jan. 2016.

Haberkorn, Gideon. "Debugging the Mind: The Rhetoric of Humor and the Poetics of Fantasy." Alton and Spruiell, pp. 160–88.

Haberkorn, Gideon, and Verena Reinhardt. "Magic, Adolescence, and Education on Terry Pratchett's Discworld." *Supernatural Youth: The Rise of the Teen Hero in Literature and Popular Culture*, edited by Jes Battis, Lexington Books, 2011, pp. 41–60.

Hand, Elizabeth. "The Uses of Disenchantment." Review of *Cheek by Jowl:*

Bibliography

Essays, by Ursula K. Le Guin, *The Magician's Book: A Skeptic's Adventures in Narnia,* by Laura Miller, and *The Magicians,* by Lev Grossman. *Fantasy & Science Fiction,* vol. 117, no. 1–2, 2009, pp. 40–9. *Gale Academic Onefile,* link.gale.com/apps/doc/A207540294/AONE?u=ocul_mcmaster&sid=AONE&xid=510733c9. Accessed 25 May 2016.

Heilman, Elizabeth E., editor. *Critical Perspectives on Harry Potter.* 2nd ed. Routledge, 2009.

——, editor. *Harry Potter's World: Multidisciplinary Critical Perspectives.* Routledge, 2003.

Helfenbein, Robert J., and Sydney K. Brown. "Conjuring Curriculum, Conjuring Control: A Reading of Resistance in *Harry Potter and the Order of the Phoenix.*" *Curriculum Inquiry,* vol. 38, no. 4, 2008, pp. 499–513. *Wiley Online Library,* doi: 10.1111/j.1467-873X.2008.00431.x. Accessed 20 Jan. 2016.

Himes, Amanda E. "Lev Grossman's *The Magicians*: Narnia Under Fire?" *Intégrité: A Faith and Learning Journal,* vol. 14, no. 1, 2015, pp. 59–65. *Missouri Baptist University,* https://www.mobap.edu/wp-content/uploads/2013/01/Integrite-Spring2015.pdf. Accessed 17 March 2016.

Himes, J.B. "Questioning God(s) of Other Worlds in Lev Grossman's *The Magicians.*" *Intégrité: A Faith and Learning Journal,* vol. 14, no. 1, 2015, pp. 59–65. *Missouri Baptist University,* https://www.mobap.edu/wp-content/uploads/2013/01/Integrite-Spring2015.pdf. Accessed 17 March 2016.

Hitchcock, Peter. "Slumming." *Passing: Identity and Interpretation in Sexuality, Race, and Religion,* edited by Maria Carla Sanchez and Linda Schlossberg, New York UP, 2001, pp. 160–86.

Hodkinson, Phil, and Heather Hodkinson. "The Significance of Individuals' Dispositions in Workplace Learning: A Case Study of Two Teachers." *Journal of Education and Work,* vol. 17, no. 2, 2004, pp. 167–82. *Taylor & Francis Online,* doi: 10.1080/136390 80410001677383. Accessed 5 Mar. 2021.

Hopkins, Lisa. "Harry Potter and the Acquisition of Knowledge." Anatol, pp. 25–34.

Hume, Kathryn. *Fantasy and Mimesis: Responses to Reality in Western Literature.* Methuen, 1984.

Hunt, Peter. "Children's Literature and Childhood." *An Introduction to Childhood Studies,* 2nd ed, edited by Mary Jane Kehily, Open UP, 2009, pp. 50–69.

——. *An Introduction to Children's Literature.* Oxford UP; 1994.

——. "Terry Pratchett." *Alternative Worlds in Fantasy Fiction,* edited by Hunt and Millicent Lenz, Bloomsbury, 2005, pp. 86–121.

Hunt, Peter, and Karen Sands. "The View from the Center: British Empire and Post-Empire Children's Literature." *Voices of the Other: Children's Literature and the Postcolonial Context,* edited by Roderick McGillis, Garland Publishing, 2000, pp. 39–53.

Jackson, Rosemary. *Fantasy: The Literature of Subversion.* Methuen, 1981.

Kassem, Derek, Lisa Murphy, and Elizabeth Taylor. "Creating Childhood." Kassem, Murphy, and Taylor, pp. 1–2.

——, editors. *Key Issues in Childhood and Youth Studies.* Routledge, 2010.

Kemmis, Stephen, and Christine Edwards-Groves. "The Politics of Education: Reproduction and Transformation." *Understanding Education: History, Politics and Practice,* Springer, 2018, pp. 65–114.

Kempf, Arlo. "Anti-Colonial Historiography: Interrogating Colonial Education." Dei and Kempf, pp. 129–58.

Kincaid, Paul. "Review Essay: Starting the Conversation." Review of *Rhetorics of Fantasy,* by Farah Mendlesohn. *Journal of the Fantastic in the Arts,* vol. 20, no. 2, 2009, pp. 262–69. *JSTOR,* www.jstor.org/stable/24352250. Accessed 17 Jun. 2019.

Bibliography

Kirkpatrick, Robert. Introduction. *The Encyclopedia of Boys' School Stories*, edited by Kirkpatrick, Ashgate, 2000, pp. 1–11.

Kittredge, Katherine. "The Girl-Hero for the New Millennia: Alice's Great-Great-Granddaughters in Post-Gender Fantasy Worlds." *The Wiley Blackwell Companion to Contemporary British and Irish Literature, Volume II*, 1st ed., edited by Richard Bradford, John Wiley & Sons, 2021, pp. 671–81.

Kiyama, Judy Marquez, and Cecilia Rios-Aguilar, editors. *Funds of Knowledge in Higher Education: Honouring Students' Cultural Experiences and Resources as Strengths*, Routledge, 2018.

Kiyama, Judy Marquez et al., "Funds of Knowledge as a Culturally Responsive Pedagogy in Higher Education." Kiyama and Rios-Aguilar, pp. 175–88.

Kochhar-Lindgren, Gray. "Tell It Slant: Of Gods, Philosophy and Politics in Terry Pratchett's Discworld." Alton and Spruiell, pp. 81–91.

Kohn, Alfie. *The Case Against Standardized Testing: Raising the Scores, Ruining the Schools*. Heinemann, 2000.

Koshy, Reeba Sara. "Magic Is Might: Understanding the Nature of Magic in Literature." *Literary Herald*, vol. 2, no. 4, 2017, pp. 479–86. *TLHjournal.com*, http://tlhjournal.com/uploads/products/58.reeba-sara-koshy-article.pdf. Accessed 16 Feb. 2021.

Kramer, Kelly. "A Common Language of Desire: *The Magicians*, Narnia, and Contemporary Fantasy." *Mythlore*, vol. 35, no. 2, 2017, pp. 153–69. *Mythlore*, https://dc.swosu.edu/mythlore/vol35/iss2/10/. Accessed 15 Jan. 2019.

Kucich, John. "Cross-Class Performativity and Organic Order in Dickens and Gaskell." *Victorian Studies*, vol. 55, no. 3, 2012, pp. 471–99. *JSTOR*, www.jstor.org/stable/10.2979/victorianstudies.55.3.471. Accessed 22 Sep. 2020.

Lacoss, Jann. "Of Magicals and Muggles: Reversals and Revulsions at Hogwarts." Whited *Ivory*, pp. 67–88.

Langton, Marcia, et al. Introduction. *Honour Among Nations? Treaties and Agreements with Indigenous People*, edited by Langton, Tehan, Palmer, and Kathryn Shain, Melbourne UP, 2004, pp. 1–26.

Lave, Jean, and Etienne Wenger. "Legitimate Peripheral Participation in Communities of Practice." *Supporting Lifelong Learning, Volume I*, edited by Roger Harrison, Fiona Reeve, Ann Hanson, and Julie Clarke, Routledge Falmer, 2002, pp. 111–26.

Lavoie, Chantel. "Safe as Houses: Sorting and School Houses at Hogwarts." Anatol, pp. 35–49.

Lehmann, Wolfgang. "Habitus Transformation and Hidden Injuries: Successful Working-class University Students." *Sociology of Education*, vol. 87, no. 1, 2014, pp. 1–15. *JSTOR*, www.jstor.org/stable/43186795. Accessed 12 Feb. 2020.

———. "In a Class of Their Own: How Working-Class Students Experience University." *Contemporary Debates in the Sociology of Education*, edited by Rachel Brooks et al., Palgrave Macmillan, 2013, pp. 93–111.

———. "Working-class Students, Habitus, and the Development of Student Roles: A Canadian Case Study." *British Journal of Sociology of Education*, vol. 33, no. 4, 2012, pp. 527–46. *Taylor & Francis*, doi: 10.1080/01425692.2012.668834. Accessed 12 Feb. 2020.

Lenzer, Gertrude. "Children's Studies: Beginnings and Purposes." *The Lion and the Unicorn*, vol. 25, no. 2, 2001, pp. 181–86. *Project Muse*, doi: 10.1353/uni.2001.0022. Accessed 28 May 2018.

Lynch, Kathleen. *The Hidden Curriculum: Reproduction in Education, a Reappraisal*. Falmer, 1989.

MacCann, Donnarae. "The Sturdy Fabric of Cultural Imperialism: Tracing Its Patterns in Contemporary Children's Novels." *Children's Literature*, vol. 33, 2005, pp. 185–208. *Project Muse*, doi.org/10.1353/chl.2005.0018. Accessed 17 Jun. 2019.

Bibliography

Maier, Sarah E. "Educating Harry Potter: A Muggle's Perspective on Magic and Knowledge in the Wizard World of J.K. Rowling." *Scholarly Studies in Harry Potter: Applying Academic Methods to a Popular Text,* edited by Cynthia Whitney Hallet, Edwin Mellen, 2005, pp. 7–28.

Manners Smith, Karen. "Harry Potter's Schooldays: J.K. Rowling and the British Boarding School Novel." Anatol, pp. 69–87.

Martin, Jane. "What Should We Do with a Hidden Curriculum When We Find One?" Giroux and Purpel, pp. 122–40.

Martins, Ana Rita. "Magic and Witchcraft in Terry Pratchett's Discworld's the Witches Novels." *Revista Abusões,* vol. 1, no. 1, 2016, pp. 99–126. *UERJ Electronic Publications Portal,* http://dx.doi.org/10.12957/abusoes.2016.25722. Accessed 17 Feb. 2021.

McDaniel, Kathryn N. "Harry Potter and the Ghost Teacher: Resurrecting the Lost Art of Lecturing." *The History Teacher,* vol. 43, no. 2, 2010, pp. 289–95. *JSTOR,* www.jstor.org/stable/40543295. Accessed 18 Sep. 2015.

McGillis, Roderick. "The Wee Free Men: Politics and the Art of Noise." Alton and Spruiell, pp. 15–25.

McGovern, Margot. *Divine Madness: Identifying, Analysing and Developing the Campus Clique Crime Novel.* 2013. Flinders University, PhD dissertation. *Flinders University Theses,* https://theses.flinders.edu.au/view/3351caeb-6e78-4b6d-a80d-48426eabd86f/1. Accessed 17 March 2016.

Meaghan, Diane E., and François R. Casas. "Bias in Standardized Testing and the Misuse of Test Scores: Exposing the Achilles Heel of Educational Reform." Moll, pp. 35–50.

Mendlesohn, Farah. "Crowning the King: Harry Potter and the Construction of Authority." Whited *Ivory,* pp. 159–81.

———. *Rhetorics of Fantasy,* Wesleyan UP, 2008.

———. "Thematic Criticism." *The Cambridge Companion to Fantasy Literature,* edited by Edward James and Mendlesohn, Cambridge UP, 2012, pp. 125–33.

Mickenberg, Julia L., and Lynna Vallone, editors. *The Oxford Handbook of Children's Literature,* Oxford UP, 2011.

Milton, Andrew K. *The Normal Accident Theory of Education: Why Reform and Regulation Won't Make Schools Better.* Rowman and Littlefield, 2014.

Moll, Luis C., et al. "Funds of Knowledge for Teaching: Using a Qualitative Approach to Connect Homes and Classrooms." *Theory Into Practice,* vol. 31, no. 2, 1992, pp. 132–41. *JSTOR,* www.jstor.org/stable/1476399. Accessed 11 Feb. 2021.

Moll, Marita. "Large Scale Educational Assessment: The New Face of Testing." Moll, pp. 11–6.

Moll, Marita, editor. *Passing the Test: The False Promise of Standardized Testing.* Canadian Centre for Policy Alternatives, 2004.

Monfils, Lora F., et al. "Teaching to the Test." Firestone et al., pp. 37–61.

Moodie, Gavin. "Identifying Vocational Education and Training." *Journal of Vocational Education and Training,* vol. 54, no. 2, 2002, pp. 249–66. *Taylor & Francis Online,* doi: 10.1080/13636820200200197. Accessed 5 Mar. 2021.

Moran, Mary Jeannette. "'Balance Is the Trick': Feminist Relationality in *The Amazing Maurice* and the Tiffany Aching Series." *The Lion and the Unicorn,* vol. 42, no. 3, 2018, pp. 259–80. *Project MUSE,* https://doi.org/10.1353/uni.2018.0027. Accessed 17 Feb. 2021.

Nagy, Philip. "The Three Roles of Assessment: Gatekeeping, Accountability, and Instructional Diagnosis." *Canadian Journal of Education,* vol. 25, no. 4, 2000, pp. 262–79. *JSTOR,* www.jstor.org/stable/1585850. Accessed 19 Oct. 2019.

Natov, Roni. "Harry Potter and the Extraordinariness of the Ordinary." Whited *Ivory,* pp. 125–39.

Nester, Robbi. "Do You Believe in Magic?

Bibliography

the Novels of Lev Grossman." *Hollins Critic*, vol. 49, no. 1, 2012, n.p. *Gale Academic OneFile*, link.gale.com/apps/doc/A282823387/AONE?u=ocul_mcmaster&sid=AONE&xid=7bf8b048. Accessed 25 May 2016.

Nguyen, Thai-Huy, and Bach Mai Dolly Nguyen. "Is the 'First-Generation Student' Term Useful for Understanding Inequality? The Role of Intersectionality in Illuminating the Implications of an Accepted—Yet Challenged—Term." *Review of Research in Education*, vol. 42, 2018, pp. 146–76. *AERA*, doi: 10.3102/0091732X18759280. Accessed 12 Feb. 2020.

Nikolajeva, Maria. "Harry Potter and the Secrets of Children's Literature." Heilman *Critical*, pp. 225–41.

———. *Power, Voice and Subjectivity in Literature for Young Readers*. Routledge, 2009.

Nodelman, Perry. *The Hidden Adult: Defining Children's Literature*. JHU Press, 2008.

———. "The Other: Orientalism, Colonialism, and Children's Literature." *Children's Literature Association Quarterly*, vol. 17, no. 1, 1992, pp. 29–35. *Project Muse*, doi.org/10.1353/chq.0.1006. Accessed 19 Jun. 2019.

Noone, Kristin, and Emily Lavin Leverett, editors. *Terry Pratchett's Ethical Worlds: Essays on Identity and Narrative in Discworld and Beyond*. McFarland, 2020.

Northedge, Andy. "Organizing Excursions Into Specialist Discourse Communities: A Sociocultural Account of University Teaching." *Learning for Life in the 21st Century: Sociocultural Perspectives on the Future of Education*, edited by Gordon Wells and Guy Claxton, Blackwell, 2002, pp. 252–64.

Nuttall, Alice. "Be a Witch, Be a Woman: Gendered Characterisation of Terry Pratchett's Witches." *Terry Pratchett's Narrative Worlds: From Giant Turtles to Small Gods*, edited by Marion Rana, Palgrave Macmillan, 2018, pp. 23–36.

O'Keefe, Deborah. *Readers in Wonderland: The Liberating Worlds of Fantasy Fiction*. A&C Black, 2004.

Ostrove, Joan M., and Susan M. Long. "Social Class and Belonging: Implications for College Adjustment." *The Review of Higher Education*, vol. 30, no. 4, 2007, pp. 363–89. *Project Muse*, doi: 10.1353/rhe.2007.0028. Accessed 12 Feb. 2020.

Ostry, Elaine. "Accepting Mudbloods: The Ambivalent Social Vision of J.K. Rowling's Fairy Tales." Anatol, pp. 89–101.

Pandey, Siddharth. "Emplacing Tasks of Magic: Hand, Land, and the Generation of Fantasy Taskscape in Terry Pratchett's *Tiffany Aching* Series." *GeoHumanities*, vol. 6, no. 1, 2020, pp. 39–50. *Taylor & Francis Online*, doi: 10.1080/2373566X.2020.1735474. Accessed 17 Feb. 2021.

Park, Julia. "Class and Socioeconomic Identity in Harry Potter's England." Anatol, pp. 179–90.

Pascarella, Ernest T., et al. "First-generation College Students: Additional Evidence on College Experiences and Outcomes." *The Journal of Higher Education*, vol. 75, no. 3, 2004, pp. 249–84. *Scholars Portal*, doi: 10.1080/0022 1546.2004.11772256. Accessed 11 Feb. 2021.

Pesold, Ulrike. *The Other in the School Stories: A Phenomenon in British Children's Literature*. Brill, 2017.

Pinsent, Pat. "The Education of a Wizard: Harry Potter and His Predecessors." Whited *Ivory*, pp. 27–50.

———. "Theories of Genre and Gender: Change and Continuity in the School Story." *Modern Children's Literature: An Introduction*, edited by Catherine Butler and Kimberley Reynolds, Reynolds Macmillan, 2014, pp. 105–20.

Popham, W. James. "Teaching to the Test?" *Educational Leadership*, vol. 58, no. 6, 2001, pp. 16–20. *A Shepherd's D*, http://www.ascd.org/publications/educational-leadership/mar01/vol58/num06/Teaching-to-the-Test%C2%A2.aspx. Accessed 27 Sep. 2019.

Bibliography

Porenius, Linnea. *Sökandet Efter Mening I En Postmodern Värld: Om Questmotivet I Lev Grossmans Fantasybok the Magicians*, 2020. Lund University, student paper. *LUP Student Papers*, https://lup.lub.lu.se/luur/download?func=downloadFile&recordOId=9006110&fileOId=9006111. Accessed 16 Feb. 2021.

Pratt, Mary Louise. *Imperial Eyes*, 2nd ed., Routledge, 2008.

Pring, Richard, et al. *Education for All: The Future of Education and Training for 14–19 Year-Olds*. Routledge, 2009.

Prout, Alan. Introduction. *The Future of Childhood: Towards the Interdisciplinary Study of Children*. Routledge Falmer, 2005, pp. 1–5.

Pugh, Tison, and David L. Wallace. "Heteronormative Heroism and Queering the School Story in J.K. Rowling's Harry Potter Series." *Children's Literature Association Quarterly*, vol. 31, no. 3, 2006, pp. 260–81. *Project Muse*, doi: 10.1353/chq.2006.0053. Accessed 4 Oct. 2017.

Rana, Marion. "'The Less You Lot Have Ter Do with These Foreigners, the Happier Yeh'll Be': Cultural and National Otherness in J.K. Rowling's *Harry Potter* Series." *International Research in Children's Literature*, vol. 4, no. 1, 2011, pp. 45–58. *EUP Journals*, doi: 10.3366/ircl.2011.0006. Accessed 8 Sep. 2020.

Reams, Jack. *Characterization in Fiction*. 2015. Texas State University, Honors thesis. *Digital Library Texas State*, https://digital.library.txstate.edu/handle/10877/5627. Accessed 26 Jul. 2020.

Reed, John R. *Old School Ties: The Public Schools of British Literature*. Syracuse UP, 1964.

Reimer, Mavis. "Traditions of the School Story." *The Cambridge Companion to Children's Literature*, edited by M.O. Grenby and Andrea Immel, Cambridge UP, 2009, pp. 209–25.

Richards, Jeffrey. "The School Story." *Stories and Society: Children's Literature in Its Social Context*, edited by Dennis Butts, Springer, 1992, pp. 1–21.

Rios-Aguilar, Cecilia, and Judy Marquez Kiyama. "A Complementary Framework: Funds of Knowledge and the Forms of Capital." Kiyama and Rios-Aguilar, pp. 7–24.

Rios-Aguilar, Cecilia, et al. "Funds of Knowledge for the Poor and Forms of Capital for the Rich? A Capital Approach to Examining Funds of Knowledge." *Theory and Research in Education*, vol. 9, no. 2, 2011, pp. 163–84. *Sage*, doi: 10.1177/1477878511409776. Accessed 12 Feb. 2020.

Rose, Jacqueline. Introduction. *The Case of Peter Pan*, by Rose, U Pennsylvania P, 1993, pp. 1–11.

Rosen, Sonia M. "Harry Potter as Modern Day Youth Activist: What Americans Can Learn from One Young Brit." *Proceedings of Accio 2008: A Harry Potter Conference*, edited by Phyllis Morris and Diana Patterson, Accio UK, 2008, pp. 200–08.

Rowlands, Julie, and Trevor Gale. "Shaping and Being Shaped: Extending the Relationship Between Habitus and Practice." *Practice Theory and Education: Diffractive Readings in Professional Practice*, edited by J. Lynch et al., Routledge, 2016, pp. 91–107.

Rowling, J.K. Interview with PotterCast, Part 1. *The Leaky Cauldron.org*, 23 Dec. 2007, http://www.the-leaky-cauldron.org/2007/12/23/transcript-of-part-1-of-pottercast-s-jk-rowling-interview/. Accessed 8 Feb. 2021.

Sandner, David. "Theorizing the Fantastic: Editing Fantastic Literature: A Critical Reader and the Six Stages of Fantasy Criticism." *Journal of the Fantastic in the Arts*, vol. 16, no. 4, 2006, pp. 277–301. *JSTOR*, https://www.jstor.org/stable/43310263.

Santaulària i Capdevila, M. Isabel. "Age and Rage in Terry Pratchett's 'witches' Novels." *European Journal of English Studies*, vol. 22, no. 1, 2018, pp. 59–75. *Taylor & Francis Online*, doi: 10.1080/

Bibliography

13825577.2018.1427201. Accessed 17 Feb. 2021.

Sattaur, Jennifer. "Harry Potter: A World of Fear." *The Journal of Children's Literature Studies*, vol. 3, no. 1, 2006, pp. 1–14. *EBShepherd'sOhost*. Accessed 27 May 2008.

Sawyer, Andy. "Narrativium and Lies-to-Children: 'Palatable Instruction' in 'The Science of Discworld.'" *Journal of the Fantastic in the Arts*, Vol. 13, No. 1, 2002, Pp. 62–81. *JSTOR*, Https://www.jstor.org/stable/43308563. Accessed 22 Apr. 2021.

Sayer, Karen. "The Witches." *Terry Pratchett: Guilty of Literature*, edited by Andrew M. Butler, Edward James, and Farah Mendlesohn, Old Earth Books, 2004, pp. 131–52.

Schaap, Harmen, Liesbeth Baartman, and Elly de Bruijn. "Students' Learning Processes During School-Based Learning and Workplace Learning in Vocational Education: A Review." *Vocations and Learning*, vol. 5, 2012, pp. 99–117. *Springer*, doi: 10.1007/s12186-011-9069-2. Accessed 5 Mar. 2021.

Schmitz, Patrick. "'True Music in the Words': A Comparative Analysis of the Function of Music in Tolkien's *The Lord of the Rings* and Rothfuss' *Kingkiller Chronicle*." *Music in Tolkien's Work and Beyond*, edited by Julian Eilmann and Friedhelm Schneidewind, Walking Tree Publishers, 2019.

Schorr, Roberta Y., and William A. Firestone. "Conclusion." Firestone et al., pp. 159–68.

Schroer, Sarah. *Bringing the Magic Back to Structuralist Approaches in Fantasy Literature*. 2020. Dalarna University, MA thesis. *DiVa Portal*, http://www.diva-portal.org/smash/record.jsf?pid=diva2%3A1451061&dswid=7960. Accessed 26 Jul. 2020.

Sims, Sue. Introduction. *The Encyclopedia of Girls' School Stories*, edited by Sims and Hilary Clare, Ashgate, 2000, pp. 1–18.

Sinclair, Lian. "Magical Genders: The Gender(s) of Witches in the Historical Imagination of Terry Pratchett's Discworld." *Mythlore*, vol. 33, no. 2, 2015, pp. 5–18. *SWOSU Digital Commons*, https://dc.swosu.edu/mythlore/vol33/iss2/4. Accessed 17 Feb. 2021.

Skeggs, Beverley. "Gender Reproduction and Further Education: Domestic Apprenticeships." *British Journal of Sociology of Education*, vol. 9, no. 2, 1988, pp. 131–49. *JSTOR*, https://www.jstor.org/stable/1393030. Accessed 5 Mar. 2021.

Skulnick, Rebecca, and Jesse Goodman. "The Civic Leadership of *Harry Potter*: Agency, Ritual, and Schooling." Heilman *Harry*, pp. 261–77.

Smith, William C. "An Introduction to the Global Testing Culture." Smith, pp. 7–23.

Smith, William C., editor. *The Global Testing Culture: Shaping Education Policy, Perceptions, and Practice*, edited by Smith, Symposium Books, 2016.

Steege, David K. "Harry Potter, Tom Brown, and the British School Story: Lost in Transit?" Whited *Ivory*, pp. 140–56.

Steinbrück, Maxi. "(Non-)Formal Education in Terry Pratchett's Discworld Novels: Mort's Apprenticeship, Tiffany's Coming of Age, Susan's Learning Path and the Unseen University." *Terry Pratchett's Narrative Worlds: From Giant Turtles to Small Gods*, edited by Marion Rana, Palgrave Macmillan, 2018, pp. 93–114.

Stetsenko, Anna, and Igor M. Arievitch. "Vygotskian Collaborative Project of Social Transformation: History, Politics, and Practice in Knowledge Construction." *Collaborative Projects: An Interdisciplinary Study*, edited by Andy Blunden, Brill, 2014, pp. 217–38.

Stuber, Jenny M. *Inside the College Gates: How Class and Culture Matter in Higher Education*. Lexington Books, 2011.

Stypczynski, Brent. "Wolf in Professor's Clothing: J.K. Rowling's Werewolf as Educator." *Journal of the Fantastic in the Arts*, vol. 20, no. 1, 2009, pp. 57–69.

Bibliography

JSTOR, www.jstor.org/stable/4352314. Accessed 18 Sep. 2015.

Subramanian, Aishwarya. "'The Whole Country Below Them': Gazing Imperially on Narnia from Above." *Space and Culture*, vol. 23, no. 4, 2020, pp. 370–81. *Sage*, doi.org/10.1177/1206331219845306. Accessed 8 Feb. 2021.

Sunderland, Jane. *Language, Gender and Children's Literature*. Continuum, 2011.

Suttie, Megan. *The Magicians and North American Education*. 2016. McMaster University, MA thesis. *MacSphere*, http://hdl.handle.net/11375/20523.

Swinfen, Ann. *In Defence of Fantasy: A Study of the Genre in English and American Literature Since 1945*. Routledge & Kegan Paul, 1984.

Taylor, Alison, et al. "Service-Learning and First-Generation Students: A Conceptual Exploration of the Literature." *Journal of Experiential Education*, vol. 42, no. 4, 2019, pp. 349–63. *Sage*, doi: 10.1177/1053825919863452. Accessed 30 Jan. 2020.

Thésée, Gina. "A Tool of Massive Erosion: Scientific Knowledge in the Neo-Colonial Enterprise." Dei and Kempf, pp. 24–42.

Thomas, R. Murray. "Education in the South Pacific: The Context for Development." *Comparative Education*, vol. 29, no. 3, 1993, pp. 233–48. *JSTOR*, www.jstor.org/stable/3099326. Accessed 2 Jul. 2019.

Tiffin, Chris, and Alan Lawson, editors. *De-Scribing Empire: Post-Colonialism and Textuality*, Routledge, 1994.

———. "Introduction: The Textuality of Empire." Tiffin and Lawson, pp. 1–11.

Tikkanen, Tapio. *Hero, Shadow and Trickster; Three Archetypes in the Kingkiller Chronicle*. 2018. University of Oulu, MA thesis. *Jultika*, http://jultika.oulu.fi/Record/nbnfioulu-201811153046. Accessed 26 Jul. 2020.

Tomková, Juliana. *Implications of Names in the Name of the Wind by Patrick Rothfuss*. 2016. Masarykova Univerzita, MA thesis. *MUNI*, https://is.muni.cz/th/hr22v/?lang=en. Accessed 26 Jul. 2020.

Traub, Ross. Introduction. *Standardized Testing in Canada: A Survey of Standardized Achievement Testing by Ministries of Education and School Boards*. Canadian Education Association, 1994, pp. 5–8.

Tribunella, Eric L. "*Tom Brown* and the Schoolboy Crush: Boyhood Desire, Hero Worship, and the Boys' School Story." Mickenberg and Vallone, pp. 455–73.

Trites, Roberta Seelinger. *Disturbing the Universe: Power and Repression in Adolescent Literature*. U Iowa P, 2000.

Tykhomyrova, Olena. "The Witch and the Memory in Terry Pratchett's Tiffany Aching Series." *History, Memory and Nostalgia in Literature and Culture*, edited by Regina Rudaitytė, Cambridge Scholars, 2018, pp. 256–63.

Vallance, Elizabeth. "Hiding the Hidden Curriculum: An Interpretation of the Language of Justification in Nineteenth-Century Educational Reform." Giroux and Purpel, pp. 9–27.

Varholy, Cristine M. "'Rich Like a Lady': Cross-Class Dressing in the Brothels and Theatres of Early Modern London." *Journal for Early Modern Cultural Studies*, vol. 8, no. 1, 2008, pp. 4–34. *JSTOR*, www.jstor.org/stable/40339588. Accessed 22 Sep. 2020.

Vinci, Tony M. "Mourning the Human: Working Through Trauma and the Posthuman Body in Lev Grossman's the Magicians Trilogy." *Journal of the Fantastic in the Arts*, vol. 28, no. 3, 2017, pp. 368–87. *JSTOR*, www.jstor.org/stable/26508549. Accessed 15 Jan. 2019.

———. "Posthumanist Magic: Beyond the Boundaries of Humanist Ethics in Lev Grossman's *The Magicians*." *Posthumanism in Young Adult Fiction: Finding Humanity in a Posthuman World*, edited by Anita Tarr and Donna R. White, UP of Mississippi, 2018, pp. 227–46.

Volante, Louis. "Teaching to the Test:

Bibliography

"What Every Educator and Policymaker Should Know." *Canadian Journal of Educational Administration and Policy*, vol. 35, 2004, n.p. *University of Calgary Journal Housing*, http://136.159.200.199/index.php/cjeap/article/view/42715. Accessed 27 Sep. 2019.

Waetjen, Jarrod, and Timothy A. Gibson. "Harry Potter and the Commodity Fetish: Activating Corporate Readings in the Journey from Text to Commercial Intertext." *Communication and Critical/Cultural Studies*, vol. 4, no. 1, 2007, pp. 3–26. *Scholars Portal*, doi: 10.1080/14791420601151289. Accessed 27 Aug. 2020.

Wallace, Jo-Ann. "De-Scribing *The Water Babies*: 'The Child' in Post-Colonial Theory." Tiffin and Lawson, pp. 171–84.

Walpole, MaryBeth. "Socioeconomic Status and College: How SES Affects College Experiences and Outcomes." *The Review of Higher Education*, vol. 27, no. 1, 2003, pp. 45–73. *Project Muse*, doi: 10.1353/rhe.2003.0044. Accessed 12 Feb. 2020.

Watral, Breeanna. *More Than the Parts That Form Them: Medievalism and Comfortable Alienation in J.R.R. Tolkien's the Hobbit and Patrick Rothfuss' Kingkiller Chronicle*. 2015. Dominican University, Honors thesis. *Constellation*, http://hdl.handle.net/10969/939. Accessed 26 Jul. 2020.

Webb, Caroline. *Fantasy and the Real World in British Children's Literature: The Power of Story*. Routledge, 2014.

Westman, Karin E. "Blending Genres and Crossing Audiences: *Harry Potter* and the Future of Literary Fiction." Mickenberg and Vallone, pp. 93–112.

Whited, Lana A. "McGonagall's Prophecy Fulfilled: The Harry Potter Critical Library." *The Lion and the Unicorn*, vol. 27, no. 3, 2003, pp. 416–25. *Project Muse*, doi: 10.1353/uni.2003.0045. Accessed 8 Jul. 2016.

Whited, Lana A., editor. *The Ivory Tower and Harry Potter: Perspectives on a Literary Phenomenon*. U of Missouri P, 2002.

Williams, L. Kaitlin. *"Change the Story, Change the World": Gendered Magic and Educational Ideology in Terry Pratchett's Discworld*. 2015. Appalachian State University, MA thesis. *NC Docks*, https://libres.uncg.edu/ir/asu/listing.aspx?styp=ti&id=18343.

Wong, Einar Christopher. *The Magic of Hogwarts: A Critical Examination of Teachers in Harry Potter*. 2014. University of British Columbia, MA thesis. *UBC Open Collections*, https://open.library.ubc.ca/cIRcle/collections/ubctheses/24/items/1.0166889. Accessed 20 Jan. 2016.

"Words from the Master." *The Annotated Pratchett File*, collected and edited by Leo Breebaart and Mike Kew, version 9.0.6, last updated 24 Aug. 2016, https://www.lspace.org/books/apf/words-from-the-master.html.

Wrigley, Terry. "The Testing Regime of Childhood: Up Against the Wall." Kassem, Murphy, and Taylor, pp. 136–48.

Young, Helen. *Race and Popular Fantasy Literature: Habits of Whiteness*. Routledge, 2016.

Zipes, Jack. *The Magic Spell: Radical Theories of Folk and Fairytales*. U Kentucky P, 2002.

Zoller Booth, Margaret, and Grace Marie Booth. "What American Schools Can Learn from Hogwarts School of Witchcraft and Wizardry." *Phi Delta Kappan*, vol. 85, no. 4, 2003, pp. 310–15. *JSTOR*, www.jstor.org/stable/20441534. Accessed 18 Sep. 2015.

Index

aetonormativity 5, 127, 151–159, 163
Akata Witch 165–166
Anglophilia 5, 105–106, 162, 166
apprenticeships 5, 127–128, 133–139, 142, 153–154, 158

capital (cultural, economic, social) 4, 19–22, 52, 55–58, 68–69, 70–92, 108, 161; and educational attainment 80, 82–84, 161; as gatekeeping 73–74, 78–79, 81–82, 84–85
care work 5, 142–146, 149–151, 158, 162
Carnival theory 4, 62–63, 65–67, 93, 153, 161, 169n5
The Chronicles of Narnia 96, 98, 100–103
class-passing 86–87, 91–92; *see also* cross-class performance; reverse slumming
colonialism *see* imperialism
critical literacy 17, 121–124
cross-class performance 4, 73, 85–92, 161

defamiliarization 15–17, 160–161
Deonn, Tracy *see Legendborn*
didacticism 10, 15, 45–46
Discworld 5, 125–127, 128; education on 128–129, 142; the Witches of 126–127, 132–133, 141–143; *see also* "Tiffany Aching" Quintet

emancipatory literary studies 6, 163–164, 166

Fillory and Further 96–100, 104, 119–124, 161–162

gender 5, 7–8, 25–27, 126–127, 140, 142–145, 148–151, 156, 159, 162–163, 167n6
Grossman, Lev *see The Magicians Trilogy*

Harry Potter 3–4, 23–24, 33–67, 69, 126–127, 160; blood status in 54–58, 61, 66–67, 160; careers in 57–61, 64–67, 160; exams in 35, 37, 39–42, 43, 46, 64
hidden curriculum 18–19, 21–25
high-stakes testing 37–38, 44–45, 62

imperialism 4–5, 95–98, 101, 110–119, 123, 162, 174n6; and children's literature 102–103, 104, 120–121; and education 104, 109–110, 112, 119, 123

The Kingkiller Chronicle 4, 68–94, 161; tuition in 76–82; University admittance in 74–78, 89–90

Legendborn 166

The Magicians Trilogy 4, 95–101, 104–124, 161–162; Brakebills as imperial centre in 104–110, 112–119, 162; conceptualizations of magic in 110–114, 118

NEWTs 35–38, 61, 64–65

Okorafor, Nnedi *see Akata Witch*
OWLs 35–39, 42–44, 46–52, 56–61, 66–67, 160

peripheral participation 5, 127, 136–139, 140–141, 158

Index

portal fantasies 4–5, 98–104, 106–107, 119–124, 162
Pratchett, Terry *see* Discworld; "Tiffany Aching" Quintet

reverse slumming 86–90, 92 *see also* class-passing; cross-class performance
Rothfuss, Patrick *see* *The Kingkiller Chronicle*
Rowling, J.K. *see* Harry Potter

school stories 8–14, 129–131, 160; definition of 10–13, 23; socialization through 13–14, 23
social mobility 73, 79, 84–85, 92–93, 161
standardized testing 3–4, 35–38, 53–54, 160–161; as gatekeeping 35, 38, 50, 52–54, 56–7, 61, 65–67, 160; *see also* NEWTs; OWLs

"teaching to the test" 44–52
thematic criticism 17–18, 23, 160
"Tiffany Aching" Quintet 5, 125–159; fantastic school stories in 128–134, 162; *see also* Discworld

under-represented students 71–72, 90–91

vocational education 135, 139, 141, 143–144, 158
vocational habitus 128, 139–142, 144–148, 151, 158, 162

Wizard's Hall 2, 7–9, 25–31

Yolen, Jane *see* *Wizard's Hall*

www.ingramcontent.com/pod-product-compliance
Ingram Content Group UK Ltd.
Pitfield, Milton Keynes, MK11 3LW, UK
UKHW042008140426
5217IPUK00015B/1048